Social Change in Modern Society

SOCIAL CHANGE IN MODERN SOCIETY

Geetanjali

CENTRUM PRESS
NEW DELHI-110002 (INDIA)

CENTRUM PRESS
H.O.: 4360/4, Ansari Road, Daryaganj,
New Delhi-110002 (India)
Tel: 23278000, 23261597, 23255577, 23286875
B.O.: No. 1015, Ist Main Road, BSK IIIrd Stage,
IIIrd Phase, IIIrd Block, Bangalore-560085 (INDIA)
Tel: 080-41723429
Email: centrumpress@gmail.com
Visit us at: www.centrumpress.com

Social Change in Modern Society

First Edition, 2011

ISBN 978-93-80921-69-3

PRINTED IN INDIA

Printed at Tarun Offset Printers, Delhi-110053

Contents

Preface

Social change is a change in society over time. The key characteristics in social change are: a constant state of change; the changes take place both as a planned act and of their own volition and the changes are controversial and vary in the importance. For example; changes in hairstyle and fashion are often controversial but aren't of great significance. An example of social change is the Women Suffrage movement when women joined together to demand the right to be treated as citizens with a focus on the right to vote. Women marched and gave speeches to bring attention to their plight of being treated as less than citizens.

Social change has always been the product of times of change, and the unmatched dynamism of our period is already reflected in the revitalization of theories of change. In this book is to take stock of and to reappraise the whole legacy of sociological thinking about change, from the classical to the contemporary, providing the intellectual tools necessary for a critical and rational grasp of our own turbulent times.

Intended primarily as an advanced book for upper-division and graduate students, as well as researchers, this book covers the grand visions of social and historical change which have dominated the field since the 19th century. It provides indispensable analytic discussions of the concepts focal to contemporary debates such as "social process, "development, "progress, "Social Time, "Historical Tradition, "Modernity, "Post-modernity, and "Globalization.

Author

1

Sociology and Sociological Perspective

THE SOCIOLOGICAL PERSPECTIVES

In sociology, sociological perspectives, theories, or paradigms are complex theoretical and methodological frameworks used to analyse and explain objects of social study. Theory is informed by epistemological discussions as to the most reliable and valid methods to use in the conduct of social science. Perspectives also relate to core assumptions regarding the ontological nature of the social world. Theory is thus informed by historical debates over positivism and antipositivism, debates over the primacy of structure and agency, as well as debates relating to other fundamental key concepts in the social sciences and humanities in general.

LIST OF SOCIOLOGICAL THEORIES

Franzgoh's Theory

Some of the major general sociological theories include:

- *Conflict theory*: Focuses on the ability of some groups to dominate others, or resistance to such domination.
- *Critical theory*: Aims to critique and change society, not simply to document and understand it.
- *Ethnomethodology*: Examines how people make sense out of social life in the process of living it, as if each were a researcher engaged in enquiry.
- *Feminist theory*: Focuses on how gender inequality has shaped social life.

- *Functionalism*: Focuses on how elements of society need to work together to have a fully functioning whole.
- *Interpretive sociology*: This theoretical perspective, based on the work of Max Weber, proposes that social, economic and historical research can never be fully empirical or descriptive as one must always approach it with a conceptual apparatus.
- *Network theory*: A structural approach to sociology, most closely associated with the work of Harrison White, that views norms and behaviours as embedded in chains of social relations.
- *Social phenomenology*: The social phenomenology of Alfred Schütz influenced the development of the social constructionism and ethnomethodology.
- *Positivism*: Social positivists believe that social processes should be studied in terms of cause and effect using 'the' scientific method.
  - *Also*: Sociological positivism
- Postcolonial theory
- *Rational choice theory*: Models social behaviour as the interaction of utility maximizing individuals.
- *Social constructionism*: Is a sociological theory of knowledge that considers how social phenomena develop in particular social contexts.
- *Structural functionalism*: Also known as a social systems paradigm, addresses the functions that various elements of the social system perform in regard to the entire system.
- *Symbolic interactionism*: Examines how shared meanings and social patterns are developed in the course of social interactions.
  - *Dramaturgical perspective*: A specialized symbolic interactionism paradigm developed by Erving Goffman, seeing life as a performance

Criminology

- Differential association theory

- Labeling theory
- Rational choice theory
- Social disorganization theory
- Social learning theory
- Strain theory
- Subcultural theory

Social Movements

Sociologists have developed various theories about social movements.

Chronologically they include:

- Collective behaviour/collective action theories
- Relative deprivation theory
- Value-added theory
- Resource mobilization/Political process theory
- Frame analysis theory
- New social movement theory
- New cultural theory

Sociology of Science and Technology

Sociologists have been active in developing theories about the nature of science and technology:

- "Institutional" sociology of science
- Sociology of scientific knowledge
  - Social construction of technology -variant of SSK focusing on technology studies.
- Actor-network theory
- Normalization Process Theory

SOCIOLOGY AS A SOCIAL SCIENCES

The relationship between sociology and the other social sciences is in reality relationship between sectors of different disciplines, not between whole disciplines. Sociology is one of the most open disciplines towards other disciplines. If specialists in a subdiscipline tend to cite mostly or exclusively specialists in the same subdiscipline, and if relatively few authors cite outside their own subdiscipline, then as a whole the discipline has a low degree of internal coherence. It could be compared to watertight compartments or containers in large ships. In this case, the real loci of research are the specialties. If, by contrast, a significant proportion of authors, cross the borders of their specialties, the discipline as a whole can be considered an integrated territory. The analytical and alphabetical indices of most compendiums and sociology has a weak core.

The fragmentation of the discipline into isolated specialties can be seen in most sociological treatises: "We divide up the discipline into a number of topics. These stages are minimally integrated". Theoretical sociology is presented as a subfield disconnected from substantive domains: "General sociology has been relegated primarily to introductory and to a lesser extent to a sort of social theory that most practicing sociologists use but little in their work". For instance, the 22 stages represent autonomous specialties, that are only weakly related to each other.

Few of the 3 200 authors cited in that work are mentioned in more than one specialty. In the general works in sociology published in the last two decades, the most frequently cited authors are ancestors, not contemporary sociologists. With some exceptions such as Parsons, Merton, Lazarsfeld, Mills, few mentors belong to the immediately previous generation. Nowadays, sociologists in their pattern of references are like children elevated by their grandparents.

This cult of the ancestors is surprising, because "following advances in the division of labour and specialization, the works of the classics ceased to be directly useful to an average sociologist. To do correct research in a specialized branch of sociology one does not in fact have to read the works—bulky, often abstruse, and semi-philosophical in nature—written by Marx and Spencer, Simmel and Weber, Mead and Znaniecki."

The fragmentation of sociology can be explained in part by the absence of any consensus on a dominant, integrative theory, or a widely-accepted paradigm. If a consensus could be reached among sociologists, it would be that sociology has today a small, soft and old core, that is not a centripetal discipline, and that it expands in all directions. Its territory looks very much like the decaying Roman empire when most soldiers were at distant frontiers, without an army in the capital. Openess to what? To other disciplines. There is very little communication between the fifty specialized domains recognized by the International Sociological Association, and between the thirty sectors of the American Sociological Association.

If cooperation among the specialized fields is weak or absent, in revenge, a vivid traffic can be observed between each specialized sociological domain and, across disciplinary borders: the cognate specialized group of scholars belonging formally to other disciplines, particularly specialties rooted in social psychology, social demography, social anthopology, social history, social geography, social ecology, some branches of political science, political economy and socio-linguistics.

A double phenomenon appears in the sociological literature of the last two decades: a division of the discipline into non-communicating specialties, and an opening of the disciplinary frontiers to specialties from different disciplines. Bridges are built over the disciplinary borders. The circulation on these bridges is almost as important as the circulation along the internal arteries of formal sociology. The importance of this "foreign" trade can be measured.

In a study covering four decades from 1936 to 1975 it was found that sociologists cited substances in sociology journals only 58% of the time; political scientists cited only 41% of the time; scholars from their own discipline; anthropologists referred 51% of the time to their colleagues; psychologists referred 73% to their own kin, and 79% of the economists did the same.

In an analysis of journals identified as belonging to sociology and economics there was a significant shift from sociology to "interdisciplinary sociology" and from economics to "interdisciplinary economics", between 1972 and 1987. The criterion for interdisciplinarity was the proportion of cited references in the journals of the respective disciplines. An analysis by the same authors in terms of clusters of references shows a clear increase in interdisciplinary relationships. In addition to this the crossing of disciplinary borders, another important trend in the last fifteen years has been the multiplication of new hybrid journals that cross disciplines and specialties.

More than three hundred hybrid journals in English concerning sociology directly or indirectly have been established in this period, along with many others in French and German. Most of these new journals have a limited circulation and are addressed to readers in highly specialized subfields.

SPECIALIZATION TO FRAGMENTATION TO HYBRIDIZATION

The fragmentation of disciplines is generated by an inevitable and growing process of specialization. All the sciences experience such specialization. As a discipline grows, its practitioners generally become increasingly specialized and inevitably neglect other areas of the discipline. The division of physics into physics and astronomy, and the division of chemistry into organic chemistry and physical chemistry are examples in the natural sciences. In the social sciences, what was originally the study of law divided into law and political science; anthropology split into physical anthropology and cultural anthropology; and psychology broke up into psychology, social psychology, psychotherapy, and psychiatry.

Each formal discipline gradually becomes too large and unmanageable for empirical research. No theory or conceptual framework can encompass the entire territory of sociology. Talcott Parsons was the last one to attempt such a unification, but his ambition was unrealistic. Contemporary theories are influential only within their particular subdiscipline. The process of fragmentation and specialization is sooner or later followed by a process of recombination of the specialties into new hybrid domains.

These recombinations correspond to the logic of multiple and concatenated causality in the social sciences. The more renowned new hybrid domains hoist their own flags, for instance, political sociology, which is a fusion of sectors from both of its parent disciplines; social psychology, which is already autonomous; political economy, which detaches large sectors from economics and political science and smaller sectors from sociology; and historical sociology, which has revived on both sides of the Atlantic. None of these four subfields were mentioned three decades ago by N. Smelser in his Sociology and the Other Social Sciences. This absence shows the changes that have occurred since then.

It is pointless to lament about the fragmentation of sociology or any other social science, because the interaction between specialties in different disciplines is beneficial. All social sciences, sociology in particular, have grown in depth and breadth through exchanges with cognate specialties born into other disciplines. What some scholars perceive as dispersion is in reality an expansion of knowledge and an inevitable trend.

In the history of social sciences, the progression from fragmentation to specialization to hybridization has taken one of the following six forms:

- Scissiparity of disciplines, by division in two parts, like amoebae, by bifurcation. The history of the sciences is a long chain of divisions. One of the oldest, going back to Aristotle, is the separation of philosophy and political theory. One of the most recent is the divorce of cognitive science from traditional psychology.
- Changing boundaries of formal disciplines. The growth of specialties at the interstices between disciplines has as a consequence the shrinking of the borders of the parent disciplines. When social psychology became independent, old psychology had lost an enormous territory. One of the borders of economics retracted when political economy was emancipated. Anthropology has seen its frontiers retract as a result of modernization, industrialization and urbanization; consequently urban studies expanded. The margins of political science are in perpetual change. In some areas of natural and social

sciences, enormous icebergs detach themselves from the ice-floe.

- Migration of individual scholars from one formal discipline to another, or to a new territory. The founders of sociology have moved away from philosophy, such as Durkheim, or from history, such as Max Weber, or from economics, such as Pareto.
- The convergence of two domains in a new hybrid field, consisting in the recombination of fragments of sciences. One of the most recent examples in medical sciences is the intermingling of fragments of cardiology with fragments of pneumonology. The nomenclature of social sciences is full of such hybrid fields, frequently at the second or third generation of hybridization.
- Outgrowth from the mother-discipline for pragmatic reasons, to the point of being grafted into another formal discipline. For instance sociology of medicine, the most populated sociological subdiscipline, is today located more often in hospitals than in departments of sociology; it has become a problem-solving subdiscipline.
- Borrowing from neighbouring disciplines, and exchanging concepts, theories, methods, practices, tools, and substance. This borrowing and lending process is an important route of hybridization. All the social sciences share concepts, theories and methods. The contribution of sociology to this treasury is impressive. Sociology has devised and exported many more concepts to neighbouring disciplines than have borrowed from it. Most theories formulated in a discipline sooner or later spread to other disciplines. The diffusion of theories across disciplinary borders is one of the arguments that could be invoked by those who advocate more interdisciplinary strategies in the social sciences. The borrowing and lending of methods among disciplines have different itineraries than those for the spread

of concepts and theories. An inventory of contributions to the methodology in social sciences, the most productive disciplines were until recently psychology, econometrics, social psychology and statistics. For concepts and theories, the most creative disciplines are sociology, political science, economics, anthropology and philosophy.

A distinction must be made between interdisciplinary amalgamation and hybridization thought recombination of specialties belonging to different disciplines. A "unified sociology" existed only in the early phase of sociological development. Hybridization of specialties came later, after the maturation of the process of the internal fragmentation of disciplines.

The word "interdisciplinary" is misleading when used to describe contemporary trends, because today only specialties overlap, not entire disciplines. The word "hybridization" may seem to be imported from biology, but it has been used by social scientists such as Piaget and Lazarsfeld.

Sociometric studies show that many specialists are more in touch with colleagues in other disciplines than with colleagues in their own disciplines. The "invisible college" described by Robert Merton, Diana Crane, and other sociologists of science is an eminent multispeciality institution because it ensures communication not only from one university to another and across all national borders, but also, between specialists attached administratively to different disciplines. The networks of cross-disciplinary influence are obliterating the old classification of the social sciences.

RECOMBINATION OF SOCIOLOGICAL SPECIALTIES WITH SPECIALTIES IN OTHER SOCIAL SCIENCES

Sociology has exchanged concepts, theories, methods, practices and substance, most intensively with three other disciplines: political science, history and economics. The analysis here will focus on these three "parentages". The well-known dominion of social psychology can be surveyed briefly. The relationships between sociology and social geography have long been difficult and poor. What happens in the absence of intermingling? Other specialties intervene in the empty space, as in case of ecological geography. Because of space constraints, I have to forgo the overlapping areas between sociology and social anthropology, social demography, ethnology and sociolinguistics, but the comments on the process of fragmentation of disciplines, on multiplication of specialties, and on recombination of the specialties in new hybrid fields are also applicable to them.

Relations with Political Science

A double phenomenon can be observed in the relationship between sociology and political science. First, there is a weak communication within each of these two disciplines among the multiple specialized fields: an impermeability between the specialized research subfields that belong formally to the same discipline.

The disciplines appear like watertight compartments in large ships. Typically, there is relatively little scholarly exchange between a student of the American Congress and a specialist in Middle Eastern politics, between a political philosopher and an expert in statistical analysis, between an Africanist and an expert on welfare states. However, most of these scholars are likely to have relationships with cognate specialties in neighbouring disciplines. The diversity of methodological schools contributes to the fragmentation of each discipline.

Second, across disciplinary frontiers there is a vivid traffic between special fields or subfields belonging to one discipline and the similar or cognate fields in the other discipline. A convincing way to show the importance of these cross-disciplinary bridges is to rank on two columns the fifty research committees of the ISA and the forty committees of IPSA. For each area of research in one discipline there is a homologue in the other discipline: religion, ethnicity, generations, gender, mass-communication, elites, socialization, crime, social inequality and so on. To these interminglings should be added theoretical and methodological pairs: All major schools and sects are represented in both disciplines from rationalists to marxists, and from qualitative methods to proponents of over-quantification. The relationships between sociology and political science can be observed, by counting the proportion of authors belonging to a discipline who cite substances from other disciplines. Such an analysis of footnotes in major journals shows the trade across disciplinary frontiers and the changes in trade routes over time. In terms of import-export balance, political science has borrowed from economics, sociology and social psychology, and has exported mostly to sociology.

There has been a change in the cross-fertilization of political science. In the 1950s and 1960s, sociology was the major lender to political science, making such important contributions such as group theory, political socialization, social cleavages, and systems theory. In the 1970s and 1980s, economics was the major cross-fertilizer of political science, especially with theories of public goods and collective action, game theory, social choice, and international trade theory. Psychology has been a constant exporter to political science and sociology, but at a lower level.

In the 1960s, its major contributions came from personality theory and the study of values. One domain of sociology—political sociology—and one domain of political science—comparative politics—have privileged relations, in some cases achieving a real fusion. In the history of comparative research, there was a privileged moment of cooperation and convergence between political sociology and comparative politics.

Between 1958 and 1972 that shared three characteristics: comparison by quantification, hybridization and cumulative knowledge. That a combination had never previously been achieved in the history of sociology and political science. This privileged moment also marks a break with European classical comparisons in the sociological style of Tocqueville, J.S. Mill, Marx, Weber and Pareto. The alarm over the parochial state of comparative politics—after the subjugation of all social sciences during the period of totalitarianism in Europe and before their renaissance in the United States—was raised by Roy Macridis in 1955. At the same time the Statistical Bureau of the United Nations started to publish "social statistics" on demographic variables, income, standards of living, social mobility, sanitary conditions, nutrition, housing, education, work, and criminality. These sources facilitated the encounter between political sociology and comparative politics.

In 1957, Reports on the World Social Situation began to be published by the Department of Economic and Social Affairs of the United Nations. In 1961 and 1963 on "the interrelations of social and economic development and the problem of balance", and on "social-economic patterns" are contributions that can be read profitably today by sociologists interested on developmental theories. Lipset's Political Man borrowed from all social sciences. A year later, Karl Deutsch produced his "manifesto". Both dealt with comparative indicators.

The following year an important by Ph. Cutright was published that appears in retrospect to have been prophetic. In the same year, Arthur Banks and Robert Textor published A Cross-Polity Survey in which the majority of the 57 variables are of direct interest for sociologists. Shortly after ward, the World of Political and Social Indicators, by B. Russett *et al.*, discussed 75 variables, the majority with sociological significance.

In Comparative Politics by G. Almond and G. Bingham Powell, several social sciences, particularly sociology and social anthropology, are seen in the background. From that moment on, the field of international comparisons became bifurcated, with both trends being related to political sociology. One road continues with quantitative research, in which contributors constantly use non-political factors in their analyses of the correlates of democracy and transition to democracy. An important contribution comes again from the Development Programme of the United Nations, the Human Development Report. In this publication GNP per capita is "dethroned" and is replaced by a new indicator: Purchasing Power Parity. The other road gave priority to sectoral comparisons, for instance, the eight volumes on development, published by the Princeton University Press, where politics is most of the time a dependent variable explained by social economic and cultural factors. About a thousand books and substances appear in a selected bibliography of sectoral comparisons published during the last three decades. About half of their authors belong administratively to political science, a quarter belong to sociology, and a quarter are hybrids scholars.

Comparative political sociology does not consist only in cross-national analysis. It is also a cross-disciplinary endeavor, because in comparative research one is crossing units and variables. The variables are usually more numerous than the units. The relations between variables are often more important for theoretical explanations than are discoveries of analogies and differences between nations.

In comparative political sociology, there is not a single major book that attempts to explain politics strictly by reference political variables. Of course, the amount of hybridization varies with the subject and the ability of the author to omit what should be implicitly admitted. In the last three decades, more than two hundred contemporary European and American scholars, have held a joint appointment in the departments of sociology and of political science, or have moved from one to the other. Some comparativists cannot be locked in only one of these two disciplines.

Historical Sociology and Social History

History is the most heterogeneous discipline in the social sciences, dispersed in time and space. It is divided into a nomothetic part and an ideographic part. The dispute over the role and borders of history, which in France goes back to Durkheim, Simiand and Seignobos, does not seem to have ended.

Three generations later, history has been excluded from the social sciences under the authority of an international institution: It is not numbered among the so-called nomothetic sciences covered in the first volume published by UNESCO, Main Trends in the Social and Human Sciences. Historians do not appear to have reacted vigorously to this affront. Indeed some have come to terms with it. "The progress of history in the last 50 years is the result of a series of marriages: with economics, then with demography, even with geography... with ethnology, sociology and psychoanalysis. When all is said and done, the new history sees itself as something like an auxiliary science of the other social sciences". And here we have the word "auxiliary" which was previously such a sore point, used this time by an historian.

This is clearly not the opinion of the other historians who are resolutely committed to interdisciplinarity: "History will progress only in the context of interdisciplinarity". As long as the focus is on the long time span and the comparative approach, there is agreement between Durkheim and Braudel. At a distance of 60 years, using different words, they say much the same thing: "History can be a science only in so far as it compares, and there can be no explanation without comparison... Once it starts comparing, history becomes indistinct from sociology".

Braudel is just as accommodating: "Where the long time span is concerned, the point is not simply that history and sociology tie in with each other and support each other but rather that they merge into one". However, this refers only to the part of history that compares while considering the long time span; other fields of history have very little to do with sociology. Similarly, many sociologists do not need to have recourse to history to resolve problems with which they are concerned. Durkheim and Braudel would have been more explicit if, instead of considering their disciplines as a whole, they had referred clearly to their common territory, which is now called comparative social history or historical sociology.

Once it is accepted that history and sociology overlap only in certain areas, the long territorial dispute between history and sociology will become a thing of the past. However this is only one sector of history brought face to face with a sector of another discipline. Exchanges with economics have thus generated economic history, which is of interest to enough historians and economists to provide material for several major journals. Each human activity has its historian, who, in order to perform his or her task, has to hunt in other people's lands.

On the other side of the Atlantic, as soon as their disciplines had begun to fragment, innovative historians and sociologists reached out to one another. Frederick Jackson Turner's study of the American frontier was a marriage of sociology and history with the benediction of geography. Later, sociologists such as R. Bellah and S.M. Lipset were joined by a new generation of historians, for instance Charles Tilly's and Barrington Moore. This interweaving of sociology and history continues to the present day.

"Most sociologists and historians have no clear understanding of what historical sociology really is." Unlike economics, political science, or linguistics, the distinction is not based on subject matter. Many have attempted to clarify the differences between the two disciplines, leaving no two authors in agreement. The reason for the lack of consensus is clear: The remarkable diversity of the historical sociologies, to say nothing of their parent disciplines, makes any unidimensional characterization of the issue unsatisfactory.

The comparative method is a very useful way to unify general statements of causality of historical events. One of the first to take this path was the French school in the journal Annales, which developed an approach to social history which was both sociological and comparative. Marc Bloch was one of the most influential figures in the development of this school, both in his programmatic statement.

For some historians it is impossible to assess the validity of any causal interpretation on the basis of a single case, making a comparative approach absolutely necessary for useful explanation.. Comparative history overcomes the fragmentation of specialized history. Examining similar causal processes in two or more specific contexts can illuminate the nature of the causal forces at work and improve one's understanding of the events being studied. The dialogue between the specific and the general is an important issue explored by many who discuss historical sociology. Along these lines, Peter Burke isolates two different aspects of the contributions history can make to sociology, one negative and one positive. The negative contribution entails picking away at the edifice constructed by others by showing how a theory does not fit one's society. This entails tests that are hazardous for any theory, but theories that can survive are proved to be of greater value.

The positive contribution involves working out from the general to the particular in order to construct a revised general theory. This task is especially valuable because a sociologist's generalizations often appear vacuous to an historian. Historians have invalidated without pity many beautiful theories built by sociologists and political scientists.

When posed in this fashion, the social sciences insistence on generalization can be helpful for historians. In the words of a sociologist turned-historian, "Whatever else they do, the social sciences serve as a giant warehouse of causal theories and concepts involving causal analogies; the problem is to pick one's way through the junk to the solid merchandise. "When one finds solid ground, a simple application of sociological theory to historical problems can be innovative. Peter Knapp, suggests that historians can help overcome the inattention to context of most social theory. He argues that one of the major problems in sociological theory is the implicit or explicitceteris paribus clause. Since all other factors are never the same in the real world, such theories are repeatedly disconfirmed and often appear vacuous.

"When sociologists decide that concern with theory absolves them from concern with history, their product will not only be irrelevant historically, it will not even be adequate as theory. "When theories are opened up to allow variation in the ceteris paribus, they can be applied to specific historical contexts. Historians who are most familiar with the peculiarities of "their" period or country, have much to add to social theory in this type of research. Contrary to what is generally believed, historical sociology sometimes is not based on quantified research. Nonetheless, quantification is so ubiquitous in most social sciences that it is easy for historians to misunderstand the nature of the field.

As Tilly points out, "In field after field, the leading edge of the change was some form of quantification. Because of that uniformity, many non quantitative historians mistook the prow for the whole ship.". Quantified data is for most sociologists what primary sources are for historians. If some historians cannot resist quoting diaries, some sociologists cannot resist quantifying. Both kinds of evidence have advantages and disadvantages, and each discipline can gain from making greater use of the kind of evidence most useful to the other.

In addition to a difference in method, history and sociology often are distinguished by their conceptual inventories. There are a number of sociological concepts historians can use to their advantage, such as structure, function, social role, kinship, socialization, deviance, social class and stratification, social mobility, modernization, patrons and clients, and factions. The breadth of this list makes it clear that there is much room for hybridization of subfields across the disciplinary boundaries. For instance the concept of "development" is central in several social sciences.

Relations with Eclectic Economics

To discuss the relationship between sociology and economics, it is necessary to distinguish several varieties of economists: econometricians, monodisciplinary monetarist theorists, landless theorists, and eclectic transgressors of borders. The first two varieties have well-known physiognomies. Landless theorists are economists who believe that they do not have to deal with nation-states, and tend to reduce all countries to a single model.

They travel at a stratospheric level of landless economies. One may assume that the first three varieties are outstanding contributors to scientific knowledge, since so many of them have been awarded Nobel prizes, but here only the last variety interests us because it is the only one which entertains good relations with the other social sciences. Eclectic economists denounce the reductionism advocated by other economists. Four decades ago, F.A. Hayek wrote that "the economist who is only an economist is likely to become a nuisance if not a positive danger".

For the Nobel prize laureate James Buchanan, "it become increasingly clear that the channels of effective communication do not extend throughout the discipline that we variously call "economics", and that some "economists" are able to communicate far more effectively with some scholars in the noneconomic disciplines than with those presumably within their own professional category". Another Nobel prize laureate asked: "Why should economics be interdisciplinary? The answer is, presumably, because otherwise it will make mistakes; the neglect of all but the narrowly economic interactions will lead to false conclusions that could be avoided". Many economists state that "it is necessary to reduce the use of the clause ceteris paribus, to adopt an interdisciplinary approach, that is to say to open economics to multidimensionality".

Economics is also divided, but to a lesser degree than the other social sciences. It has maintained some coherence but has had to pay a high price for this by considerably reducing its field. At one time, economics reached a fork in the path: It could have chosen intellectual expansion, and the penetration of other disciplines, at the cost of heterogeneity and diversification and at the risk of dispersal; it chose instead to remain true to itself, thereby forfeiting vast territories. Many economists consider that the choice of purity, methodological rigor and hermetic terminology was the right choice.

It is thus clear that self-sufficiency, eventually, leads to a shrinking of borders, but this does not mean general impoverishment, since the lands abandoned by economists were soon cultivated by others. Those lands now have their own departments, research centres, and professional schools. The position of economics in the constellation of the social sciences today might have been more dominant if so many economists had not withdrawn into monodisciplinarity. This situation is surprising in that "few classical sociologists have failed to assign a central place in their theories to the relationship between economy and society: from Marx and Weber to Schumpeter, Polanyi, Parsons and Smelser" not forgetting Pareto.

If many economists have locked themselves in an ivory tower, and allowed whole areas to escape from their scrutinity, other economists have advocated an "imperialistic expansion of economics into the traditional domains of sociology, political science, anthropology, law and social biology". Several of these economists are famous scholars, including several Nobel laureates. A kind of manifesto has been published in the American Economic Review:

- "It is ultimately impossible to carve off a distinct territory for economics, bordering upon but separated from other social disciplines. Economics interpenetrates them all, and is reciprocally penetrated by them. There is only one social science. What gives economics its imperialist invasive power is that our analytical categories are truly universal in applicability. Thus economics really does constitute the universal grammar of social science. But there is a flip side to this. While scientific work in anthropology and sociology and political science and the like will become increasingly in distinguishable from economics, economists will reciprocally have to become aware of their functions. Ultimately, good economics will also have to be good anthropology and sociology and political science and psychology".

This view is anachronistic, but many outstanding economists have succeeded not only in "exporting" their knowledge to other disciplines but also in "invading" them with their methods and theories and achieving innovative research.

Arrow's Social Choice and Individual Values led mathematically trained economists to apply game theory to a variety of social conflict situations. Several works, in quick succession, made such applications, including Anthony Down's An Economic Theory of Democracy, Duncan Black's

The Theory of Committees and Elections, Buchanan and Tullock's The Calculus of Consent, Riker's The Theory of Political Coalitions, and Olson's The Logic of Collective Action. Since then, many social scientists have borrowed ideas and techniques from economists and applied them to the analysis of various processes and situations.

The economists were the first in the field because they had a longer tradition of mathematical training, and used more abstract, and thus more widely applicable concepts. The other social sciences had learned statistics in order to handle the interpretation of their empirical data, but were much slower to learn advanced mathematics. In a number of important graduate schools, economists hold joint appointments with other social science departments.

Some economists continue to spread the application of their analytic techniques to outside fields. Gary Becker wrote a book on discrimination and prejudice, and in Treatise on the Family applied economic analysis to topics such as the incidence of marriage, divorce and childbearing. He was awarded the Nobel prize in Economic Sciences in 1992 for his work applying economics to different areas of human behaviour, particularly the family, a traditional stronghold of demography.

Gordon Tullock's The Economics of Non-Human Societies deals with ants, termites, bees, mole rats, sponges and slime molds. Many similar examples could be given: "The fields to which the economic approach or perspective has been applied over the last thirty or forty years include politics, sociology, ethnology, law, biology, psychology". An examination of recent issues of journals of economic literature shows that some economists explore a wide range of issues. Among these eclectic economists there are a few who behave like academic cowbirds who lay eggs in the nest of another discipline, and return immediately to their home discipline. The economist Michael Intriligator has presented in a schematic way the patterns of cross-fertilization among the behavioural sciences by identifying concepts and theories developed in economics and adopted by others. He traces in terms of input-output the itinerary of social choice theory, structural models, decision theory, organization theory, bounded rationality, utility theory, game theory, the concept of balance of power, and anomie.

The interferences between economics and political science are deeper than those between economics and sociology. Many economists are better known in political science than in economics, particularly in the domain of political economy. The new economic-sociology receives great attention, but it is not clear how it is different from the older political economy. This should be confronted with of Economic Sociology, edited by N. Smelser and R. Swedberg.

For instance, Claus Offe describes the "asymmetry" between the two disciplines: "Political economists do have an economic theory of institutions and tend to disregard this demarcation line separating spheres. Sociologists have perhaps only the rudiments of a sociological theory of what is going on in markets and firms, while the most ambitious argument that sociologists do have to offer effectively demonstrates that non-economic spheres of society are not only constituted in different ways than the economy, but that the economy itself depends on non-economic spheres".

Social Psychology

Most sociologists are not involved in the kind of research that interests most psychologists, and vice versa. For the majority of sociologists and the majority of psychologists, their respective territories are clearly separated. Nevertheless, between the two disciplines there is a condominium; social psychology, inhabited by hybrid scholars, some of whom have began their scientific activity in one of the two disciplines while others started as "hybrids".

In addition, for many sociologists who are not social psychologists, psychology is, the nearest and most important disciplinary neighbour. We can therefore be brief on this old and familiar parenthood. What Alex Inkeles wrote three decades ago is still valid today: "It would not be at all difficult to assemble a set of fifty or one hundred recent substances in social psychology, chosen half from the psychological and half from the sociological journals, which would be so much alike that no one, judging without knowledge of source or author, could with any precision discriminate those written by professional sociologists from those written by psychologists. Several considerations follow from this simple fact. Clearly, the two disciplines cannot be defined in terms of what psychologists and sociologists respectively do, since they so often do the same thing".

The growth of social psychology during the last two generations makes Durkheim's arguments in favour of the supremacy of sociology over psychology irrelevant along with the old debate about the individual-society dichotomy. "The claim to a principled distinction of sociology from psychology based on the distinction of individual from society is challenged by the substantial attention that at least some sociologists pay to individuals, by difficulties in describing psychology as the study of individuals, and by difficulties in the very conceptual distinction of individual from society".

At the early stages of the discipline's postwar history, psychology had been the most cited cognate discipline by sociologists, but during the last two decades, it was partly overtaken by political science and economics. Meanwhile social psychology has become an autonomous discipline.

Relations with Ecological Geography

As a reaction against the exaggerations of the sociologist Ellsworth Huntington, who was rightly criticized by Pitirim Sorokin in 1928, an entire generation of American sociologists was dissuaded from taking geographical factors into consideration. Even today, most sociologists and geographers are ignoring each other.

Until recently, sociologists neglected environmental and climatic factors, but many prominent hybrid scholars did not remain silent. W. Arthur Lewis noted in his Theory of Economic Growth that "it is important to identify the reasons why tropical countries have lagged during the last two hundred years in the process of modern economic growth".

Kenneth Galbraith wrote: "If one marks off a belt a couple of thousand miles in width encircling the earth at the equator one finds within it no developed countries—Everywhere the standard of living is low and the span of human life is short".

The book published by Andrew Kamarck, as the director of the Economic Development Institute of the World Bank, The Tropics and Economic Development, challenges the common perception of tropical areas. Trypanosomiasis, carried by the tsetse fly, prevented much of Africa from progressing beyond the subsistence level: "For centuries, by killing transport animals, it abetted the isolation of Tropical Africa from the rest of the world and the isolation of the various African peoples from one another".

An area of Africa larger than the United States thus had been denied to cattle. Agricultural production in humid tropics is limited by the condition of the soil, which has become laterite. Surveys by the World Health Organization and the World Food Organization estimated that parasitic worms infected over one billion people throughout the tropics and sub-tropics. Hookworm disease, characterized by anemia, weakness and fever, infected five hundred million in those areas.

These ecological factors are confirmed by a considerable amount of research in tropical areas during the several last decades by geologists, geographers, biologists, zoologists, botanists, agronomists, epidemiologists, parasitologists, climatologists, experts of the World Bank and several agencies of the United Nations, and hybrid scientists well versed in tropical agriculture, the exploitation of minerals, and sanitary conditions in those countries.

The situation has improved, just as to dozens of reports prepared by international organizations. To explain the economic under-development of tropical Africa and some other tropical areas, natural sciences and demography are brought into the picture. Dependency theory may be of some help for Latin America and Eastern Europe, though much less so for tropical Africa. The literature on the ecological parameters of the tropics can be contrasted with the literature on the transfer of flora and fauna from one temperate zone to another. For instance Alfred Crosby's, Ecological Imperialism: the Biological Expansion of Europe 900-1900, casts new light on the building of American power.

This is an example of what can happen when a discipline neglects an important topic. The vacuum left by the absence of sociological studies of this geographic-ecological-economic issue has been filled by eclectic economists and hybrid ecologists. Sociologists and geographers have met not in vast "interdisciplinary" work but in a series of individual fields such as urban studies. In the history of this hybrid in the USA, important work came from sociologists in the subfields of "human ecology", geographers influenced by sociologists and scholars in both disciplines working on spatial statistics. Once a hybrid, "urban studies" is now a department of its own at many large universities in Europe and USA.

Urban studies as a quasi-discipline includes subfields that overlap specialties in sociology, geography, and anthropology. It also encompasses architecture, which covers engineering, the natural sciences, the social sciences, the humanities and some hybrids of its own. Some architects remodeling cities, building airports, cultural or commercial centres are famous, from Rotterdam to Brasilia to Osaka. Their fame is based on facilities which span engineering, the natural sciences, the social sciences, the humanities, as well as urban planning.

Urban studies also has been influenced by economics and economic geography. This hybrid has made its major contribution in the area of location theories for agricultural, industrial, and commercial activities. Communication seems to be much better with geographers and even sociologists it is than with economists, partly because the inductive nature of much of their work makes it difficult to integrate into deductive economic theory. Other sociologists have drawn from sectors of geography in conjunction with history and economy. Stein Rokkan has suggested a conceptual framework for comparative political analysis. He weaves together Parsonian pattern variables, the sequence of various kinds of "crises", and the typically Scandinavian notion of centre-periphery relations into a geographical schema built around the main Hansa-Rhine-Italy trade routes, the notion of a country's distance from Rome, and whether a state faces seaward or is landbound. This schema is suggestive, not only because it can clarify the different political outcomes in the states of modern Europe, but also because it can help us understand why many once-powerful states have disappeared, such as Scotland, Wales, Brittany, Bohemia, Bavaria, and Aragon. Today, geography's breadth can be seen in the multiplication of hybrid subfields.

The discipline now encompasses the subfields of human geography, cultural geography, biogeography, geomorphology, climatology, medical geography, economic geography, political geography, urban geography, environmental science, regional geography, and cartography. Each subfield relates directly to specialties outside the discipline. Different interests have favoured closer contacts sometimes with one field, and sometimes with another. These outside fields have made some of geography's most important advances. As a result of all these trends, there is an incredible fragmentation that has made geography span large areas in both the natural and social sciences, with a general tendency to drift from the former to the latter.

From studying habitats, geographers have turned to studying the societies themselves. Many traditional geographers have become social scientists. As in other disciplines, interaction has kept geography on the move. Many geographers have developed their method and have penetrated other disciplines to such a degree that they have become specialist in another discipline or of one sector of another discipline. Such emigration naturally leaves the old core of the discipline empty.

At a symposium on the social sciences in Paris in 1982, a geographer asked, "With the progress of the other social sciences, what remains proper to geography? A residual part, or a boring nomenclature? Does geography still have its own domain, or is it a relic of an old division of labour? Has geography an identity and, if so, of what is it made?" As is true for the other social sciences, its identity can be found in hybrid specialties, not in disciplinary unity. The contemporary social sciences have experienced three majors trends: rapid expansion, fragmentation of formal disciplines by increasing specialization, and recombination of specialties in new hybrid domains. The social sciences have expanded enormously over the last four decades.

It is difficult to evaluate the number of substances rooted in sociology or relevant for sociologists even if one can locate the origin of the substances, and adopt criteria for what is relevant and what is not. The main difficulty comes from the ambiguity and arbitrariness of the borders of these disciplines. Between one quarter and one third of the substances cited by sociologists in the last few decades were written by economists, political scientists, psychologists, historians, geographers and other social scientists.

In 1994, the SSCI contained almost two million citations involving 400,000 authors from 15 disciplines and from many countries. Obviously, no one can master the entire spectrum of sociology. There are no paradigms in the discipline, only partial and contested theories, and moving borders. One can succeed nevertheless without too many difficulties finding one's way in the bibliographical labyrinth, because the scientific patrimony is structured in sectors, subdisciplines, areas, fields, subfields, specialties, topics and niches, in spite of the fact that the borders are blurred.

This increasing specialization within sociology is the main route of scientific advancement. Some scholars recommend an interdisciplinary approach. Just as some seem to believe that the social sciences can be neatly categorized, many others persist in pursuing interdisciplinarity. That recommendation is not realistic because it overlooks an essential phenomenon in the history of science: specialization through a process of fragmentation. To understand scientific creativity another phenomenon is even more important than the expansion of the scientific literature and the increase in specialization: the recombination of specialties into new hybrid domains, a phenomenon called the hybridization of scientific knowledge.

A hybrid scholar is a specialist who crosses the borders of her or his home discipline by integrating into his or her research: factors, variables, theories, concepts, methods and substance generated in other disciplines. Different disciplines may proceed from different foci to examine the same phenomenon. This multidisciplinarity implies a division of territories between disciplines.

On the contrary, hybridization implies an overlapping of segments of disciplines, a recombination of knowledge in new and specialized fields. Innovation in each discipline depends largely of exchanges with other fields belonging to other disciplines. At the highest levels, most researchers belong to a hybrid subdiscipline. Alternatively, they may belong to a hybrid field or subfield. An innovative recombination is a blending of fragments of sciences. When old fields grow they accumulate such masses of material in their patrimony that they split up. Each fragment of the discipline then confronts the fragments of other fields across disciplinary boundaries, losing contact with its siblings in the old discipline.

A specialist in urbanization has less in common with a sociologist studying elite recruitment than he does with a geographer doing research on the distribution of cities, who at his turn has more in common with a colleague in economics analyzing urban income inequality. Most hybrid specialties and domains recognize their genealogical roots: political economy, social psychology, social geography, historical sociology, genetic demography, psycholinguistics, political anthropology, social ecology, biogeography and many others. The hybrid specialties branch out in turn giving rise, at the second generation, to an even larger member of hybrids.

Among the ISA research committees and study groups, about half are focusing on hybrid specialties. The number of sociologists who work across disciplinary borders is so high that there is more communication between various fields of sociology and their cognates outside the discipline than there is between fields within sociology. One can find in the literature of each social science complaints about the "lack of core", like this one, concerning sociology: "the substantive core of the discipline may have dissolved". Dozens of similar testimonies could be collected. If so many scholars formulate the same diagnosis, that means that most disciplines are facing a problem of self-identity. However, if one considers that the real world cannot be cut into disciplinary pieces, this issue of disciplinary identity may appear fallacious.

It is difficult or impossible to inquire into the large social phenomena within a strictly monodisciplinary framework. Only by taking a position at the crossroads of many branches of knowledge can one explain the impact of technological advancement on structural unemployment in Western Europe, the proliferation of giant cities in the Third World, the economic decline of the United Kingdom and the economic growth of Japan, or how a child learns to speak. Whenever a question of such magnitude is raised, one finds oneself at the intersection of numerous disciplines and specialities.

All major issues cross the formal borders of disciplines: war and peace, generational change, the freedom-equality nexus, individualism in advanced societies and fundamentalism in traditional societies. Most specialists are not located in the so-called core of the discipline. They are in the outer rings, in contact with specialists from other disciplines. They borrow and lend at the frontiers; they are hybrid scholars. The notion of hybridization does not mean "two whole disciplines in a single skull", but a recombination of two or several domains of knowledge originating from different disciplines.

Most classical sociologists were interdisciplinary generalists, but in recent times, cross-disciplinary advancements have been achieved not by generalists, but by hybrid specialists. The hybrid specialist today may be, in reality, a "marginal" scholar in each of the disciplines from which he or she borrows, including his own original discipline, but such a specialist becomes central to the intersection of two or several disciplines. Today most social scientists admit that the best alternative to the difficulty of experimentation in their disciplines is the comparative method, which is one of the few ways to validate or to falsify generalizations in the "soft" sciences. The comparative method is the key to circulation among sciences. Comparative sociologists and comparative political scientists have developed methods to a greater extent than have other social scientists. One of them wrote: "There is no noncomparative sociological theory.

All scientific analyses are a subset of the general set entitled comparitive analysis... any generalized statement involving variables implies a comparison". Major social phenomena cannot be explained in a strictly monodisciplinary framework, nor in the absence of a comparative perspective. It is only by taking up a position at the crossroad of various branches of knowledge and simultaneously adopting a comparative perspective that social scientists can advance knowledge. The intersections of hybrid specialties and comparative approaches are privileged sites in the social sciences.

THEORETICAL PERSPECTIVES OF SOCIOLOGY

Sociologists have covered a broad amount of material in their accumulated studies. Some, like Karl Marx, studied broad topics related to the whole of societies. He theorized that the root of human misery lies in the uneven distribution of wealth in society. Others, like Emile Durkheim, focused on more concise topics. He concentrated much of his effort on determining why certain sects of people are more apt to commit suicide than others. Still others, like Max Weber, studied patterns in culture throughout history to determine how much a social group can affect one's life.

Though many sociologists study different topics, all use their recorded data to produce theories. These theories suggest how certain parts of the world fit together and how they work. If you break theories down further, you can sort them into three distinct categories: symbolic interactionism, functional analysis, and conflict theory. All three can use different observations to prove the same point. Firstly, symbolic interactionism. This theory initially stated that one evaluates himself based on the conduct of others. As years went on, symbolic interactionism also showed that people use symbols to encapsulate their experiences. Symbolic interaction is generally conducted at the Microsociological level. That is—it examines small scale patterns of social interaction. For example. If you think of a family member as an aunt or an uncle, you will behave in a certain way. If the person is a best friend, you will carry yourself quite differently. Without symbolic interaction, we would have no way to define relationships, and we would be reduced to a level of animal interaction.

In short, symbolic interactionists analyse how our behaviours depend on the ways we define ourselves and others. Functional analysis basically states that society is a whole made up of independent parts that work together. Emile Durkheim, was one of the most prominent sociologists associated with this view. His work noted that, although the whole of society works together, individual sects of people can be more likely to do certain things than others.

Most notable of all his studies is likely his work done on finding social factors that may contribute to the likelihood of a person committing suicide. He observed that how strong or weak social bonds are have a strong impact on suicide rate in a social group. For example, women and protestants are more apt to commit suicide because their ties to their social groups are weaker. Also, he noted that if bonds are too strong, the risk for suicide increases as well. A man who loses his spouse may be more likely to commit suicide, because he sees death as a better option than living without his wife. In this case, their feelings were deeply integrated.

Finally, there is conflict theory. This theory came as a result of Karl Marx's studies on social equality. He concluded that the key to human history is class struggle. This meant that one small group of people controls the means, while a much larger group of workers is exploited for their benefit. This, of course, was recorded at a time when worker's rights, labour laws, and capitalism were in their infancy. For the most part, workers were at the mercy of their employers. Marx suggested that if all the wealth was shared evenly, humans could coexist in harmony. These three theories not only explained human interaction when they were created many years ago, but can also be applied today to more modern situations. Take Emile Durkheim. His studies on human interaction stated that the group of people one is surrounded by determines how he carries himself. If Durkheim were alive today, and he intended to undertake a study of gangs, he would likely start out by observing what type of external factors lead to an individual's desire to join one. External forces, such as parental neglect, lack of friendship, and lack of social activity could all be considered legitimate reasons for one to join a gang.

Upon entering, Durkheim would follow several gang members and see how drastically a person's values would change in order to conform to the life-style of the gang. In short, he would show that weak bonds with family fuel a desire for strong bonds with another source—whether that source is a positive or a negative influence. The three sub levels of Theoretical Perspectives help us to better understand how sociologists go about crafting their theories, and how they will experiment to attempt to prove them.

FUNCTIONALISM

Functionalism is the oldest, and still the dominant, theoretical perspective in sociology and many other social sciences. This perspective is built upon twin emphases: application of the scientific method to the objective social world and use of an analogy between the individual organism and society.

The emphasis on scientific method leads to the assertion that one can study the social world in the same ways as one studies the physical world. Thus, Functionalists see the social world as "objectively real" as observable with such techniques as social surveys and interviews. Furthermore, their positivistic view of social science assumes that study of the social world can be value-free, in that the investigator's values will not necessarily interfere with the disinterested search for social laws governing the behaviour of social systems. Many of these ideas go back to Emile Durkheim, the great French sociologist whose writings form the basis for functionalist theory;

Durkheim was himself one of the first sociologists to make use of scientific and statistical techniques in sociological research. The second emphasis, on the organic unity of society, leads functionalists to speculate about needs which must be met for a social system to exist, as well as the ways in which social institutions satisfy those needs. A functionalist might argue, for instance, that every society will have a religion, because religious institutions have certain functions which contribute to the survival of the social system as a whole, just as the organs of the body have functions which are necessary for the body's survival.

This analogy between society and an organism focuses attention on the homeostatic nature of social systems: social systems work to maintain equilibrium and to return to it after external shocks disturb the balance among social institutions. Such social equilibrium is achieved, most importantly, through the socialization of members of the society into the basic values and norms of that society, so that consensus is reached. Where socialization is insufficient for some reason to create conformity to culturally appropriate roles and socially supported norms, various social control mechanisms exist to restore conformity or to segregate the nonconforming individuals from the rest of society. These social control mechanisms range from sanctions imposed informally—sneering and gossip, for example—to the activities of certain formal organizations, like schools, prisons, and mental institutions.

You might notice some similarities between the language used by functionalists and the jargon of "systems theorists" in computer science or biology. Society is viewed as a system of interrelated parts, a change in any part affecting all the others. Within the boundaries of the system, feedback loops and exchanges among the parts ordinarily lead to homeostasis. Most changes are the result of natural growth or of evolution, but other changes occur when outside forces impinge upon the system. A thoroughgoing functionalist, such as Talcott Parsons, the best-known American sociologist of the 1950s and 60s, conceptualizes society as a collection of systems within systems: the personality system within the small-group system within the community system within society even viewed the whole world as a system of societies. Functionalist analyses often focus on the individual, usually with the intent to show how individual behaviour is molded by broader social forces. Functionalists tend to talk about individual actors as decision-makers, although some critics have suggested that functionalist theorists are, in effect, treating individuals either as puppets, whose decisions are a predictable result of their location in the social structure and of the norms and expectations they have internalized, or sometimes as virtual prisoners of the explicit social control techniques society imposes.

In any case, functionalists have tended to be less concerned with the ways in which individuals can control their own destiny than with the ways in which the limits imposed by society make individual behaviour scientifically predictable. Robert Merton, another prominent functionalist, has proposed a number of important distinctions to avoid potential weaknesses and clarify ambiguities in the basic perspective. First, he distinguishes between manifest and latent functions: respectively, those which are recognized and intended by actors in the social system and hence may represent motives for their actions, and those which are unrecognized and, thus, unintended by the actors.

Second, he distinguishes between consequences which are positively functional for a society, those which are dysfunctional for the society, and those which are neither. Third, he distinguishes between levels of society, that is, the specific social units for which regularized patterns of behaviour are functional or dysfunctional.

Finally, he concedes that the particular social structures which satisfy functional needs of society are not indispensable, but that structural alternatives may exist which can also satisfy the same functional needs. Functionalist theories have very often been criticized as teleological, that is, reversing the usual order of cause and effect by explaining things in terms of what happens afterward, not what went before. A strict functionalist might explain certain religious practices, for instance, as being functional by contributing to a society's survival; however, such religious traditions will usually have been firmly established long before the question is finally settled of whether the society as a whole will actually survive.

Bowing to this kind of criticism of the basic logic of functionalist theory, most current sociologists have stopped using any explicitly functionalistic explanations of social phenomena, and the extreme version of functionalism expounded by Talcott Parsons has gone out of fashion. Nevertheless, many sociologists continue to expect that by careful, objective scrutiny of social phenomena they will eventually be able to discover the general laws of social behaviour, and this hope still serves as the motivation for a great deal of sociological thinking and research.

SYMBOLIC INTERACTIONISM

Symbolic interactionism, or interactionism for short, is one of the major theoretical perspectives in sociology. This perspective has a long intellectual history, beginning with the German sociologist and economist, Max Weber and the American philosopher, George H. Mead, both of whom emphasized the subjective meaning of human behaviour, the social process, and pragmatism.

Although there are a number of versions of interactionist thought, some deriving from phenomenological writings by philosophers, the following description offers a simplified amalgamation of these ideas, concentrating on points of convergence. Herbert Blumer, who studied with Mead at the University of Chicago, is responsible for coining the term, "symbolic interactionism," as well as for formulating the most prominent version of the theory. Interactionists focus on the subjective aspects of social life, rather than on objective, macro-structural aspects of social systems. One reason for this focus is that interactionists base their theoretical perspective on their image of humans, rather than on their image of society. For interactionists, humans are pragmatic actors who continually must adjust their behaviour to the actions of other actors. We can adjust to these actions only because we are able to interpret them, *i.e.*, to denote them symbolically and treat the actions and those who perform them as symbolic objects. This process of adjustment is aided by our ability to imaginatively rehearse alternative lines of action before we act.

The process is further aided by our ability to think about and to react to our own actions and even our selves as symbolic objects. Thus, the interactionist theorist sees humans as active, creative participants who construct their social world, not as passive, conforming objects of socialization. For the interactionist, society consists of organized and patterned interactions among individuals. Thus, research by interactionists focuses on easily observable face-to-face interactions rather than on macro-level structural relationships involving social institutions.

Furthermore, this focus on interaction and on the meaning of events to the participants in those events shifts the attention of interactionists away from stable norms and values towards more changeable, continually readjusting social processes. Whereas for functionalists socialization creates stability in the social system, for interactionists negotiation among members of society creates temporary, socially constructed relations which remain in constant flux, despite relative stability in the basic framework governing those relations.

These emphases on symbols, negotiated reality, and the social construction of society lead to an interest in the roles people play. Erving Goffman, a prominent social theorist in this tradition, discusses roles dramaturgically, using an analogy to the theater, with human social behaviour seen as more or less well scripted and with humans as role-taking actors. Role-taking is a key mechanism of interaction, for it permits us to take the other's perspective, to see what our actions might mean to the other actors with whom we interact. At other times, interactionists emphasize the improvisational quality of roles, with human social behaviour seen as poorly scripted and with humans as role-making improvisers. Role-making, too, is a key mechanism of interaction, for all situations and roles are inherently ambiguous, thus requiring us to create those situations and roles to some extent before we can act. Ethnomethodology, an offshoot of symbolic interactionism, raises the question of how people who are interacting with each other can create the illusion of a shared social order even when they don't understand each other fully and in fact have different points of view.

Harold Garfinkel, a pioneer in these investigations, demonstrated the problem by sending his students out to perform "experiments in trust, "called breaching experiments, in which they brought ordinary conversations to an abrupt halt by refusing to take for granted that they knew what the other person was saying, and so demanded explanations and then explanations of the explanations. More recently, ethnomethodologist researchers have performed minutely detailed analyses of ordinary conversations in order to reveal the methods by which turn-taking and other conversational maneuvers are managed.

Interactionists tend to study social interaction through participant observation, rather than surveys and interviews. They argue that close contact and immersion in the everyday lives of the participants is necessary for understanding the meaning of actions, the definition of the situation itself, and the process by which actors construct the situation through their interaction. Given this close contact, interactionists could hardly remain free of value commitments, and, in fact, interactionists make explicit use of their values in choosing what to study but strive to be objective in the conduct of their research.

Symbolic interactionists are often criticized by other sociologists for being overly impressionistic in their research methods and somewhat unsystematic in their theories. These objections, combined with the fairly narrow focus of interactionist research on small-group interactions and other social psychological issues, have relegated the interactionist camp to a minority position among sociologists, although a fairly substantial minority.

CONFLICT THEORY

The several social theories that emphasize social conflict

have roots in the ideas of Karl Marx, the great German theorist and political activist. The Marxist, conflict approach emphasizes a materialist interpretation of history, a dialectical method of analysis, a critical stance towards existing social arrangements, and a political programme of revolution or, at least, reform.

The materialist view of history starts from the premise that the most important determinant of social life is the work people are doing, especially work that results in provision of the basic necessities of life, food, clothing and shelter. Marx thought that the way the work is socially organized and the technology used in production will have a strong impact on every other aspect of society. He maintained that everything of value in society results from human labour. Thus, Marx saw working men and women as engaged in making society, in creating the conditions for their own existence.

Marx summarized the key elements of this materialist view of history as follows:

- In the social production of their existence, men inevitably enter into definite relations, which are independent of their will, namely relations of production appropriate to a given stage in the development of their material forces of production. The totality of these relations of production constitutes the economic structure of society, the real foundation, on which arises a legal and political superstructure and to which correspond definite forms of social consciousness. The mode of production of material life conditions the general process of social, political and intellectual life. It is not the consciousness of men that determines their existence, but their social existence that determines their consciousness.

Marx divided history into several stages, conforming to broad patterns in the economic structure of society. The most important stages for Marx's argument were feudalism, capitalism, and socialism. The bulk of Marx's writing is concerned with applying the materialist model of society to capitalism, the stage of economic and social development that Marx saw as dominant in 19th century Europe. For Marx, the central institution of capitalist society is private property, the system by which capital is controlled by a small minority of the population. This arrangement leads to two opposed classes, the owners of capital and the workers, whose only property is their own labour time, which they have to sell to the capitalists. Owners are seen as making profits by paying workers less than their work is worth and, thus, exploiting them.

Economic exploitation leads directly to political oppression, as owners make use of their economic power to gain control of the state and turn it into a servant of bourgeois economic interests. Police power, for instance, is used to enforce property rights and guarantee unfair contracts between capitalist and worker. Oppression also takes more subtle forms: religion serves capitalist interests by pacifying the population; intellectuals, paid directly or indirectly by capitalists, spend their careers justifying and rationalizing the existing social and economic arrangements.

In sum, the economic structure of society molds the superstructure, including ideas and the social institutions that support the class structure of society. Because the dominant or ruling class controls the social relations of production, the dominant ideology in capitalist society is that of the ruling class. Ideology and social institutions, in turn, serve to reproduce and perpetuate the economic class structure. Thus, Marx viewed the exploitative economic arrangements of capitalism as the real foundation upon which the superstructure of social, political, and intellectual consciousness is built. Marx's view of history might seem completely cynical or pessimistic, were it not for the possibilities of change revealed by his method of dialectical analysis. Marx was an optimist. He believed that any stage of history based on exploitative economic arrangements generated within itself the seeds of its own destruction. For instance, feudalism, in which land owners exploited the peasantry, gave rise to a class of town-dwelling merchants, whose dedication to making profits eventually led to the bourgeois revolution and the modern capitalist era. Similarly, the class relations of capitalism will lead inevitably to the next stage, socialism. The class relations of capitalism embody a contradiction: capitalists need workers, and vice versa, but the economic interests of the two groups are fundamentally at odds. Such contradictions mean inherent conflict and instability, the class struggle. Adding to the instability of the capitalist system are the inescapable needs for ever-wider markets and ever-greater investments in capital to maintain the profits of capitalists. Marx expected that the resulting economic cycles of expansion and contraction, together with tensions that will build as the working class gains greater understanding of its exploited position will eventually culminate in a socialist revolution.

Despite this sense of the unalterable logic of history, Marxists see the need for social criticism and for political activity to speed the arrival of socialism, which, not being based on private property, is not expected to involve as many contradictions and conflicts as capitalism. Marxists believe that social theory and political practice are dialectically intertwined, with theory enhanced by political involvement and with political practice necessarily guided by theory. Intellectuals ought, therefore, to engage in praxis, to combine political criticism and political activity. Theory itself is seen as necessarily critical and value-laden, since the prevailing social relations are based upon alienating and dehumanizing exploitation of the labour of the working classes.

Marx's ideas have been applied and reinterpreted by scholars for over a hundred years, starting with Marx's close friend and collaborator, Friedrich Engels, who supported Marx and his family for many years from the profits of the textile factories founded by Engels 'father, while Marx shut himself away in the library of the British Museum. Later, Vladimir I. Lenin, leader of the Russian revolution, made several influential contributions to Marxist theory. In recent years Marxist theory has taken a great variety of forms, notably the world-systems theory proposed by Immanuel Wallerstein and the comparative theory of revolutions put forward by Theda

Skocpol. Marxist ideas have also served as a starting point for many of the modern feminist theorists. Despite these applications, Marxism of any variety is still a minority position among American sociologists.

OTHER CURRENT THEORIES

Feminism

Feminism, though not a unified theory, is among the most influential of current theoretical perspectives. Focusing their analyses on gender inequalities and on the institution of patriarchy, feminists have sought to understand society from the standpoint of women. Feminists have criticized all three of the traditionally dominant theoretical perspectives—functionalism, symbolic interactionism, and conflict theory—as biased towards male points of view.

However, the feminist movement has also had its limitations. Most feminists have been white middle-class women, and feminist literature from the early days of the movement often neglected the concerns of working-class women and women of colour. In recent years, however, some feminists have begun to analyse the ways that race, class, and gender inequalities intersect. For instance, Patricia Hill Collins in her book, Black Feminist Thought, argues that the common experiences of African American women have given them a unique perspective on social theory.

Feminists come in a variety of theoretical stripes. Early feminists divided themselves up into liberal, radical, or socialist camps, depending on their political points of view. Today, many feminist sociologists continue to draw heavily on the conflict theory tradition, while many others have been influenced by symbolic interactionism. A few even call themselves functionalists or rational choice theorists.

Rational Choice and Exchange Theory

Another perspective gaining popularity in recent years is known as Rational Choice Theory. Sociologists in this tradition have drawn heavily on the work of economists and political scientists in their analyses of the ways that economic incentives and other material considerations affect the choices people make. Some of the earliest sociological work of this type was known as Exchange Theory, exemplified in the works of George Homans and Peter Blau. More recently, James S. Coleman, with his monumental book, Foundations of Social Theory, emerged as the leading sociologist in the field. Despite the name "rational choice," much of the sociological work in this tradition has focused on probing the limits of rationality and on devising mathematical models of the conditions needed for maintaining trust and solidarity within a social group.

Phenomenology, Ethnomethodology, Social Construction Theory and Feminist Standpoint Theory

Yet another approach to sociological theory which has been gaining in popularity is Phenomenology. The approach is based on the ideas of German philosopher Edmund Husserl, who insisted that the phenomena we encounter in sensory perceptions are the ultimate source of all knowledge His perspective was brought to the United States by sociologist Alfred Schutz and then was developed further by Harold Garfinkel, whose work on Ethnomethodology was described in the part on Symbolic Interactionism above.

Another important development in phenomenological thinking can be found in the works of Peter Berger and Thomas Luckmann, whose landmark book, The Social Construction of Reality has been widely influential, especially among contemporary feminists. Prominent theorist Dorothy Smith draws heavily on Social Construction Theory, and also the ideas of Garfinkel and others, in her presentation of Feminist Standpoint Theory, arguing that sociological theory as constructed by men gives a distorted picture of women's experiences, and that any theory which ignores the perspectives of women is necessarily incomplete.

Post-Structuralism and Postmodernsim

Finally, Post-Structuralism and Postmodernism, perspectives developed on the French intellectual scene, have had considerable influence on American sociologists in recent years. Derived from both the Marxist tradition and the works of anthropologist Claude Lévi-Strauss—who developed a "structuralist" theory of culture—these theoretical schools seek to account for the apparent disintegration of modern culture over the past several decades. Such as Jacques Derrida and Jean Baudrillard, perhaps the best known is Michel Foucault, a historian and philosopher.

Tracing the historical changes in societal attitudes towards punishment, mental illness, and sexuality, among other topics, he argued that knowledge and power have become inextricably entwined. Foucault stressed the disciplinary nature of power, and argued that scientific discourse as one such discipline may itself need to be questioned. Sociologists in this tradition seek not only to study the world differently, but to make the production of sociological knowledge, and thus our own situatedness within structures of knowledge and power, part of the study. American sociologists influenced by this tradition sometimes call their work Discourse Analysis or Cultural Studies.

Other Individual Theorists

This quick review of the current sociological theories are some major theorists with their own influential perspectives. Jürgen Habermas, a leading German sociologist, Anthony Giddens, a leading British sociologist, and American sociologist Randall Collins are all noted for having constructed theories which synthesize ideas drawn from several theoretical traditions.

For introductory students, the point is not to memorize all these names, but to be aware of the multiple points of view and the often contentious theoretical differences among contemporary sociologists. Sociology is in a theoretical ferment, as sociologists seek new ways to understand the formidable complexity of the social world.

SOCIAL RESEARCH

Social research is the scientific study of society. More

specifically, social research examines a society's attitudes, assumptions, beliefs, trends, stratifications and rules. The scope of social research can be small or large, ranging from the self or a single individual to spanning an entire race or country. Popular topics of social research include poverty, racism, class issues, sexuality, voting behaviour, gender constructs, policing and criminal behaviour.

Social research determines the relationship between one or more variables. For example, sex and income level are variables. Social scientists will look for underlying concepts and cause-and-effect relationships of a social issue. Before even beginning research, scientists must formulate a research question.

For example, a researcher might ask if there is a relationship between a person's sex and his or her income level. Do men have higher incomes than women? Are women most likely to be poor? A third variable, race, can be added to the question. Then the social scientist can pose a research question: Does race and sex affect a person's income level? Social scientists will then collect data, organize and analyse information and create a report of their findings.

People conducting social research must also consider ethics, biases and the reliability and validity of the research they're conducting. They must decide which form of sampling to use, how to measure information, how to analyse data and present their findings. Research can be conducted using surveys, reports, observation, questionnaires, focus groups, historical accounts, personal diaries and census statistics. There are two types of research: qualitative research and quantitative research.

Qualitative research is inductive, meaning the researcher creates hypotheses and abstractions from collected data. Most data is collected via words or pictures and mostly from people. Researchers are interested in how people make sense of their lives and in the research process itself.

Quantitative research is the complete opposite and most often involves numbers and set data. Quantitative data is efficient but focuses only on the end result, not the process itself, as qualitative research does. Quantitative data is precise and is often the result of surveys or questionnaires. Even though social research is most often conducted by social scientists or sociologists, it is an interdisciplinary study crossing into subjects like criminology, the study of crime; politics, the study of power; economics, the study of money and business; psychology, study of the mind; philosophy, study of beliefs and morals; and anthropology, the study of culture.

2

Culture and Society

SOCIAL ISSUES IN THE NEWS

"Cows with Gas" the headline said. In India, cows are considered sacred by that nation's major religion, Hinduism. They are also an important source of milk and fertilizer. It is no surprise that India has almost 300 million cows, the highest number in the world, and that they roam freely in Indian cities and towns. But one problem of this abundance of cows is the methane gas they excrete as they burp and belch.

They emit so much methane that scientists think Indian cows, along with some 180 million sheep and goats, are a significant source of global warming. One reason Indian livestock emit so much methane, aside from their sheer numbers, is that they are underfed and undernourished; better diets would reduce their methane emission. However, India is such a poor country that the prospect of a better diet for livestock remains years away, and the problem of cows with gas will continue for some time to come.

The idea of cows with too much gas, or any gas at all, roaming city streets is probably not very appealing, but cow worship is certainly a part of India's culture. This news story provides just one of many examples of the importance of cultural differences for beliefs and behaviours. Here is a more pleasing example. When you are in love, what can be more natural and enjoyable than kissing? This simple act is the highlight of countless movies and television shows where two people meet each other, often not liking each other at first, but then slowly but surely fall madly in love and have their first magical kiss. What we see on the screen reflects our own interest in kissing. When we reach puberty, many of us yearn for our first kiss. That kiss is as much a part of growing up as almost anything else we can think of, and many of us can remember when, where, and with whom our first kiss occurred. Kissing certainly seems a natural, enjoyable act to most of us, but anthropological evidence indicates it might not be so natural after all.

In societies such as the Balinese and Tinguian of Oceania, the Chewa and Thonga of Africa, and the Siriono of South America, kissing is unknown, as the people there think it is unhealthy and disgusting. When the Thonga first saw Europeans kissing, they retorted, "Look at them-they eat each other's saliva and dirt".

Even in modern societies, kissing is not always considered desirable. Until fairly recently, the Japanese abhorred kissing and did not even have a word for it until they created kissu from the English kiss, and even today older Japanese frown on kissing in public. Reflecting the traditional Japanese view, when Rodin's famous statue The Kiss arrived in Japan in the 1920s as part of a European art show, the Japanese hid it behind a curtain. In other societies, people do kiss, but their type of kissing differs greatly from what we are used to. In one of these, people kiss the mouth and the nose simultaneously, while people in a few other societies kiss only by sucking the lips of their partners.

CULTURE AND THE SOCIOLOGICAL PERSPECTIVE

As this evidence on kissing suggests, what seems to us a very natural, even instinctual act turns out not to be so natural and biological after all. Instead, kissing seems best understood as something we learn to enjoy from our culture, or the symbols, language, beliefs, values, and artifacts that are part of a society.

Because society, Sociology and the Sociological Perspective, refers to a group of people who live in a defined territory and who share a culture, it is obvious that culture is a critical component of any society. If the culture we learn influences our beliefs and behaviours, then culture is a key concept to the sociological perspective. Someone who grows up in the United States differs in many ways, some of them obvious and some of them not so obvious, from someone growing up in China, Sweden, South Korea, Peru, or Nigeria.

Culture influences not only language but the gestures we use when we interact, how far apart we stand from each other when we talk, and the values we consider most important for our children to learn, to name just a few. Without culture, we could not have a society. The profound impact of culture becomes most evident when we examine behaviours or conditions that, like kissing, are normally considered biological in nature. Consider morning sickness and labour pains, both very familiar to pregnant women before and during childbirth, respectively.

These two types of discomfort have known biological causes, and we are not surprised that so many pregnant women experience them. But we would be surprised if the husbands of pregnant women woke up sick in the morning during their wives' pregnancies or experienced severe abdominal pains while their wives gave birth. These men are neither carrying nor delivering a baby, and there is no logical-that is, biological-reason for them to suffer either type of discomfort. And yet anthropologists have discovered several societies in which men about to become fathers experience precisely these symptoms. They are nauseous during their wives' pregnancies, and they experience labour pains while their wives give birth.

The term couvade refers to these symptoms, which do not have any known biological origin. Yet the men feel them nonetheless, because they have learned from their culture that they should feel these types of discomfort. And because they should feel these symptoms, they actually do so. Perhaps their minds are playing tricks on them, but that is often the point of culture. As sociologists William I. and Dorothy Swaine Thomas once pointed out, if things are perceived as real, then they are real in their consequences. These men learn how they should feel as budding fathers, and thus they feel this way.

Unfortunately for them, the perceptions they learn from their culture are real in their consequences. The example of drunkenness further shows how cultural expectations influence a behaviour that is commonly thought to have biological causes. In the United States, when people drink too much alcohol, they become intoxicated and their behaviour changes. Most typically, their inhibitions lower and they become loud, boisterous, and even rowdy. We attribute these changes to alcohol's biological effect as a drug on our central nervous system, and scientists have documented how alcohol breaks down in our body to achieve this effect.

This explanation of alcohol's effect is OK as far as it goes, but it turns out that how alcohol affects our behaviour depends on our culture. In some societies anthropologists have studied, people drink alcohol until they pass out, but they never get loud or boisterous; they might not even appear to be enjoying themselves. In other societies, they drink lots of alcohol and get loud but not rowdy. In some societies, including our own, people lose sexual inhibitions as they drink, but in other societies they do not become more aroused. The anthropological evidence is very clear: alcohol as a drug does affect human behaviour, but culture influences the types of effects that occur. We learn from our culture how to behave when drunk just as we learn how to behave when sobre.

CULTURE VERSUS BIOLOGY

These examples suggest that human behaviour is more the result of culture than it is of biology. This is not to say that biology is entirely unimportant. As just one example, humans have a biological need to eat, and so they do. But humans are much less under the control of biology than any other animal species, including other primates such as monkeys and chimpanzees.

These and other animals are governed largely by biological instincts that control them totally. A dog chases any squirrel it sees because of instinct, and a cat chases a mouse for the same reason. Different breeds of dogs do have different personalities, but even these stem from the biological differences among breeds passed down from one generation to another. Instinct prompts many dogs to turn around before they lie down, and it prompts most dogs to defend their territory. When the doorbell rings and a dog begins barking, it is responding to ancient biological instinct. Because humans have such a large, complex central nervous system, we are less controlled by biology.

The critical question then becomes, how much does biology influence our behaviour? Predictably, scholars in different disciplines answer this question in different ways. Most sociologists and anthropologists would probably say that culture affects behaviour much more than biology does. In contrast, many biologists and psychologists would give much more weight to biology. Advocating a view called sociobiology, some scholars say that several important human behaviours and emotions, such as competition, aggression, and altruism, stem from our biological makeup. Sociobiology has been roundly criticized and just as staunchly defended, and respected scholars continue to debate its premises. Why do sociologists generally favour culture over biology? Two reasons stand out.

First, and as kissing and the other examples show, many behaviours differ dramatically among societies in ways that show the strong impact of culture. Second, biology cannot easily account for why groups and locations differ in their rates of committing certain behaviours. For example, what biological reason could explain why suicide rates west of the Mississippi River are higher than those east of it or why the U.S. homicide rate is so much higher than Canada's? Various aspects of culture and social structure seem much better able than biology to explain these differences.

Many sociologists also warn of certain implications of biological explanations. First, they say, these explanations implicitly support the status quo. Because it is difficult to change biology, any problem with biological causes cannot be easily fixed. Consider evidence that women do worse than men on the math SAT exam and are less likely to be mathematically gifted. Some researchers attribute this difference to women's lower testosterone levels or to their brain structures. Suppose either explanation is true. What, then, can we do to improve women's math SAT scores? Operate on their brains? Give them more testosterone? Obviously either option is morally unethical and practically impossible.

If these are the only options, then there is little hope for improving women's math ability, and gender inequality in math will continue. Suppose instead, as many educators think, that the gender math difference stems from social and cultural factors, including the way girls and boys are brought up, the amount of attention teachers pay to them, and gender stereotyping in children's books. None of these factors will be easy to change, but at least it is more possible to change them than to change biological conditions. Sociology's perspective on gender and math performance thus promises at least some hope in reducing gender inequality in math performance. A second possible implication of biological explanations that concerns some sociologists harkens back to an earlier time.

This was a time when perceived biological differences among races and religions were used to justify forced sterilization and mass violence, including genocide, against certain groups. As just one example, in the early 1900s, some 70,000 people, most of them poor and many of them immigrants or African Americans, were involuntarily sterilized in the United States as part of the eugenics movement, which said that certain kinds of people were biologically inferior and must not be allowed to reproduce.

The Nazi Holocaust a few decades later used a similar eugenics argument to justify its genocide against Jews, Catholics, gypsies, and gays. With this history in mind, some scholars fear that biological explanations of human behaviour might still be used to support views of biological inferiority.

THE ELEMENTS OF CULTURE

Culture was defined earlier as the symbols, language, beliefs, values, and artifacts that are part of any society. As this definition suggests, there are two basic components of culture: ideas and symbols on the one hand and artifacts on the other. The first type, called nonmaterial culture, includes the values, beliefs, symbols, and language that define a society. The second type, called material culture, includes all the society's physical objects, such as its tools and technology, clothing, eating utensils, and means of transportation. These elements of culture are discussed next.

SYMBOLS

Every culture is filled with symbols, or things that stand for something else and that often evoke various reactions and emotions. Some symbols are actually types of nonverbal communication, while other symbols are in fact material objects. As the symbolic interactionist perspective Sociology and the Sociological Perspective emphasizes, shared symbols make social interaction possible. Let's look at nonverbal symbols first. A common one is shaking hands, which is done in some societies but not in others. It commonly conveys friendship and is used as a sign of both greeting and departure. Probably all societies have nonverbal symbols we call gestures, movements of the hand, arm, or other parts of the body that are meant to convey certain ideas or emotions. However, the same gesture can mean one thing in one society and something quite different in another society.

In the United States, for example, if we nod our head up and down, we mean yes, and if we shake it back and forth, we mean no. In Bulgaria, however, nodding means no, while shaking our head back and forth means yes! In the United States, if we make an "O" by putting our thumb and forefinger together, we mean "OK," but the same gesture in certain parts of Europe signifies an obscenity. "Thumbs up" in the United States means "great" or "wonderful," but in Australia it means the same thing as extending the middle finger in the United States. Certain parts of the Middle East and Asia would be offended if they saw you using your left hand to eat, because they use their left hand for bathroom hygiene. Some of our most important symbols are objects. Here the U.S. flag is a prime example. For most Americans, the flag is not just a piece of cloth with red and white stripes and white stars against a field of blue. Instead, it is a symbol of freedom, democracy, and other American values and, accordingly, inspires pride and patriotism. During the Vietnam War, however, the flag became to many Americans a symbol of war and imperialism. Some burned the flag in protest, prompting angry attacks by bystanders and negative coverage by the news media. Other objects have symbolic value for religious reasons. Three of the most familiar religious symbols in many nations are the cross, the Star of David, and the crescent moon, which stand for Christianity, Judaism, and Islam, respectively.

Whereas many cultures attach no religious significance to these shapes, for many people across the world they evoke very strong feelings of religious faith. Recognizing this, hate groups have often desecrated these symbols. As these examples indicate, shared symbols, both nonverbal communication and tangible objects, are an important part of any culture but also can lead to misunderstandings and even hostility. These problems underscore the significance of symbols for social interaction and meaning.

LANGUAGE

Perhaps our most important set of symbols is language. In English, the word chair means something we sit on. In French, the word chaise means the same thing. As long as we agree how to interpret these words, a shared language and thus society are possible. By the same token, differences in languages can make it quite difficult to communicate.

For example, imagine you are in a foreign country where you do not know their language and they do not know yours. Worse yet, you forgot to bring your dictionary that translates their language into yours, and vice versa, and your iPhone battery has died. You become lost. How will you get help? What will you do? Is there any way to communicate your plight? As this scenario suggests, language is crucial to communication and thus to any society's culture. Children learn language from their culture just as they learn about shaking hands, about gestures, and about the significance of the flag and other symbols. Humans have a capacity for language that no other animal species possesses. Our capacity for language in turn helps make our complex culture possible. In the United States, some people consider a common language so important that they advocate making English the official language of certain cities or states or even the whole country and banning bilingual education in the public schools.

Critics acknowledge the importance of English but allege that this movement smacks of anti-immigrant prejudice and would help destroy ethnic subcultures. In 2009, voters in Nashville, Tennessee, rejected a proposal that would have made English the city's official language and required all city workers to speak in English rather than their native language. Language, of course, can be spoken or written. One of the most important developments in the evolution of society was the creation of written language. Some of the preindustrial societies that anthropologists have studied have written language, while others do not, and in the remaining societies the "written" language consists mainly of pictures, not words.

This variation with data from 186 preindustrial societies called the Standard Cross-Cultural Sample, a famous data set compiled several decades ago by anthropologist George Murdock and colleagues from information that had been gathered on hundreds of preindustrial societies around the world. In Figure, we see that only about one-fourth of the SCCS societies have a written language, while about equal proportions have no language at all or only pictures.

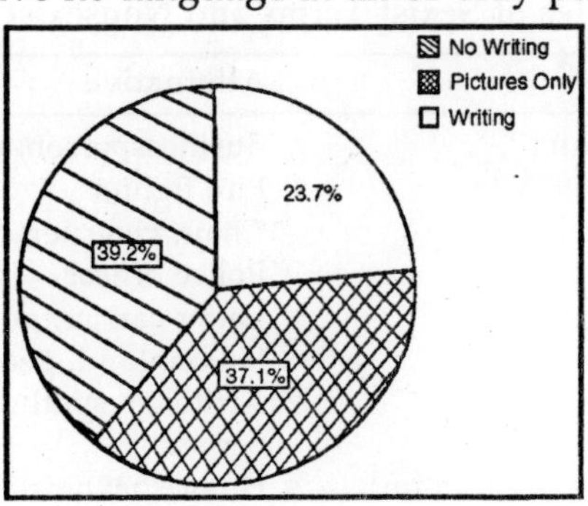

Fig. The Presence of Written Language
(Percentage of Societies)

To what extent does language influence how we think and how we perceive the social and physical worlds? The famous but controversial Sapir-Whorf hypothesis, named after two linguistic anthropologists, Edward Sapir and Benjamin Lee Whorf, argues that people cannot easily understand concepts and objects unless their language contains words for these items. Language thus influences how we understand the world around us. For example, people in a country such as the United States that has many terms for different types of kisses are better able to appreciate these different types than people in a country such as Japan, which, as we saw earlier, only fairly recently developed the word kissu for kiss. Another illustration of the Sapir-Whorf hypothesis is seen in sexist language, in which the use of male nouns and pronouns shapes how we think about the world. In older children's books, words like fireman and mailman are common, along with pictures of men in these jobs, and critics say they send a message to children that these are male jobs, not female jobs. If a teacher tells a second-grade class, "Every student should put his books under his desk" the teacher obviously means students of both sexes but may be sending a subtle message that boys matter more than girls. For these reasons, several guidebooks promote the use of nonsexist language. Table, "Examples of Sexist Terms and Nonsexist Alternatives" provides examples of sexist language and nonsexist alternatives.

Table. Examples of Sexist Terms and Nonsexist Alternatives

Term	Alternative
Businessman	Businessperson, executive
Fireman	Fire fighter
Chairman	Chair, chairperson
Policeman	Police officer
Mailman	Letter carrier, postal worker
Mankind	Humankind, people
Man-made	Artificial, synthetic
Waitress	Server
He (as generic pronoun)	He or she; he/she; s/he
"A professor should be devoted to his students	"Professors should be devoted to their students"

The use of racist language also shows the Sapir-Whorf hypothesis. An old saying goes, "Sticks and stones may break my bones, but names will never hurt me." That may be true in theory but not in reality. Names can hurt, especially names that are racial slurs, which African Americans growing up before the era of the civil rights movement routinely heard. The Sapir-Whorf hypothesis, the use of these words would have affected how whites perceived African Americans. More generally, the use of racist terms may reinforce racial prejudice and racial stereotypes.

NORMS

Cultures differ widely in their norms, or standards and expectations for behaving. We already saw that how people behave when drunk stems from society's expectations of how they should behave when drunk. Norms of drunken behaviour influence how we behave when we drink too much. Norms are often divided into two types, formal norms and informal norms. Formal norms, also called mores and laws, refer to the standards of behaviour considered the most important in any society.

Examples in the United States include traffic laws, criminal codes, and, in a college context, student behaviour codes addressing such things as cheating and hate speech. Informal norms, also called folkways and customs, refer to standards of behaviour that are considered less important but still influence how we behave. Many norms differ dramatically from one culture to the next. Some of the best evidence for cultural variation in norms comes from the study of sexual behaviour. Among the Pokot of East Africa, for example, women are expected to enjoy sex, while among the Gusii a few hundred miles away, women who enjoy sex are considered deviant. In Inis Beag, a small island off the coast of Ireland, sex is considered embarrassing and even disgusting; men feel that intercourse drains their strength, while women consider it a burden. Even nudity is considered terrible, and people on Inis Beag keep their clothes on while they bathe. The situation is quite different in Mangaia, a small island in the South Pacific.

Here sex is considered very enjoyable, and it is the major subject of songs and stories. While many societies frown on homosexuality, others accept it. Among the Azande of East Africa, for example, young warriors live with each other and are not allowed to marry.

During this time, they often have sex with younger boys, and this homosexuality is approved by their culture. Among the Sambia of New Guinea, young males live separately from females and engage in homosexual behaviour for at least a decade. It is felt that the boys would be less masculine if they continued to live with their mothers and that the semen of older males helps young boys become strong and fierce. Other evidence for cultural variation in norms comes from the study of how men and women are expected to behave in various societies. For example, many preindustrial societies are simple hunting and gathering societies. In most of these, men tend to hunt and women tend to gather.

Many observers attribute this gender difference to at least two biological differences between the sexes. First, men tend to be bigger and stronger than women and are thus better suited for hunting. Second, women become pregnant and bear children and are less able to hunt. Yet a different pattern emerges in some hunting and gathering societies. Among a group of Australian aborigines called the Tiwi and a tribal society in the Philippines called the Agta, both sexes hunt. After becoming pregnant, Agta women continue to hunt for most of their pregnancy and resume hunting after their child is born. Some of the most interesting norms that differ by culture govern how people stand apart when they talk with each other.

In the United States, people who are not intimates usually stand about three to four feet apart when they talk. If someone stands more closely to us, especially if we are of northern European heritage, we feel uncomfortable. Yet people in other countries-especially Italy, France, Spain, and many of the nations of Latin America and the Middle East-would feel uncomfortable if they were standing three to four feet apart. To them, this distance is too great and indicates that the people talking dislike each other. If a U.S. native of British or Scandinavian heritage were talking with a member of one of these societies, they might well have trouble interacting, because at least one of them will be uncomfortable with the physical distance separating them.

Rituals

Different cultures also have different rituals, or established procedures and ceremonies that often mark transitions in the life course. As such, rituals both reflect and transmit a culture's norms and other elements from one generation to the next. Initiation and commencement ceremonies in colleges and universities are familiar examples of time-honoured rituals. In many societies, rituals help signify one's gender identity.

For example, girls around the world undergo various types of initiation ceremonies to mark their transition to adulthood. Among the Bemba of Zambia, girls undergo a month-long initiation ceremony called the chisungu, in which girls learn songs, dances, and secret terms that only women know. In some cultures, special ceremonies also mark a girl's first menstrual period.

Such ceremonies are largely absent in the United States, where a girl's first period is a private matter. But in other cultures the first period is a cause for celebration involving gifts, music, and food. Boys have their own initiation ceremonies, some of them involving circumcision. That said, the ways in which circumcisions are done and the ceremonies accompanying them differ widely.

In the United States, boys who are circumcised usually undergo a quick procedure in the hospital. If their parents are observant Jews, circumcision will be part of a religious ceremony, and a religious figure called a moyel will perform the circumcision. In contrast, circumcision among the Maasai of East Africa is used as a test of manhood.

If a boy being circumcised shows signs of fear, he might well be ridiculed. Are rituals more common in preindustrial societies than in modern ones such as the United States? Consider the Nacirema, studied by anthropologist Horace

Miner more than 50 years ago. In this society, many rituals have been developed to deal with the culture's fundamental belief that the human body is ugly and in danger of suffering many diseases. Reflecting this belief, every household has at least one shrine in which various rituals are performed to cleanse the body. Often these shrines contain magic potions acquired from medicine men.

The Nacirema are especially concerned about diseases of the mouth. Miner writes, "Were it not for the rituals of the mouth, they believe that their teeth would fall out, their gums bleed, their jaws shrink, their friends desert them, and their lovers reject them". Many Nacirema engage in "mouth-rites" and see a "holy-mouth-man" once or twice yearly. Spell Nacirema backward and you will see that Miner was describing American culture. As his satire suggests, rituals are not limited to preindustrial societies. Instead, they function in many kinds of societies to mark transitions in the life course and to transmit the norms of the culture from one generation to the next.

Changing Norms and Beliefs

Our examples show that different cultures have different norms, even if they share other types of practices and beliefs. It is also true that norms change over time within a given culture. Two obvious examples here are hairstyles and clothing styles. When the Beatles first became popular in the early 1960s, their hair barely covered their ears, but parents of teenagers back then were aghast at how they looked. If anything, clothing styles change even more often than hairstyles. Hemlines go up, hemlines go down.

Lapels become wider, lapels become narrower. This colour is in, that colour is out. Hold on to your out-of-style clothes long enough, and eventually they may well end up back in style. A more important topic on which norms have changed is abortion and birth control. Despite the controversy surrounding abortion today, it was very common in the ancient world. Much later, medieval theologians generally felt that abortion was not murder if it occurred within the first several weeks after conception. This distinction was eliminated in 1869, when Pope Pius IX declared abortion at any time to be murder. In the United States, abortion was not illegal until 1828, when New York state banned it to protect women from unskilled abortionists, and most other states followed suit by the end of the century.

However, the sheer number of unsafe, illegal abortions over the next several decades helped fuel a demand for repeal of abortion laws that in turn helped lead to the Roe v. Wade Supreme Court decision in 1973 that generally legalized abortion during the first two trimesters. Contraception was also practiced in ancient times, only to be opposed by early Christianity.

Over the centuries, scientific discoveries of the nature of the reproductive process led to more effective means of contraception and to greater calls for its use, despite legal bans on the distribution of information about contraception. In the early 1900s, Margaret Sanger, an American nurse, spearheaded the growing birth-control movement and helped open a birth-control clinic in Brooklyn in 1916. She and two other women were arrested within 10 days, and Sanger and one other defendant were sentenced to 30 days in jail.

Efforts by Sanger and other activists helped to change views on contraception over time, and finally, in 1965, the U.S. Supreme Court ruled in Griswold v. Connecticut that contraception information could not be banned. As this brief summary shows, norms about contraception changed dramatically during the last century. Other types of cultural beliefs also change over time. Since the 1960s, the U.S. public has changed its views about some important racial and gender issues.

The percentage of Americans who would vote for a qualified black person as president rose almost 20 points from the early 1970s to the middle of 1996, when the GSS stopped asking the question. If beliefs about voting for an African American had not changed, Barack Obama would almost certainly not have been elected in 2008. Several years of the GSS, shows that the percentage saying that women should take care of running their homes and leave running the country to men declined from almost 36% in the early 1970s to only about 15% in 1998, again, when the GSS stopped asking the question. Values are another important element of culture and involve judgments of what is good or bad and desirable or undesirable. A culture's values shape its norms. In Japan, for example, a central value is group harmony.

The Japanese place great emphasis on harmonious social relationships and dislike interpersonal conflict. Individuals are fairly unassertive by American standards, lest they be perceived as trying to force their will upon others. When interpersonal disputes do arise, Japanese do their best to minimize conflict by trying to resolve the disputes amicably. Lawsuits are thus uncommon; in one case involving disease and death from a mercury-polluted river, some Japanese who dared to sue the company responsible for the mercury poisoning were considered bad citizens.

Individualism in the United States

In the United States, of course, the situation is quite different. The American culture extols the rights of the individual and promotes competition in the business and sports worlds and in other areas of life. Lawsuits over the most frivolous of issues are quite common and even expected. Phrases like "Look out for number one!" abound.

If the Japanese value harmony and group feeling, Americans value competition and individualism. Because the Japanese value harmony, their norms frown on self-assertion in interpersonal relationships and on lawsuits to correct perceived wrongs. Because Americans value and even thrive on competition, our norms promote assertion in relationships and certainly promote the use of the law to address all kinds of problems. This difference between the two nations' cultures with data from the 2002 World Values Survey which was administered to random samples of the adult populations of more than 80 nations around the world. One question asked in these nations was, "On a scale of one to ten, please indicate your views on competition. "The percentages of Americans and

Japanese who responded with a "one" or "two" to this question, indicating they think competition is very beneficial. Americans are about three times as likely as Japanese to favour competition.

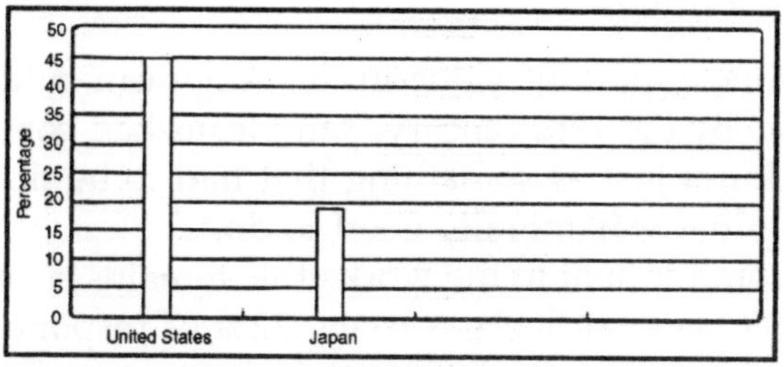

Fig. Percentage That Thinks Competition Is Very Beneficial

The Japanese value system is a bit of an anomaly, because Japan is a modern nation with very traditional influences. Its emphasis on group harmony and community is more usually thought of as a value found in preindustrial societies, while the U.S. emphasis on individuality is more usually thought of as a value found in modern cultures.

Anthropologist David Maybury-Lewis describes this difference as follows: "The heart of the difference between the modern world and the traditional one is that in traditional societies people are a valuable resource and the interrelations between them are carefully tended; in modern society things are the valuables and people are all too often treated as disposable.

"In modern societies, continues Maybury-Lewis, individualism and the rights of the individual are celebrated and any one person's obligations to the larger community are weakened. Individual achievement becomes more important than values such as kindness, compassion, and generosity. Other scholars take a less bleak view of modern society, where they say the spirit of community still lives even as individualism is extolled.

In American society, these two simultaneous values sometimes create tension. In Appalachia, for example, people view themselves as rugged individuals who want to control their own fate. At the same time, they have strong ties to families, relatives, and their neighbours. Thus their sense of independence conflicts with their need for dependence on others.

The Work Ethic

Another important value in the American culture is the work ethic. By the 19th century, Americans had come to view hard work not just as something that had to be done but as something that was morally good to do.

The commitment to the work ethic remains strong today: in the 2008 General Social Survey, 72% of respondents said they would continue to work even if they got enough money to live as comfortably as they would like for the rest of their lives.

Cross-cultural evidence supports the importance of the work ethic in the United States. Using earlier World Values Survey data, The percentage of people in United States and three other nations from different parts of the world-Mexico, Poland, and Japan-who take "a great deal of pride" in their work. More than 85% of Americans feel this way, compared to much lower proportions of people in the other three nations.

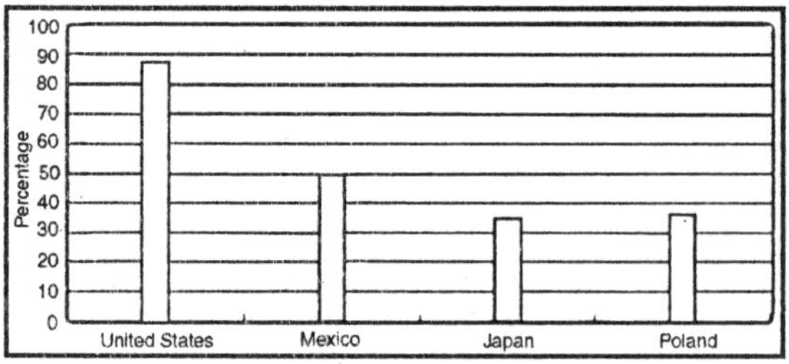

Fig. Percentage of People Who Take a Great Deal of Pride in Their Work

Closely related to the work ethic is the belief that if people work hard enough, they will be successful. Here again the American culture is especially thought to promote the idea that people can pull themselves up by their "bootstraps" if they work hard enough. The WVS asked whether success results from hard work or from luck and connections. The proportions of people in the four nations just examined who most strongly thought that hard work brings success. Once again we see evidence of an important aspect of the American culture, as U.S. residents were especially likely to think that hard work brings success.

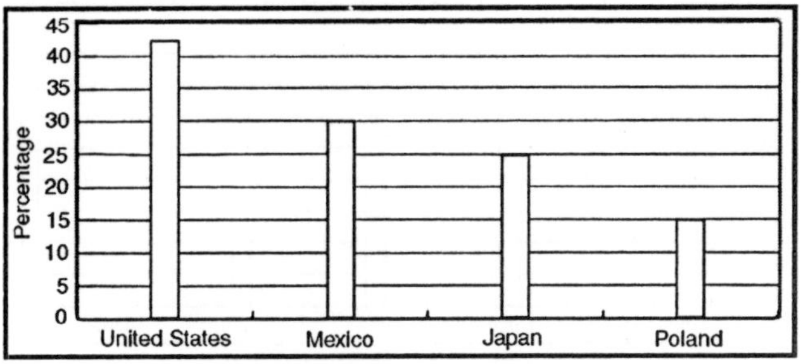

Fig. Percentage of People Who Think Hard Work Brings Success

If Americans value the work ethic and also believe hard work brings success, then they should be more likely than people in most other nations to believe that poverty stems from not working hard enough. True or false, Sociology and the Sociological Perspective.

WVS percentages of respondents who said the most important reason people are poor is due to "laziness and lack of willpower." As expected, Americans are much more likely to attribute poverty to not working hard enough.

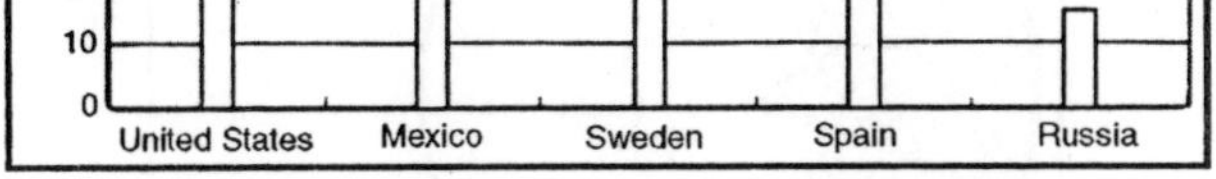

Fig. Percentage of People Who Attribute Poverty to Laziness and Lack of Willpower

We could discuss many other values, but an important one concerns how much a society values employment of women outside the home. The WVS asked respondents whether they agree or disagree that "when jobs are scarce men should have more right to a job than women." U.S. residents are more likely than those in nations with more traditional views of women to disagree with this statement.

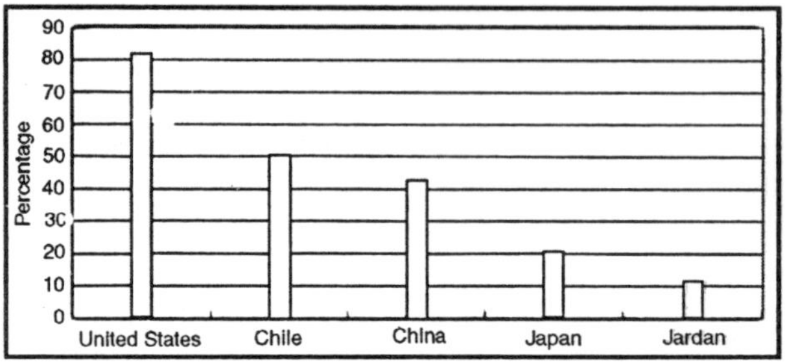

Fig. Percentage of People Who Disagree That Men Have More Right to a Job Than Women When Jobs are Scarce

ARTIFACTS

The last element of culture is the artifacts, or material objects, that constitute a society's material culture. In the most simple societies, artifacts are largely limited to a few tools, the huts people live in, and the clothing they wear. One of the most important inventions in the evolution of society was the wheel. The very few of the societies in the SCCS use wheels to move heavy loads over land, while the majority use human power and about one-third use pack animals.

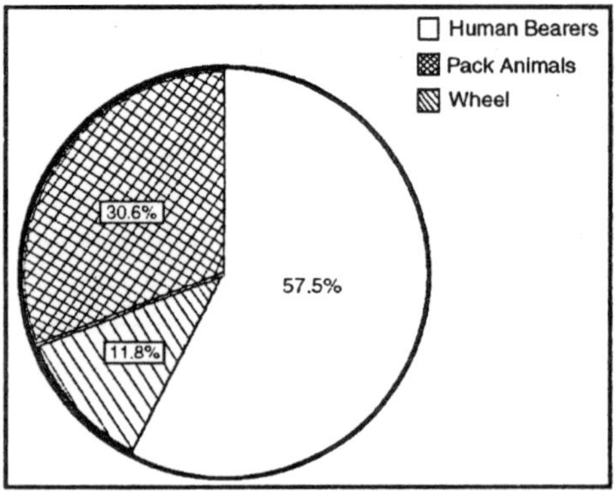

Fig. Primary Means of Moving Heavy Loads

Although the wheel was a great invention, artifacts are obviously much more numerous and complex in modern industrial societies. Because of technological advances during the past two decades, many such societies may be said to have a wireless culture, as smartphones, netbooks and laptops, and GPS devices now dominate so much of modern life.

The artifacts associated with this culture were unknown a generation ago. Technological development created these artifacts and also new language to describe them and the functions they perform. Today's wireless artifacts in turn help reinforce our own commitment to wireless technology as a way of life, if only because children are now growing up with them, often even before they can read and write.

Sometimes people in one society may find it difficult to understand the artifacts that are an important part of another society's culture. If a member of a tribal society who had never seen a cell phone, or who had never even used batteries or electricity, were somehow to visit the United States, she or he would obviously have no idea of what a cell phone was or of its importance in almost everything we do these days.

Conversely, if we were to visit that person's society, we might not appreciate the importance of some of its artifacts. In this regard, consider once again India's cows. People from India consider cows holy, and they let cows roam the streets of many cities. In a nation where hunger is so rampant, such cow worship is difficult to understand, at least to Americans, because a ready source of meat is being ignored.

Anthropologist Marvin Harris advanced a practical explanation for India's cow worship. Millions of Indians are peasants who rely on their farms for their food and thus their existence. Oxen and water buffalo, not tractors, are the way they plow their fields. If their ox falls sick or dies, farmers may lose their farms.

Because, as Harris observes, oxen are made by cows, it thus becomes essential to preserve cows at all costs. In India, cows also act as an essential source of fertilizer, to the tune of 700 million tons of manure annually, about half of which is used for fertilizer and the other half of which is used as fuel for cooking. Cow manure is also mixed with water and used as flooring material over dirt floors in Indian households. For all of these reasons, cow worship is not so puzzling after all, because it helps preserve animals that are very important for India's economy and other aspects of its way of life. If Indians exalt cows, many Jews and Muslims feel the opposite about pigs: they refuse to eat any product made from pigs and so obey an injunction from the Old Testament of the Bible and from the Koran.

Harris thinks this injunction existed because pig farming in ancient times would have threatened the ecology of the Middle East. Sheep and cattle eat primarily grass, while pigs eat foods that people eat, such as nuts, fruits, and especially grains. In another problem, pigs do not provide milk and are much more difficult to herd than sheep or cattle. Next, pigs do not thrive well in the hot, dry climate in which the people of the Old Testament and Koran lived.

Finally, sheep and cattle were a source of food back then because beyond their own meat they provided milk, cheese, and manure, and cattle were also used for plowing. In contrast, pigs would have provided only their own meat. Because sheep and cattle were more "versatile" in all of these ways, and because of the other problems pigs would have posed, it made sense for the eating of pork to be prohibited.

In contrast to Jews and Muslims, at least one society, the Maring of the mountains of New Guinea, is characterized by "pig love." Here pigs are held in the highest regard. The Maring sleep next to pigs, give them names and talk to them, feed them table scraps, and once or twice every generation have a mass pig sacrifice that is intended to ensure the future health and welfare of Maring society.

Harris explains their love of pigs by noting that their climate is ideally suited to raising pigs, which are an important source of meat for the Maring. Because too many pigs would overrun the Maring, their periodic pig sacrifices help keep the pig population to manageable levels. Pig love thus makes as much sense for the Maring as pig hatred did for people in the time of the Old Testament and the Koran.

CULTURAL DIVERSITY

Cultural diversity is the variety of human societies or cultures in a specific region, or in the world as a whole. There is a general consensus among mainstream anthropologists that humans first emerged in Africa about two million years ago. Since then they have spread throughout the world, successfully adapting to widely differing conditions and to periodic cataclysmic changes in local and global climate.

The many separate societies that emerged around the globe differed markedly from each other, and many of these differences persist to this day. As well as the more obvious cultural differences that exist between people, such as language, dress and traditions, there are also significant variations in the way societies organize themselves, in their shared conception of morality, and in the ways they interact with their environment.

By analogy with biodiversity, which is thought to be essential to the long-term survival of life on earth, it can be argued that cultural diversity may be vital for the long-term survival of humanity; and that the conservation of indigenous cultures may be as important to humankind as the conservation of species and ecosystems is to life in general.

The General Conference of UNESCO took this position in 2001"...cultural diversity is as necessary for humankind as biodiversity is for nature "This position is rejected by some people, however, on several grounds. Firstly, like most evolutionary accounts of human nature, the importance of cultural diversity for survival may be an untestable hypothesis, which can neither be proved nor disproved. Secondly, it can be argued that it is unethical deliberately to conserve "less developed" societies, because this will deny people within those societies the benefits of technological and medical advances enjoyed by those of us in the "developed" world.

In the same way it is unethical to promote poverty in underdeveloped nations as cultural diversity it is also unethical to promote all religious practices simply because they contribute to cultural diversity. Particularly, there are some practices that are recognized by the WHO and UN as unethical: Female Genital Mutilation, Sati, polygamy, child brides, human sacrifice, etc. Some individuals, particularly those with strong religious beliefs, maintain that it is in the best interests of individuals and of humanity as a whole that all people adhere to a specific model for society or specific aspects of such a model. For example, evangelical missionary organisations such as the New Tribes Mission actively work to support social changes that some observers would consider detrimental to cultural diversity by seeking out remote tribal societies to convert them to Christianity; and Islamic groups strategically buy up land in Papua New Guinea.

Cultural diversity is tricky to quantify, but a good indication is thought to be a count of the number of languages spoken in a region or in the world as a whole. By this measure, there are signs that we may be going through a period of precipitous decline in the world's cultural diversity. Research carried out in the 1990s by David Crystal suggested that at that time, on average, one language was falling into disuse every two weeks. He calculated that if that rate of language death were to continue, then by the year 2100 more than 90% of the languages currently spoken in the world will have gone extinct. Overpopulation, immigration and imperialism are reasons that have been suggested to explain any such decline.

CULTURAL HERITAGE

The Universal Declaration on Cultural Diversity adopted by UNESCO in 2001 is regarded as a legal instrument recognizing for the first time, cultural diversity as "common heritage of humanity" and considers its safeguarding to be a concrete and ethical imperative inseparable from respect for human dignity.

There is also the Convention for the Safeguarding of the Intangible Cultural Heritage ratified on June 20, 2007 by 78 States which said:

- The intangible cultural heritage, transmitted from generation to generation is constantly recreated by communities and groups in response to their environment, their interaction with nature and their history, and gives them a sense of identity and continuity, thus promoting respect for cultural diversity and human creativity.

Cultural diversity was also promoted by the Montreal Declaration of 2007, and by the European Union. The idea of a global multicultural heritage covers several ideas, which are not exclusive. In addition to language, diversity can also include religious or traditional practice.

DEFENCE

The defence of cultural diversity can take several meanings:

- *A balance to be achieved*: thus, the idea of defence of cultural diversity through the promotion of actions in favour of "cultural minorities" said to be disadvantaged;
- Preservation of "cultural minorities" thought to be endangered;
- In other cases, one speaks of "cultural protection", which refers to the concept of "cultural exception", which is mainly used in France under the title "French exception". This makes the link between the social vision of culture and the vision inherent in its commercialisation. The cultural exception highlights the specificity of cultural products and services, including special recognition by the European Union in its Declaration on Cultural Diversity. In this context, the objective is to defend against what is seen as a "commodification"- considered harmful to a "disadvantaged" culture—supporting its development through grants, promotion operations, etc., also known as "cultural protectionism".
- This defence may also refer to incorporating "cultural rights" provisions, conducted unsuccessfully in the early 1990s in Europe, into a layer of human rights.

Cultural Uniformity

Cultural diversity is presented as the antithesis of cultural uniformity. Some fear this hypothesis of a trend towards cultural uniformity.

To support this argument they emphasize different aspects:

- The disappearance of many languages and dialects, regarding for example the languages of France, without legal status or protection.
- Anxiety of people on the preservation of their traditions as in New Zealand, coastal regions in Australia, North America, Central America;
- Increasing cultural preeminence of the United States through the distribution of its products in film, television, music, clothing and nutritional products promoted in audio-visual media, consumer products virtually standardized on the planet.

There are several international organizations that work towards protecting threatened societies and cultures, including Survival International and UNESCO. The UNESCO Universal Declaration on Cultural Diversity, adopted by 185 Member States in 2001, represents the first international standard-setting instrument aimed at preserving and promoting cultural diversity and intercultural dialogue.

The European Commission-funded Network of Excellence on "Sustainable Development in a Diverse World"builds upon the UNESCO Declaration to investigate the relationship between cultural diversity and sustainable development.

CULTURAL DIVERSITY IN INDIA

Cultural Diversity in India has a history of thousands of years. People have been living in India since the Stone Age. People from different regions of the world came to India. They became one with the Indian culture. From this has evolved the composite Indian Culture. All of us living in different parts of the country are Indians.

Though there is a variety in our languages, literature and art, as Indians, we all are one. It is this diversity which has created a sense of unity among the Indians. This diversity has enriched our social life. Indian Languages: Many languages are spoken in India. Hindi and English are the two languages used in our country. Marathi is the state language of Maharashtra. Festival Celebrations: People such as Hindus,

Muslims, Buddhists, Sikhs, Christians, Jains, and Parsis etc. belonging to different live in India. Different festivals are celebrated in India with lots of joys and happiness. Agriculture is the main occupation in our country.

Many of our festivals are related to agriculture and environment. In Maharashtra, Dassera, Diwalil, Holi in Punjab Baisakhi, in Andhra Pradesh Eruvak Punnam, in Tamil nadu Pongal and in Kerala Onam are celebrated. Ramzaam—Id, Christmas, Buddha Pornima, Samvatsari, and Pateti are also important festivals. What ever religious festival all Indians happily participate in it. They greet one another, It increase the feeling of unity among them. Costumes and food: We find diversity in the clothing and food habits of Indians.

Clothing depends upon the climate, physical feature and traditions of the respective regions. There is diversity in our foods habits too, due to climatic conditions crops and other geographical factors. For e.g. the people of Punjab eat dalroti whereas people living in the coastal areas eat rice and fish. Shelter: In respective of constructions of houses also there is diversity. In the rural areas, many houses have wattle and daub walls.

Some houses have tiled roofs. In areas of heavy rainfall, the houses have slopping roofs. In the places with scanty rains have houses with terraced roofs. In big cities, multistorey buildings are seen. Sports and games: Many kinds of games are played in India since ancient times. We play different games such as tip—cat, chess, wrestling, phugadi, malkhamb, lagori, kabadi and kho-kho.

Modern games are such as hockey and cricket are the two popular games played in India. Sports and games have an important place in out life. They help values like cooperation and solidarity Sport spirit it is more important than winning or losing. Art: Different arts such as dance, handicrafts, painting and sculpture have flourished in India. Since days of old, India had different styles of music. There are two main styles of Indian classical music. They are Hindustani music and Carnatic music. There is much folk music played in India. In India, the tradition of dances is very ancients. We have different variety of folk dances some ancient times; various types of handicrafts have developed in India. The art of painting and sculpture has long tradition. It is originated from the Stone age period. For e.g. Ajanta Ellora caves our country have rich historical heritage. Historical monuments are the wealth of our country. Very few countries in the world have such history and ancients culture.

DEVELOPMENT OF MODERN SOCIETY

Since the origins of sociology during the 19th century, sociologists have tried to understand how and why modern society developed. Part of this understanding involves determining the differences between modern societies and non-modern ones. This stage has already alluded to some of these differences. We look at the development of modern society more closely. One of the key differences between simple and modern societies is the emphasis placed on the community versus the emphasis placed on the individual. As we saw earlier, although community and group commitment remain in modern society, and especially in subcultures like the Amish, in simple societies they are usually the cornerstone of social life. In contrast, modern society is more individualistic and impersonal. Whereas the people in simple societies have close daily ties, in modern societies we have many relationships where we barely know the person. Commitment to the group and community become less important in modern societies, and individualism becomes more important. Sociologist Ferdinand Tönnies long ago characterized these key characteristics of simple and modern societies with the German words Gemeinschaft and Gesellschaft.

Gemeinschaft means human community, and Tönnies said that a sense of community characterizes simple societies, where family, kin, and community ties are quite strong. As societies grew and industrialized and as people moved to cities, Tönnies said, social ties weakened and became more impersonal. Tönnies called this situation a Gesellschaft and found it dismaying. Other sociologists have distinguished societies just as to their type of economy and technology. One of the most useful schemes distinguishes the following types of societies: hunting and gathering, horticultural, pastoral, agricultural, and industrial. Some scholars add a final type, postindustrial, to the end of this list. We now outline the major features of each type in turn. Table, "Summary of Societal Development" summarizes these features.

Table. Summary of Societal Development

Type of Society	Key Characteristics
Hunting and gathering	These are small, simple societies in which people hunt and gather food. Because all people in these societies have few possessions, the societies are fairly galitarian, and the degree of inequality is very low.
Horticultural and pastoral	Horticultural and pastoral societies are larger than hunting and gathering societies. Horticultural societies grow rops with simple tools, while pastoral societies raise livestock. Both types of societies are wealthier than hunting and gathering societies, and they also have more inequality and greater conflict than hunting and gathering societies.
Agricultural	These societies grow great numbers of crops, thanks to the use of plows, oxen, and other devices. Compared to horticultural and pastoral societies, they are wealthier and have a higher degree of conflict and of inequality.
Industrial	Industrial societies feature factories and machines. They are wealthier than agricultural societies and have a greater sense of individualism and a lower degree of inequality.
Postindustrial	These societies feature information technology and service jobs. Higher education is especially important in these societies for economic success.

HUNTING AND GATHERING SOCIETIES

Beginning about 250,000 years ago, hunting and gathering societies are the oldest ones we know of; few of them remain today, partly because modern societies have encroached on their existence. As the name "hunting and gathering" implies, people in these societies both hunt for food and gather plants and other vegetation. They have few possessions other than some simple hunting and gathering equipment.

To ensure their mutual survival, everyone is expected to help find food and also to share the food they find. To seek their food, hunting and gathering peoples often move from place to place. Because they are nomadic, their societies tend to be quite small, often consisting of only a few dozen people. Beyond this simple summary of the type of life these societies lead, anthropologists have also charted the nature of social relationships in them.

One of their most important findings is that hunting and gathering societies are fairly egalitarian. Although men do most of the hunting and women most of the gathering, perhaps reflecting the biological differences between the sexes discussed earlier, women and men in these societies are roughly equal. Because hunting and gathering societies have few possessions, their members are also fairly equal in terms of wealth and power, as virtually no wealth exists.

HORTICULTURAL AND PASTORAL SOCIETIES

Horticultural and pastoral societies both developed about 10,000-12,000 years ago. In horticultural societies, people use a hoe and other simple hand tools to raise crops. In pastoral societies, people raise and herd sheep, goats, camels and other domesticated animals and use them as their major source of food and also, depending on the animal, as a means of transportation.

Some societies are either primarily horticultural or pastoral, while other societies combine both forms. Pastoral societies tend to be at least somewhat nomadic, as they often have to move to find better grazing land for their animals. Horticultural societies, on the other hand, tend to be less nomadic, as they are able to keep growing their crops in the same location for some time. Both types of societies often manage to produce a surplus of food from vegetable or animal sources, respectively, and this surplus allows them to trade their extra food with other societies. It also allows them to have a larger population size than hunting and gathering societies.

Horticultural societies often produced an excess of food that allowed them to trade with other societies and also to have more members than hunting and gathering societies. Accompanying the greater complexity and wealth of horticultural and pastoral societies is greater inequality in terms of gender and wealth than is found in hunting and gathering societies.

In pastoral societies, wealth stems from the number of animals a family owns, and families with more animals are wealthier and more powerful than families with fewer animals. In horticultural societies, wealth stems from the amount of land a family owns, and families with more land are more wealthy and powerful.

One other side effect of the greater wealth of horticultural and pastoral societies is greater conflict. Sharing of food is a key norm in hunting and gathering societies. In horticultural and pastoral societies, however, their wealth, and more specifically their differences in wealth, leads to disputes and even fighting over land and animals. Whereas hunting and gathering peoples tend to be very peaceful, horticultural and pastoral peoples tend to be more aggressive.

AGRICULTURAL SOCIETIES

Agricultural societies developed some 5,000 years ago in the Middle East, thanks to the invention of the plow. When pulled by oxen and other large animals, the plow allowed for much more cultivation of crops than the simple tools of horticultural societies permitted. The wheel was also invented about the same time, and written language and numbers began to be used.

The development of agricultural societies thus marked a watershed in the development of human society. Ancient Egypt, China, Greece, and Rome were all agricultural societies, and India and many other large nations today remain primarily agricultural. We have already seen that the greater food production of horticultural and pastoral societies led them to become larger than hunting and gathering societies and to have more trade and greater inequality and conflict. Agricultural societies continue all of these trends.

First, because they produce so much more food than horticultural and pastoral societies, they often become quite large, with their numbers sometimes reaching into the millions.

Second, their huge food surpluses lead to extensive trade, both within the society itself and with other societies.

Third, the surpluses and trade both lead to degrees of wealth unknown in the earlier types of societies and thus to unprecedented inequality, exemplified in the appearance for the first time of peasants, people who work on the land of rich landowners.

Finally, agricultural societies' greater size and inequality also produce more conflict. Some of this conflict is internal, as rich landowners struggle with each other for even greater wealth and power, and peasants sometimes engage in revolts. Other conflict is external, as the governments of these societies seek other markets for trade and greater wealth. If gender inequality became somewhat greater in horticultural and pastoral societies than in hunting and gathering ones, it became very pronounced in agricultural societies.

An important reason for this is the hard, physically taxing work in the fields, much of it using large plow animals, that characterizes these societies. Then, too, women are often pregnant in these societies, because large families provide more bodies to work in the fields and thus more income.

Because men do more of the physical labour in agricultural societies-labour on which these societies depend-they have acquired greater power over women. In the Standard Cross-Cultural Sample, agricultural societies are much more likely than hunting and gathering ones to believe men should dominate women.

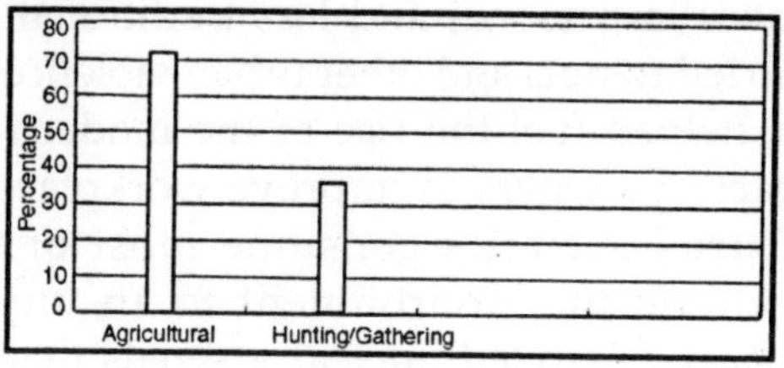

Fig. Type of Society and Presence of Cultural Belief That Men Should Dominate Women

INDUSTRIAL SOCIETIES

Industrial societies emerged in the 1700s as the development of machines and then factories replaced the plow and other agricultural equipment as the primary mode of production. The first machines were steam- and water-powered, but eventually, of course, electricity became the main source of power. The growth of industrial societies marked such a great transformation in many of the world's societies that we now call the period from about 1750 to the late 1800s the Industrial Revolution.

This revolution has had enormous consequences in almost every aspect of society, some for the better and some for the worse. On the positive side, industrialization brought about technological advances that improved people's health and expanded their life spans. As noted earlier, there is also a greater emphasis in industrial societies on individualism, and people in these societies typically enjoy greater political freedom than those in older societies.

Compared to agricultural societies, industrial societies also have lower economic and gender inequality. In industrial societies, people do have a greater chance to pull themselves up by their bootstraps than was true in earlier societies, and "rags to riches" stories continue to show the opportunity available under industrialization. On the negative side, industrialization meant the rise and growth of large cities and concentrated poverty and degrading conditions in these cities, as the novels of Charles Dickens poignantly remind us.

This urbanization changed the character of social life by creating a more impersonal and less traditional Gesellschaft society. It also led to riots and other urban violence that, among other things, helped fuel the rise of the modern police force and forced factory owners to improve workplace conditions. Today industrial societies consume most of the world's resources, pollute the environment to an unprecedented degree, and have compiled nuclear arsenals that could undo thousands of years of human society in an instant.

POSTINDUSTRIAL SOCIETIES

We are increasingly living in what has been called the information technology age as wireless technology vies with machines and factories as the basis for our economy. Compared to industrial economies, we now have many more service jobs, ranging from housecleaning to secretarial work to repairing computers. Societies in which this is happening are moving from an industrial to a postindustrial phase of development.

In postindustrial societies, then, information technology and service jobs have replaced machines and manufacturing jobs as the primary dimension of the economy. If the car was the sign of the economic and social times back in the 1920s, then the smartphone or netbook/laptop is the sign of the economic and social future in the early years of the 21st century.

If the factory was the dominant workplace at the beginning of the 20th century, with workers standing at their positions by conveyor belts, then cell phone, computer, and software companies are dominant industries at the beginning of the 21st century, with workers, almost all of them much better educated than their earlier factory counterparts, huddled over their wireless technology at home, at work, or on the road. In short, the Industrial Revolution has been replaced by the Information Revolution, and we now have what has been called an information society. As part of postindustrialization in the United States, many manufacturing companies have moved their operations from U.S. cities to overseas sites.

Since the 1980s, this process has raised unemployment in cities, many of whose residents lack the college education and other training needed in the information sector. Partly for this reason, some scholars fear that the information age will aggravate the disparities we already have between the "haves" and "have-nots" of society, as people lacking a college education will have even more trouble finding gainful employment than they do now. In the international arena, postindustrial societies may also have a leg up over industrial or, especially, agricultural societies as we move ever more into the information age.

IMPORTANT POINTS

- Culture involves the symbols, language, norms, values, and artifacts that characterize any society and that shape the thoughts, behaviours, and attitudes of the members of the society.
- Scholars continue to debate the relative importance of biology and culture for human behaviour. Sociologists favour culture over biology for several reasons, including the cultural variations existing around the world, the inability of biological explanations to account for many differences in groups' rates of behaviour, and the support of biological explanations of behaviour for the status quo.
- Symbols are an important part of culture and help members of a society interact. They include both objects and nonverbal means of communication. Failure to understand the meanings of symbols can make it difficult to interact.
- Language is another important element of culture and fundamental to communication. If the Sapir-

Whorf hypothesis is correct, language shapes the thoughts and perceptions of society's members.

- A culture's norms and values influence how people behave. When we look around the world, we see several dramatic illustrations of cross-cultural variation in norms and values. In Japan, for example, harmony is a central value, while in the United States individualism and competition prevail.
- Artifacts are the final element of culture and may prove puzzling to people outside a given culture. However, artifacts often make much sense from the perspective of the people living amid a given culture.
- Cultural relativism and ethnocentrism are two sides of the same coin in the issue of cultural diversity. Many societies have cultural practices that may surprise and even dismay us, and it's often difficult to decide whether we should accept or instead condemn these practices.
- As societies moved beyond the hunting and gathering stage, they became larger and more impersonal and individualistic and were characterized by increasing inequality and conflict.
- Hunting and gathering societies developed about 250,000 years ago. In these societies, people share the food they have, and an ethos of cooperation prevails. Women and men are fairly equal, and little economic inequality exists because these societies have so little to begin with.
- Horticultural and pastoral societies developed about 10,000-12,000 years ago. Horticultural societies depend on the hoe and other simple tools to cultivate fields, while pastoral societies raise grazing animals. The surplus of food in these societies prompts some trade with other societies and increases inequality within their own societies.
- Agricultural societies developed about 5,000 years ago after the invention of the plow and other devices that allowed them to raise crops in unprecedented

amounts. Their huge food surpluses lead to very large societies, increased trade with other societies, and extreme degrees of inequality.

- Industrial societies developed about 250 years ago after several inventions allowed work to become more mechanized. The Industrial Revolution has had important consequences, some good and some bad, in virtually every area of society.
- Postindustrial societies have begun in the last few decades with the advent of the computer and an increasing number of service jobs. While it's too soon to know the consequences of the advent of postindustrialization, there are signs it will have important implications for the nature of work and employment in modern society.

3

Socialization and Social Interaction

THE IMPORTANCE OF SOCIALIZATION

Being socialized is an important part of a happy life for any person, and dogs are no different. Humans can adapt easily to different situations throughout life, but dogs aren't that pliable. They critical time for their development is in the first 4 months of life. Their experiences in this period will literally affect the rest of their lives.

The best way to avoid having a dog with issues is to expose them to as many stimuli as possible during this time and to minimize any negative stimuli. The easiest way to expose your puppy to stimuli is to simply get them out into the world. Many people worry about letting out puppies with out all their shots, but you can solve this problem by controlling their exposure.

Let only immunized dogs play with them, and don't take them to any public dog runs. It's also great to let plenty of people and children of all types to pet your puppy. This gets the little one used to all kinds of humans which makes for an easy-going dog later in life. It is equally important to minimize negative stimuli. Most importantly, never spank your puppy. If you want to discipline them, clap your hands to startle them when they're doing something wrong. Also make use of pee pads and deterrent sprays to help the house breaking process. You shouldn't hit them or let anyone else strike them unless you want a dog that fears humans later in life.

EXPLAINING SOCIALIZATION

Because socialization is so important, scholars in various fields have tried to understand how and why it occurs, with different scholars looking at different aspects of the process. Their efforts mostly focus on infancy, childhood, and adolescence, which are the critical years for socialization, but some have also looked at how socialization continues through the life course. Let's examine some of the major theories of socialization, which are summarized in Table, "Theory Snapshot".

Table. Theory Snapshot

Theory	Major Figure(s)	Major Assumptions
Looking-glass self	Charles Horton Cooley	Children gain an impression of how people perceive them as the children interact with them. In effect, children "see" themselves when they interact with other people, as if they are looking in a mirror. Individuals use the perceptions that others have of them to develop judgments and feelings about themselves.
Taking the role of the other	George Herbert Mead	Children pretend to be other people in their play and in so doing learn what these other people expect of them. Younger children take the role of significant others, or the people, most typically parents and siblings, who have the most contact with

		them; older children when they play sports and other games take on the roles of other people and internalize the expectations of the generalized other, or society itself.
Psychoanalytic	Sigmund Freud	The personality consists of the id, ego, and superego. If a child does not develop normally and the superego does not become strong enough to overcome the id, antisocial behaviour may result.
Cognitive development	Jean Piaget	Cognitive development occurs through four stages. The final stage is the formal operational stage, which begins at age 12 as children begin to use general principles to resolve various problems.
Moral development	Lawrence Kohlberg, Carol Gilligan	Children develop their ability to think and act morally through several stages. If they fail to reach the conventional stage, in which adolescents realise that their parents and society have rules that should be followed because they are morally right to

		follow, they might well engage in harmful behaviour. Whereas boys tend to use formal rules to decide what is right or wrong, girls tend to take personal relationships into account.
Identity development	Erik Erikson	Identity development encompasses eight stages across the life course. The fifth stage occurs in adolescence and is especially critical because teenagers often experience an identity crisis as they move from childhood to adulthood.

SOCIOLOGICAL EXPLANATIONS: THE DEVELOPMENT OF THE SELF

One set of explanations, and the most sociological of those we discuss, looks at how the self, or one's identity, self-concept, and self-image, develops. These explanations stress that we learn how to interact by first interacting with others and that we do so by using this interaction to gain an idea of who we are and what they expect of us.

Charles Horton Cooley

Among the first to advance this view was Charles Horton Cooley, who said that by interacting with other people we gain an impression of how they perceive us. In effect, we "see" ourselves when we interact with other people, as if we are looking in a mirror when we are with them. Cooley developed his famous concept of the looking-glass self to summarize this process. Cooley said we first imagine how we appear to others and then imagine how they think of us and, more specifically, whether they are evaluating us positively or negatively. We then use these perceptions to develop judgments and feelings about ourselves, such as pride or embarrassment. Sometimes errors occur in this complex process, as we may misperceive how others regard us and develop misguided judgments of our behaviour and feelings.

For example, you may have been in a situation where someone laughed at what you said, and you thought they were mocking you, when in fact they just thought you were being funny. Although you should have interpreted their laughter positively, you interpreted it negatively and probably felt stupid or embarrassed.

Whether errors occur or not, the process Cooley described is especially critical during childhood and adolescence, when our self is still in a state of flux. Imagine how much better children on a sports team feel after being cheered for making a great play or how children in the school band feel after a standing ovation at the end of the band's performance. If they feel better about themselves, they may do that much better next time. For better or worse, the reverse is also true. If children do poorly on the sports field or in a school performance and the applause they hoped for does not occur, they may feel dejected and worse about themselves and from frustration or anxiety perform worse the next time around. Yet it is also true that the looking-glass-self process affects us throughout our lives.

By the time we get out of late adolescence and into our early adult years, we have very much developed our conception of our self, yet this development is never complete. As young, middle-aged, or older adults, we continue to react to our perceptions of how others are viewing us, and these perceptions influence our conception of our self, even if this influence is often less than was true in our younger years. Whether our social interaction is with friends, relatives, coworkers, supervisors, or even strangers, our self continues to change.

George Herbert Mead

Another scholar who discussed the development of the

self was George Herbert Mead, Sociology and the Sociological Perspective. Mead's main emphasis was on children's playing, which he saw as central to their understanding of how people should interact. When they play, Mead said, children take the role of the other. This means they pretend to be other people in their play and in so doing learn what these other people expect of them.

For example, when children play house and pretend to be their parents, they treat their dolls the way they think their parents treat them. In so doing, they get a better idea of how they are expected to behave. Another way of saying this is that they internalize the expectations other people have of them. Younger children, said Mead, take the role of significant others, or the people, most typically parents and siblings, who have the most contact with them.

Older children take on the roles of other people and learn society's expectations as a whole. In so doing they internalize the expectations of what Mead called the generalized other, or society itself. This whole process, Mead wrote, involves several stages. In the imitation stage, infants can only imitate behaviour without really understanding its purposes. If their parents rub their own bellies and laugh, 1-year-olds may do likewise.

After they reach the age of 3, they are in the play stage. Here most of their play is by themselves or with only one or two other children, and much of it involves pretending to be other people: their parents, teachers, superheroes, television characters, and so forth. In this stage they begin taking the role of the other. Once they reach age 6 or 7, or roughly the time school begins, the games stage begins, and children start playing in team sports and games.

The many players in these games perform many kinds of roles, and they must all learn to anticipate the actions of other members of their team. In so doing, they learn what is expected of the roles all team members are supposed to play and by extension begin to understand the roles society wants us to play, or to use Mead's term, the expectations of the generalized other. Mead felt that the self has two parts, the "I" and the "me".

"The "I" is the creative, spontaneous part of the self, while the "me" is the more passive part of the self stemming from the internalized expectations of the larger society. These two parts are not at odds, he thought, but instead complement each other and thus enhance the individual's contributions to society. Society needs creativity, but it also needs at least some minimum of conformity. The development of both these parts of the self is important not only for the individual but also for the society to which the individual belongs.

SOCIAL-PSYCHOLOGICAL EXPLANATIONS

A second set of explanations is more psychological, as it focuses on the development of personality, cognitive ability, and morality.

Sigmund Freud and the Unconscious Personality

Whereas Cooley and Mead focused on interaction with others in explaining the development of the self, the great psychoanalyst Sigmund Freud focused on unconscious, biological forces that he felt shape individual personality. Freud thought that the personality consists of three parts: the id, the ego, and the superego.

The id is the selfish part of the personality and consists of biological instincts that all babies have, including the need for food and, more generally, the demand for immediate gratification. As babies get older, they learn that not all their needs can be immediately satisfied and thus develop the ego, or the rational part of the personality.

As children get older still, they internalize society's norms and values and thus begin to develop their superego, which represents society's conscience. If a child does not develop normally and the superego does not become strong enough, the individual is more at risk for being driven by the id to commit antisocial behaviour. Freud's basic view that an individual's personality and behaviour develop from within conflicts with sociology's emphasis on the social environment. That is not to say his view is wrong, but it is to say that it neglects the many very important influences highlighted by sociologists. In another problem, Freud's views on women reflected the sexism of the Victorian era in which he lived. He thought that having and raising babies was women's natural, desired role in life and that women who desired careers were mentally ill because they had not adjusted to this role. Freud's views on women were heavily criticized by the contemporary women's movement at its outset in the 1960s.

Piaget and Cognitive Development

Children acquire a self and personality, but they also learn how to think and reason. The way they acquire such cognitive development was the focus of research by Swiss psychologist Jean Piaget. Piaget thought that cognitive development occurs through four stages and that proper maturation of the brain and socialization were necessary for adequate development. The first stage is the sensorimotor stage, in which infants cannot really think or reason and instead use their hearing, vision, and other senses to discover the world around them. The second stage is the preoperational stage, lasting from about age 2 to age 7, in which children begin to use symbols, especially words, to understand objects and simple ideas.

The third stage is the concrete operational stage, lasting from about age 7 to age 11 or 12, in which children begin to think in terms of cause and effect but still do not understand underlying principles of fairness, justice, and related concepts. The fourth and final stage is the formal operational stage, which begins about the age of 12. Here children begin to think abstractly and use general principles to resolve various problems.

Recent research supports Piaget's emphasis on the importance of the early years for children's cognitive development. Scientists have found that brain activity develops rapidly in the earliest years of life, and that stimulation from a child's social environment enhances this development. Conversely, a lack of stimulation impairs it, and children whose parents or other caregivers routinely play with them and talk, sing, and read to them have much better neurological and cognitive development than other children.

By providing a biological basis for the importance of human stimulation for children, this research underscores both the significance of interaction and the dangers of social isolation. For both biological and social reasons, socialization is not fully possible without extensive social interaction.

Kohlberg, Gilligan, and Moral Development

An important part of children's reasoning is their ability to distinguish right from wrong and to decide on what is morally correct to do. Psychologist Lawrence Kohlberg said that children develop their ability to think and act morally through several stages. In the preconventional stage, young children equate what is morally right simply to what keeps them from getting punished.

In the conventional stage, adolescents realise that their parents and society have rules that should be followed because they are morally right to follow, not just because disobeying them leads to punishment. At the postconventional stage, which occurs in late adolescence and early adulthood, individuals realise that higher moral standards may supersede those of their own society and even decide to disobey the law in the name of these higher standards.

If people fail to reach at least the conventional stage, Kohlberg said, they do not develop a conscience and instead might well engage in harmful behaviour if they think they will not be punished. Incomplete moral development, Kohlberg concluded, was a prime cause of antisocial behaviour. One problem with Kohlberg's research was that he studied only boys. That raises the question of whether girls go through similar stages of moral development. Carol Gilligan concluded that they do not. Whereas boys tend to use formal rules to decide what is right or wrong, she wrote, girls tend to take personal relationships into account.

If people break a rule because of some important personal need or because they are trying to help someone, then their behaviour may not be wrong. To use other terminology, males tend to use impersonal, universalistic criteria for moral decision making, whereas females tend to use more individual, particularistic criteria. An example from children's play may show the difference between these two forms of moral reasoning. If boys are playing a sport, say basketball, and a player says he was fouled, they may disagree-sometimes heatedly-over how much contact occurred and whether it indeed was enough to be a foul. In contrast, girls in a similar situation may decide in the interest of having everyone get along to call the play a "do-over."

ERIKSON AND IDENTITY DEVELOPMENT

We noted earlier that the development of the self is not limited to childhood but instead continues throughout the life span. More generally, although socialization is most important during childhood and adolescence, it, too, continues throughout the life span.

Psychologist Erik Erikson explicitly recognized this central fact in his theory of identity development. This sort of development, he said, encompasses eight stages of life across the life course. In the first four stages, occurring in succession from birth to age 12, children ideally learn trust, self-control, and independence and also learn how to do tasks whose complexity increases with their age. If all this development goes well, they develop a positive identity, or self-image.

The fifth stage occurs in adolescence and is especially critical, said Erikson, because teenagers often experience an identity crisis. This crisis occurs because adolescence is a transition between childhood and adulthood: adolescents are leaving childhood but have not yet achieved adulthood. As they try to work through all the complexities of adolescence, teenagers may become rebellious at times, but most eventually enter young adulthood with their identities mostly settled.

Stages 6, 7, and 8 involve young adulthood, middle adulthood, and late adulthood, respectively. In each of these stages, people's identity development is directly related to their family and work roles. In late adulthood, people reflect on their lives while trying to remain contributing members of society. Stage 8 can be a particularly troubling stage for many people, as they realise their lives are almost over.

AGENTS OF SOCIALIZATION

Several institutional and other sources of socialization exist and are called agents of socialization. The first of these, the family, is certainly the most important agent of socialization for infants and young children.

THE FAMILY

Should parents get the credit when their children turn out to be good kids and even go on to accomplish great things in life? Should they get the blame if their children turn out to be bad? No parent deserves all the credit or blame for their children's successes and failures in life, but the evidence indicates that our parents do affect us profoundly. In many ways, we even end up resembling our parents in more than just appearance.

The reason we turn out much like our parents, for better or worse, is that our families are such an important part of our socialization process. When we are born, our primary caregivers are almost always one or both of our parents. For several years we have more contact with them than with any other adults. Because this contact occurs in our most formative years, our parents'interaction with us and the messages they teach us can have a profound impact throughout our lives, as indicated by the stories of Sarah Patton Boyle and Lillian Smith presented earlier.

The ways in which our parents socialize us depend on many factors, two of the most important of which are our parents'social class and our own biological sex. Melvin Kohn found that working-class and middle-class parents tend to socialize their children very differently. Kohn reasoned that working-class parents tend to hold factory and other jobs in which they have little autonomy and instead are told what to do and how to do it. In such jobs, obedience is an important value, lest the workers be punished for not doing their jobs correctly. Working-class parents, Kohn thought, should thus emphasize obedience and respect for authority as they raise their children, and they should favour spanking as a primary way of disciplining their kids when they disobey. In contrast, middle-class parents tend to hold white-collar jobs where autonomy and independent judgment are valued and workers get ahead by being creative. These parents should emphasize independence as they raise their children and should be less likely than working-class parents to spank their kids when they disobey.

Sociology Making a Difference

Understanding Racial Socialization

In a society that is still racially prejudiced, African American parents continue to find it necessary to teach their children about African American culture and to prepare them for the bias and discrimination they can expect to encounter. Scholars in sociology and other disciplines have studied this process of racial socialization. One of their most interesting findings is that African American parents differ in the degree of racial socialization they practice: some parents emphasize African American identity and racial prejudice to a considerable degree, while other parents mention these topics to their children only minimally.

The reasons for these differences have remained unclear. Sociologist Jason E. Shelton analysed data from a national random sample of African Americans to determine these reasons, in what he called "one of the most comprehensive analyses to date of racial socialization strategies among African Americans". Among other questions, respondents were asked whether "in raising your children, have you done or told them things to help them know what it means to be Black.

"They were also asked whether" there are any other things you've done or told your children to help them know how to get along with White people. "In his major results, Shelton found that respondents were more likely to practice racial socialization if they were older, female, and living outside the South; if they perceived that racial discrimination was a growing problem and were members of civil rights and other organizations aimed at helping African Americans; and if they had higher incomes.

These results led Shelton to conclude that "African Americans are not a culturally monolithic group, "as they differ in" the parental sessions they impart to their children about race relations". Further, the parents who do practice racial socialization "do so in order to demystify and empower their offspring to seize opportunities in the larger society".

Shelton's study helps us to understand the factors accounting for differences in racial socialization by African American parents, and it also helps us understand that the parents who do attempt to make their children aware of U.S. race relations are merely trying, as most parents do, to help their children get ahead in life. By increasing our understanding of these matters, Shelton's research has helped make a difference.

If parents' social class influences how they raise their children, it is also true that the sex of their children affects how they are socialized by their parents. Many studies find that parents raise their daughters and sons quite differently as they interact with them from birth. As suggested, explore this suffice it to say here that parents help their girls learn how to act and think "like girls" and they help their boys learn how to act and think "like boys." That is, they help their daughters and sons learn their gender.

For example, they are gentler with their daughters and rougher with their sons. They give their girls dolls to play with, and their sons guns. Girls may be made of "sugar and spice and everything nice" and boys something quite different, but their parents help them greatly, for better or worse, to turn out that way. To the extent this is true, our gender stems much more from socialization than from biological differences between the sexes, or so most sociologists probably assume. To return to a question posed earlier, if Gilligan is right that boys and girls reach moral judgments differently, socialization matters more than biology for how they reach these judgments.

As the "Learning From Other Societies" box shows, various cultures socialize their children differently. We can also examine cross-cultural variation in socialization with data from the World Values Survey, which was administered to almost six dozen nations. The percentage of people in several countries who think it is "especially important for children to learn obedience at home." Here we see some striking differences in the value placed on obedience.

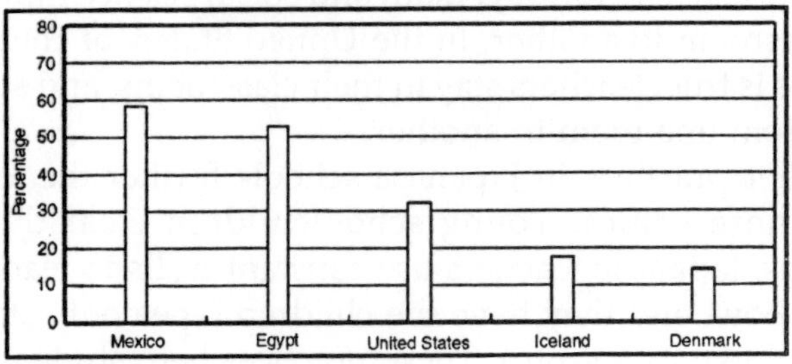

Fig. Percentage Believing That Obedience is Especially Important for a Child to Learn

Learning from Other Societies

Children and Socialization in Japan

This stage ends with the observation that American children need to be socialized with certain values in order for our society to be able to address many of the social issues, including hate crimes and violence against women, facing it. As we consider the socialization of American children, the experience of Japan offers a valuable session.

Culture and Society that Japan's culture emphasizes harmony, cooperation, and respect for authority in Japan's culture. Socialization in Japan is highly oriented towards the teaching of the values just listed, with much of it stressing the importance of belonging to a group and dependence, instead of individual autonomy and independence. This is especially true in Japanese schools, which, as two sociologists write, "stress the similarity of all children, and the importance of the group". From the time they begin school, Japanese children learn to value their membership in their homeroom, or kumi, and they spend several years in the same kumi. Each kumi treats its classroom as a "home away from home," as the children arrange the classroom furniture, bring in plants and other things from their own homes, and clean the classroom every day. At recess one kumi will play against another. In an interesting difference from standard practice in the United States, a kumi in junior high school will stay in its classroom while the teachers for, say, math and social science move from one classroom to another. In the United States, of course, the opposite is true: teachers stay in their classrooms, and students move from one room to another.

Other practices in Japanese schools further the learning of Japanese values. Young schoolchildren wear the same uniforms. Japanese teachers use constant drills to teach them how to bow, and they have the children repeatedly stand up and sit down as a group. These practices help students learn respect for authority and help to enhance the sense of group belonging that the kumi represents.

Whereas teachers in the United States routinely call on individual students to answer a question, Japanese teachers rarely do this. Rather than competing with each other for a good grade, Japanese schoolchildren are evaluated just as to the performance of the kumi as a whole. Because decision making within the kumi is done by consensus, the children learn the need to compromise and to respect each other's feelings. Because the members of a kumi spend so much time together for so many years, they develop extremely close friendships and think of themselves more as members of the kumi than as individuals.

They become very loyal to the kumi and put its interests above their own individual interests. In these and other ways, socialization in Japanese schools helps the children and adolescents there learn the Japanese values of harmony, group loyalty, and respect for authority. If American children learned these values to a greater degree, it would be easier to address violence and other issues facing the United States.

SCHOOLS

Schools socialize children by teaching them their formal curriculum but also a hidden curriculum. The formal curriculum is the "three Rs": reading, writing, and arithmetic.

But there is also a hidden curriculum that schools impart, and that is the cultural values of the society in which the schools are found. To help you understand the hidden curriculum, pretend you could wave a magic wand and start your own society.

Because you would probably want children to grow up loving their country and respecting your authority, you realise their schooling needs to help them grow up this way. What would you do in the schools to make sure this happens? First, because you want children to grow up respecting your authority, it is important for them to respect authority in general.

You would thus have them sit in rows and learn from kindergarten on that they should do whatever their teacher and principal tell them. Second, you would make sure that their history sessions emphasize only positive things about the country's past. Of course, because you just invented this country with a magic wand, it has no past, so you make it up.

Naturally, you want to pretend that the country had a great past-that it was a land that promised freedom and opportunity to people moving to it from poor, oppressed countries overseas, for example, and that many people indeed were able to find this opportunity and become quite successful. Third, you would probably want schoolchildren to learn songs that extolled your country's virtues.

At a minimum, these songs would talk about the freedom in your country and about its natural beauty. Ideally, children would sing these songs every day, or at least once or twice a week. After several years of coming to school and learning to obey their teachers and principal, of learning about how great their country was in the past, and of singing songs praising their country, you would have gone a long way towards socializing the children in your society to love their country and to respect your authority.

Now this has been magic wand time, but weren't you raised in a society that sounds suspiciously like this one? Wasn't your schooling similar to the type just described? No one deliberately went out to brainwash you once you started kindergarten, of course, but the processes and consequences of your early schooling were still quite similar to the more conspiratorial type just described. There is not necessarily anything wrong with that, but it does show, for better or worse, that schools are an important agent of socialization.

As the especially true in Japan, where schooling helps instill the traditional Japanese values of harmony, group loyalty, and respect for authority. Besides the values and beliefs just discussed, schools also teach us through their tests and grading to be competitive. Implicitly, they teach us that failure-in this case poor grades-stems from not studying hard enough and, more generally, from not trying hard enough.

This process reinforces the blaming-the-victim ideology. Again, no one conspires for this to happen, but it happens nonetheless. Schools are also a significant source of gender socialization, as even in this modern day, teachers and curriculum send out various messages that reinforce the qualities traditionally ascribed to females and males, and students engage in recess and other extracurricular activities that do the same thing.

PEERS

When you were a 16-year-old, how many times did you complain to your parent, "All of my friends are. Why can't I? It isn't fair!" As this all-too-common example indicates, our friends play a very important role in our lives. This is especially true during adolescence, when peers influence our tastes in music, clothes, and so many other aspects of our lives, as the now common image of the teenager always on a cell phone reminds us. But friends are important during other parts of the life course as well.

We rely on them for fun, for emotional comfort and support, and for companionship. That is the upside of friendships. The downside is called peer pressure, with which you are undoubtedly familiar. Suppose it is Friday night and you are studying for a big exam on Monday. Your friends come by and ask you to go with them to get a pizza and the beverage of your choice. You would probably agree to go with them, partly because you really dislike studying on a Friday night, but also because there is at least some subtle pressure on you to do so. As this example indicates, our friends can influence us in many ways. During adolescence, their interests can affect our own interests in film, music, and other aspects of popular culture. More ominously, adolescent peer influences have been implicated in underage drinking, drug use, delinquency, and hate crimes.

After we reach our 20s and 30s, our peers become less important in our lives, especially if we get married. Yet even then our peers do not lose all their importance, as married couples with young children still manage to get out with friends now and then. Scholars have also begun to emphasize the importance of friendships with coworkers for emotional and practical support and for our continuing socialization.

THE MASS MEDIA

The mass media are another agent of socialization. Television shows, movies, popular music, magazines, Web sites, and other aspects of the mass media influence our political views; our tastes in popular culture; our views of women, people of colour, and gays; and many other beliefs and practices. In an ongoing controversy, the mass media are often blamed for youth violence and many other of our society's ills.

The average child sees thousands of acts of violence on television and in the movies before reaching young adulthood. Rap lyrics often seemingly extol very ugly violence, including violence against women. Commercials can greatly influence our choice of soda, shoes, and countless other products. The mass media also reinforce racial and gender stereotypes, including the belief that women are sex objects and suitable targets of male violence.

In the General Social Survey, about 28% of respondents said that they watch four or more hours of television every day, while another 46% watch 2-3 hours daily. The mass media certainly are an important source of socialization unimaginable a half-century ago.

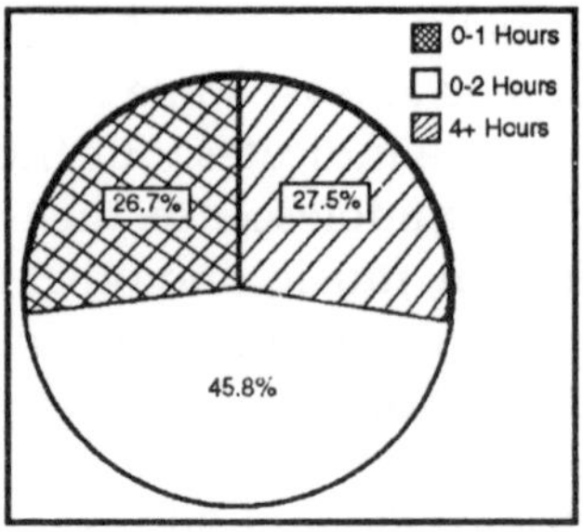

Fig. Average Number of Hours of Television Watched Daily

As the mass media socialize children, adolescents, and even adults, a key question is the extent to which media violence causes violence in our society. Studies consistently uncover a strong correlation between watching violent television shows and movies and committing violence.

However, this does not necessarily mean that watching the violence actually causes violent behaviour: perhaps people watch violence because they are already interested in it and perhaps even committing it. Scholars continue to debate the effect of media violence on youth violence.

In a free society, this question is especially important, as the belief in this effect has prompted calls for monitoring the media and the banning of certain acts of violence. Civil libertarians argue that such calls smack of censorship that violates the First Amendment to the Constitution, whole others argue that they fall within the First Amendment and would make for a safer society. Certainly the concern and debate over mass media violence will continue for years to come.

RELIGION

One final agent of socialization is religion Education and Religion. Although religion is arguably less important in people's lives now than it was a few generations ago, it still continues to exert considerable influence on our beliefs, values, and behaviours.

Here we should distinguish between religious preference and religiosity. Both these aspects of religion can affect your values and beliefs on religious and nonreligious issues alike, but their particular effects vary from issue to issue. Consider the emotionally charged issue of abortion. People hold very strong views on abortion, and many of their views stem from their religious beliefs. Yet which aspect of religion matters the most, religious preference or religiosity? General Social Survey data help us answer this question.

It turns out that religious preference, if we limit it for the sake of this discussion to Catholics versus Protestants, does not matter at all: Catholics and Protestants in the GSS exhibit roughly equal beliefs on the abortion issue, as about one-third of each group thinks abortion should be allowed for any reason.

However, religiosity matters a lot: GSS respondents who pray daily are only about half as likely as those who rarely or never pray to think abortion should be allowed.

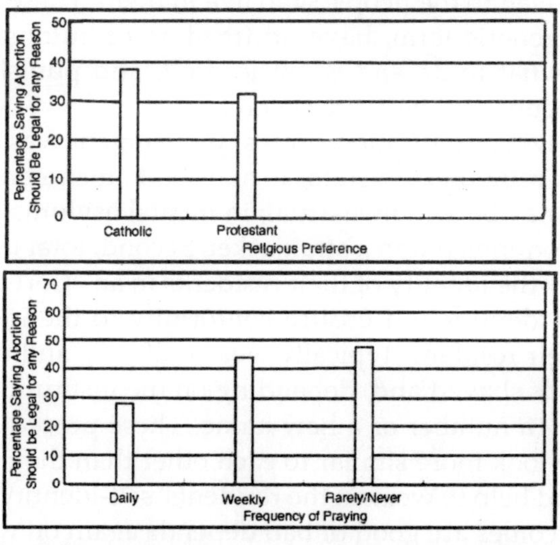

Fig. Religious Preference, Religiosity, and Belief that Abortion should be Legal for Any Reason

RESOCIALIZATION AND TOTAL INSTITUTIONS

Some people live in settings where their lives are so controlled that their values and beliefs change drastically. This change is so drastic, in fact, that these people are in effect resocialized. Such resocialization occurs in what Erving

Goffman called total institutions. As their name implies, these institutions have total control over the lives of the people who live in them. Several types of total institutions exist: mental asylums, Nazi concentration camps, military boot camps, convents, and monasteries. Some scholars would also say that criminal prisons are total institutions, as they exhibit some of the same processes found in the other types.

As this list implies, total institutions can be used for good or bad purposes. Resocialization is not necessarily good or bad in and of itself; what is more important is the ends to which it is put. Whether we are talking about total institutions that are good or bad, they all share certain processes and procedures that make them total institutions.

The most important characteristic is that they have total control over the lives of their inmates, patients, or whatever name is given to the people who live in them. These residents, to use a generic term, have no freedom or autonomy. They are told what to do and when to do it, and punishment for rule infraction can be quite severe.

In Nazi concentration camps, punishment was torture or death; in religious cloisters, it may be banishment; in boot camp, it may be a court-martial; in mental asylums, it may be solitary confinement in a straitjacket. Second, total institutions take away the identity of their residents in an effort to weaken their self-identity and ensure conformity to the institutions' rules. Their residents typically wear uniforms and often have their heads shaved and, depending on the institution, may be known by a number or a new name. These procedures make everyone look more similar to each other than they otherwise would and help to weaken the residents' self-identity. Whether these outcomes are good or bad depends again on which total institution we have in mind.

Third, total institutions subject their residents to harsh treatment and, quite often, abuse, although the nature of this abuse, and whether it occurs at all, obviously depends on which total institution we have in mind. Nazis starved concentration camp inmates, tortured them, stripped them naked, conducted hideous experiments on them, and, of course, exterminated millions. Literature on mental asylums is filled with examples of abuses of the patients living there. Drill sergeants have also been known for harshly treating new recruits: some observers defend this practice as necessary for military discipline and readiness, while others consider it to be unjustified abuse. Resocialization is often accompanied via a degradation ceremony, an encounter in which a total institution's resident is humiliated, often in front of the institution's other residents or officials.

A drill sergeant may call a physically unconditioned male recruit a "girl" or "lady" and question his manhood in front of other recruits. In a mental asylum or prison, an inmate may be stripped naked and checked in their private areas for lice and other vermin. Shaving the heads of new military recruits or prison inmates is another example of a degradation ceremony.

Resocialization also occurs in groups that are not institutional settings. Alcoholics Anonymous is one such group, as it tries to change the alcoholics' value system by having them internalize several principles about how to live one's life. The goal here, of course, is to have the alcoholic stop drinking and to continue to refrain from drinking. Some religious cults also resocialize their members and continue to spark much controversy in today's society.

SOCIAL INTERACTIONS

If socialization results from our social interaction with others, it is also true that we learn how to interact from our socialization. Among other things, we learn how far apart to stand when talking to someone else, we learn to enjoy kissing, we learn how to stand and behave in an elevator, and we learn to shake hands when greeting someone.

DRAMATURGY AND IMPRESSION MANAGEMENT

From a sociological standpoint, much of our social interaction can be understood by likening it to a performance in a play. As with so many things, Shakespeare said it best when he wrote,

- All the world's a stage,
- And all the men and women merely players.
- They have their exits and their entrances;
- And one man in his time plays many parts.

From this perspective, each individual has many parts or roles to play in society, and many of these roles specify how we should interact in any given situation. These roles exist before we are born, and they continue long after we die. The culture of society is thus similar to the script of a play. Just as actors in a play learn what lines to say, where to stand on the stage, how to position their bodies, and so many other things, so do we learn as members of society the roles that specify how we should interact.

This fundamental metaphor was developed and popularized by sociologist Erving Goffman in what he called a dramaturgical approach. By this he meant that we can understand social interaction as if it were a theatrical performance. People who interact are actors on a stage, the things they say and do are equivalent to the parts actors play, and the people who observe their interaction are equivalent to the audience at a play.

Beyond these aspects of his theatrical analogy, Goffman also stressed that the presentation of self guides social interaction just as it guides behaviour in a play. Actors in a play, he wrote, aim to act properly, which at a minimum means they need to say their lines correctly and in other ways carry out their parts as they were written. They try to convey the impression of their character the playwright had in mind when the play was written and the director has in mind when the play is presented.

Such impression management, Goffman wrote, also guides social interaction in everyday life. When people interact, they routinely try to convey a positive impression of themselves to the people with whom they interact. Our behaviour in a job interview differs dramatically from our behaviour at a party. The key dimension of social interaction, then, involves trying to manage the impressions we convey to the people with whom we interact. We usually do our best, consciously or unconsciously, to manage the impressions we convey to others and so to evoke from them reactions that will please us. Goffman wrote about other aspects of social interaction that affect our efforts to manage these impressions. Again using his dramaturgical metaphor, he said that some interaction occurs in the "frontstage," or front region, while other interaction occurs in the "backstage," or back region.

In a play, of course, the frontstage is what the audience sees and is obviously the location in which the actors are performing their lines. Backstage, they can do whatever they want, and the audience will have no idea of what they are doing. Much of our everyday interaction is on the frontstage, where an audience can see everything we do and hear everything we say. But we also spend a lot of time on the backstage, by ourselves, when we can do and say things in private that we would not dare do or say in public.

How we dress is also a form of impression management. You are the same person regardless of what clothes you wear, but if you dress for a job interview as you would dress for a party, the person interviewing you would get an impression you might not want to be conveying. If you showed up for a medical visit and your physician were wearing a bathing suit, wouldn't you feel just a bit uneasy?

People convey impressions not only through how they act and dress but also through how they arrange the appearance of the settings in which they interact. A physician tries to convey an impression of a serious, knowledgeable professional not only by how she or he dresses but also by how the waiting room looks.

Usually the room is well furnished with clean, comfortable chairs and such magazines as People, Time, and Newsweek. What impression would be conveyed if the physician's office looked shabby and even had a bad odour? What if it had Playboy in it? How long would you stay in that office? Life is filled with impression management.

Compare the decor of your favourite fast-food restaurant with that of a very expensive restaurant with which you might be familiar. Compare the appearance, dress, and demeanor of the servers and other personnel in the two establishments. The expensive restaurant is trying to convey an image that the food will be wonderful and that the time you spend there will be memorable and well worth the money. The fast-food restaurant is trying to convey just the opposite impression. In fact, if it looked too fancy, you would probably think it was too expensive. Some people go to great efforts to manage the impressions they convey. You have probably done so in a job interview or on a date.

In New York City, the capital of book publishing, editors of large publishing companies and "superagents" for authors are very conscious of the impressions they convey, because much of the publishing industry depends on gossip, impressions, and the development of rapport. Editors and agents often dine together in one of a few very expensive "power" restaurants, where their presence is certain to be noted.

Publishers or senior editors who dine at these restaurants will eat only with celebrity authors, other senior editors or publishers, or important agents. Such agents rarely dine with junior editors, who are only "allowed" to eat with junior agents. To eat with someone "beneath" your standing would convey the wrong impression.

As these examples indicate, social reality is to a large extent socially constructed. It is what we make of it, and the individuals who interact help construct the reality of the situation in which they interact. Sociologists refer to this process as the social construction of reality. Although we usually come into a situation with shared understandings of what is about to happen, as the interaction proceeds the actors continue to define the situation and thus to construct its reality.

ROLES AND STATUSES

The related concepts of role and status help us further understand social interaction. Status has many meanings in the dictionary and also within sociology, but for now as suggested, define it as the position that someone occupies in society. This position is often a job title, but many other types of positions exist: parent, sibling, relative, friend, and so forth. Any one individual often occupies several different statuses at the same time, and someone can simultaneously be a banker, Girl Scout troop leader, mother, school board member, volunteer at a homeless shelter, and wife. This someone would be very busy! We call all the positions an individual occupies that person's status set. Sociologists often speak of three kinds of statuses.

The first type is ascribed status, which is the status that someone is born with and has no control over. There are relatively few ascribed statuses; the most common ones are our biological sex, race, and parents' social class and religious affiliation. The second kind of status is called achieved status, which, as the name implies, is a status you achieve, at some point after birth, sometimes through your own efforts and sometimes because good or bad luck you.

The third type of status is called a master status. This is a status that is so important that it overrides other statuses you may hold. A physical disability often becomes a master status, because if you are confined to a wheelchair, to take one type of disability, this confinement becomes more important than the other statuses you have.

For similar reasons, gender, race, and sexual orientation may also be considered master statuses, as these statuses often subject women, people of colour, and gays and lesbians, respectively, to discrimination and other problems, no matter what other statuses they may have. Whatever its type, every status is accompanied by a role, which is the behaviour expected of someone-and in fact everyone-with a certain status. You and most other people reading this book are students. Despite all the other differences among you, you have at least this one status in common.

As such, there is a role expected of you as a student: this role includes coming to class regularly and studying the best you can for exams. Because roles are the behaviour expected of people in various statuses, they help us interact because we are familiar with the roles in the first place. Suppose you are shopping in a department store. Your status is a shopper, and the role expected of you as a shopper-and of all shoppers-involves looking quietly at various items in the store, taking the ones you want to purchase to a checkout line, and paying for them. The person who takes your money is occupying another status in the store that we call a cashier.

The role expected of that cashier-and of all cashiers not only in that store but in every other store-is to accept your payment in a businesslike way and put your items in a bag. This is all very automatic, and we often perform our roles without thinking about them. That is why social interaction is possible: if we always had to think about our roles before we performed them, social interaction would be slow, tedious, and fraught with error.

It is when people violate their roles that the importance of roles is thrown into sharp relief. Suppose you were shopping in that department store just mentioned, and while you were in the checkout line the cashier asked you how your sex life has been!

Now, you might expect such an intimate question from a very close friend, because discussions of intimate matters are part of the roles close friends play, but you would definitely not expect it from a cashier you do not know.

As this example suggests, the social construction of reality rests on shared assumptions, including our understanding of the roles expected of people in a given encounter, that are easily violated if one has the nerve to do so. If they are violated, social order might well break down, as you would quickly find if you dared to ask your cashier how her or his sex life has been, or if two people sitting in the front of a large lecture hall started kissing each other passionately.

Sociologist Harold Garfinkel argued that unexpected events like these underscore how fragile social order is and remind us that people are constantly constructing the social reality of the situations in which they find themselves. He had his students perform a series of experiments, including acting like a stranger in their parents' home. Not surprisingly, their parents quickly became flustered and wondered what college was doing to their daughters and sons!

ROLES AND PERSONALITIES

Roles help us interact and help make social order possible. But they even can shape our personalities. The idea here is that if we assume a new role, the expectations of that role can change how we interact with others and the way we even think about ourselves. In short, roles can change our personalities. A telling example of this effect comes from the story of a criminal justice professor from Florida named George Kirkham.

In his classes, Kirkham would be critical of the harshness with which police treated suspects and other citizens. One day, some police officers in one of his classes said Kirkham could not begin to understand what it was like being a police officer, and they challenged him to become one. He took up the challenge by gaining admission to a police academy and going through the regular training programme for all recruits. Kirkham later recounted what happened on his first few days on the job.

In one episode, he and his veteran partner went into a bar where an intoxicated patron had been causing trouble. Kirkham politely asked the patron to go with him outside. Evidently surprised by this new police officer's politeness, the man instead swung at Kirkham and landed a blow. Kirkham could not believe this happened and was forced to subdue his assailant.

In another episode, Kirkham and his partner were checking out the drivers of a double-parked car. An ugly crowd soon gathered and began making threats. Alarmed, Kirkham opened up his car's trunk and pulled out a shotgun to keep the crowd away.

In recounting this episode, Kirkham wrote that as a professor he quickly would have condemned the police officer he had now become. In a few short days, he had turned from a polite, kind professor into a gruff, angry police officer. His role had changed and, along with it, his personality.

ROLE PROBLEMS

Roles can help our interactions run smoothly and

automatically and, for better or worse, shape our personalities, but they can also cause various kinds of problems. One such problem is role conflict, which occurs when the roles of our many statuses conflict with each other. For example, say you are a student and also a parent. Your 3-year-old child gets sick. You now have a conflict between your role as a parent and your role as a student.

To perform your role as a parent, you should stay home with your sick child. To perform your role as a student, you should go to your classes and take the big exam that had been scheduled weeks ago. What do you do? Obviously, you cannot perform both roles at the same time. To resolve role conflict, we ordinarily have to choose between one role or the other, which is often a difficult choice to make. In this example, if you take care of your child, you miss your classes and exam; if you go to your classes, you have to leave your child at home alone, an unacceptable and illegal option. Another way to resolve role conflict is to find some alternative that would meet the needs of your conflicting roles.

In our sick child example, you might be able to find someone to watch your child until you can get back from classes. It is certainly desirable to find such alternatives, but, unfortunately, they are not always forthcoming. If role conflict becomes too frequent and severe, a final option is to leave one of your statuses altogether.

In our example, if you find it too difficult to juggle your roles as parent and student, you could stop being a parent-hardly likely!-or, more likely, take time off from school until your child is older. Most of us in these circumstances would try our best to avoid having to do this. Another role-related problem is called role strain.

Here you have one status, and a role associated with it, that is causing problems because of all the demands coming to you from people in other statuses with which your own status is involved. Suppose you were a high school principal. In your one role as a principal, you come into contact with people in several different statuses: teachers, students, custodial and support staff, the superintendent, school board members, the community as a whole, and the news media. These statuses may make competing demands on you in your one role as a principal. If your high school has a dress code, for example, the students may want you to abolish it, the teachers and superintendent may want you to keep it, and maybe the school board would agree with the students. These competing factions, you certainly might experience some role strain! A third type of role problem occurs when we occupy a status whose role demands a certain type of personality that differs from the one we actually have.

Can you imagine a police officer who was afraid of guns? An athlete who was not competitive? Although most people avoid this type of role problem by not taking on a role to which their personality is ill suited, such problems occur nonetheless. For example, some people who dislike children and do not have the patience to be good parents end up being parents anyway.

In another example, your author once knew a new professor who was woefully nervous lecturing in front of students. You might wonder why he became a professor in the first place, but he probably just loved the subject matter so much that he thought he would overcome his nervousness. He did not.

SOCIALIZATION PRACTICES AND IMPROVING SOCIETY

This stage began with a news story about the beating and killing of a gay man and proceeded with the stories of two women who grew up in the South when it was racially segregated. These stories show the power of socialization, which can have both good and bad consequences.

Socialization into one's culture is necessary for any society to exist, and socialization is also necessary for any one individual to be "human" in the social sense of the term, as our discussion of feral children indicated.

Yet socialization can also result in attitudes and behaviours that most of us would rightly condemn. Socialization created the homophobic mentality that led three teenagers to beat Charlie Howard and throw him into a river, and it also created the racist mentality that Sarah Patton Boyle and Lillian Smith described in their accounts of growing up in the South. We learn to be good, cooperative members of society, but some of us also learn to hate and to think that other kinds of people are inferior and perhaps even less than human. For many of the social issues confronting the United States today-hate crimes, other crimes, violence against women, sexism, racism, and so forth-it might not be an exaggeration to say that new patterns of socialization are ultimately necessary if our society wants to be able to address these issues effectively.

Parents of young children and adolescents bear a major responsibility for making sure our children do not learn to hate and commit harm to others, but so do our schools, mass media, and religious bodies. No nation is perfect, but nations like Japan have long been more successful than the United States in raising their children to be generous and cooperative.

IMPORTANT POINTS

- Socialization is important for at least two reasons. First, it is the process by which people learn the culture of their society. Second, it is the process by which they become fully human in terms of behaviour, emotions, and cognitive ability. The unfortunate examples of feral children reinforce the importance of socialization in these respects.
- Charles Horton Cooley and George Herbert Mead both theorized about how the self develops through socialization. Cooley's concept of the looking-glass self recognized that we see ourselves when we interact with other people and through this process develop our self-image. Mead's concept of "taking the role of the other" stressed that children play at various roles and so learn what others expect of them.
- Sigmund Freud's psychoanalytic theory of personality development stressed the role of unconscious forces. Every individual is born with a selfish id and will achieve a normal personality if

the individual's ego and superego develop properly. If the id, ego, and superego are in the wrong balance, the individual may engage in antisocial or other mentally disordered behaviour.

- Jean Piaget theorized that people go through several stages of cognitive development, while Lawrence Kohlberg said the same for moral development. Carol Gilligan argued that boys and girls engage in different types of moral reasoning, with the boys' type resting on formal rules and the girls' resting more on social relationships.
- Erik Erikson discussed identity development throughout the life span while calling attention to adolescence as a stage in which many individuals experience an identity crisis.
- Several agents of socialization exist. The most important one is arguably the family, as parents socialize their children in any number of ways; children end up resembling their parents not only biologically but also sociologically. Schools, peers, the mass media, and, to some extent, religion all also play important roles in socializing not only children but also older individuals.
- Resocialization involves a dramatic change in an individual's values, beliefs, and behaviour. It is often the goal of total institutions, such as military boot camp, convents and monasteries, mental institutions, and prisons, as it was with the Nazi death camps. Total institutions often exercise arbitrary power and in many ways try to achieve total control over the individual and remove their sense of individual identity.
- Erving Goffman used a theatrical metaphor called dramaturgy to understand social interaction, which he likened to behaviour on a stage in a play. More generally, many sociologists stress the concept of roles in social interaction. Although we usually play our roles automatically, social order occasionally

breaks down when people don't play their roles. This breakdown shows the fragility of social order.

- Although roles help us interact, they can also lead to problems such as role conflict and role strain. In another problem, some individuals may be expected to carry out a role that demands a personality they do not have.

4

Groups and Organizations

SOCIAL GROUPS

A social group consists of two or more people who interact with one another and who recognize themselves as a distinct social unit. The definition is simple enough, but it has significant implications. Frequent interaction leads people to share values and beliefs. This similarity and the interaction cause them to identify with one another. Identification and attachment, in turn, stimulate more frequent and intense interaction. Each group maintains solidarity with all to other groups and other types of social systems. Groups are among the most stable and enduring of social units.

They are important both to their members and to the society at large. Through encouraging regular and predictable behaviour, groups form the foundation upon which society rests. Thus, a family, a village, a political party a trade union is all social groups. These, it should be noted are different from social classes, status groups or crowds, which not only lack structure but whose members are less aware or even unaware of the existence of the group. These have been called quasi-groups or groupings. Nevertheless, the distinction between social groups and quasi-groups is fluid and variable since quasi-groups very often give rise to social groups, as for example, social classes give rise to political parties.

PRIMARY GROUPS

If all groups are important to their members and to society, some groups are more important than others. Early in the twentieth century, Charles H. Cooley gave the name, primary groups, to those groups that he said are characterized by intimate face-to-face association and those are fundamental in the development and continued adjustment of their members. He identified three basic primary groups, the family, the child's play group, and the neighbourhoods or community among adults.

These groups, he said, are almost universal in all societies; they give to people their earliest and most complete experiences of social unity; they are instrumental in the development of the social life; and they promote the integration of their members in the larger society. Since Cooley wrote, over 65 years ago, life in the United States has become much more urban, complex, and impersonal, and the family play group and neighbourhood have become less dominant features of the social order. Secondary groups, characterized by anonymous, impersonal, and instrumental relationships, have become much more numerous.

People move frequently, often from one part of the country to another and they change from established relationships and promoting widespread loneliness. Young people, particularly, turn to drugs, seek communal living groups and adopt deviant lifestyles in attempts to find meaningful primary-group relationships. The social context has changed so much so that primary group relationship today is not as simple as they were in Cooley's time.

SECONDARY GROUPS

An understanding of the modern industrial society requires an understanding of the secondary groups. The social groups other than those of primary groups may be termed as secondary groups. They are a residual category. They are often called special interest groups. They are of the opinion that secondary groups have become almost inevitable today. Their appearance is mainly due to the growing cultural complexity. Primary groups are found predominantly in societies where life is relatively simple. With the expansion in population and territory of a society however interests become diversified and other types of relationships which can be called secondary or impersonal become necessary. Interests become differentiated. The services of experts are required. The new range of the interests demands a complex organization. Especially selected persons act on behalf of all and hence arises a hierarchy of officials called bureaucracy. These features characterize the rise of the modern state, the great corporation, the factory, the labour union, a university or a nationwide political party and so on. These are secondary groups. Ogburn and Nimkoff defines secondary groups as groups which provide experience lacking in intimacy. Frank D. Watson writes that the secondary group is larger and more formal is specialized and direct in its contacts and relies more for unity and continuance upon the stability of its social organization than does the primary group.

Characteristics of Secondary Group

Dominance of Secondary Relations

Secondary groups are characterized by indirect, impersonal, contractual and non-inclusive relations. Relations are indirect because secondary groups are bigger in size and members may not stay together. Relations are contractual in the sense they are oriented towards certain interests

Largeness of the Size

Secondary groups are relatively larger in size. City, nation, political parties, trade unions and corporations, international associations are bigger in size. They may have thousands and lakhs of members. There may not be any limit to the membership in the case of some secondary groups.

Membership

Membership in the case of secondary groups is mainly voluntary. Individuals are at liberty to join or to go away from the groups. However there are some secondary groups like the state whose membership is almost involuntary.

No Physical Basis

Secondary groups are not characterized by physical proximity. Many secondary groups are not limited to any definite area. There are some secondary groups like the Rotary Club and Lions Club which are international in character.

The members of such groups are scattered over a vast area. Specific ends or interest: Secondary groups are formed for the realization of some specific interests or ends. They are called special interest groups. Members are interested in the groups because they have specific ends to aim at. Indirect communication: Contacts and communications in the case of secondary groups are mostly indirect.

Mass media of communication such as radio, telephone, television, newspaper, movies, magazines and post and telegraph are resorted to by the members to have communication. Communication may not be quick and effective even. Impersonal nature of social relationships in secondary groups is both the cause and the effect of indirect communication.

Nature of Group Control

Informal means of social control are less effective in regulating the relations of members. Moral control is only secondary. Formal means of social control such as law, legislation, police, court etc. are made of to control the behaviour of members.

The behaviour of the people is largely influenced and controlled by public opinion, propaganda, rule of law and political ideologies. Group structure: The secondary group has a formal structure. A formal authority is set up with designated powers and a clear-cut division of labour in which the function of each is specified in relation to the function of all. Secondary groups are mostly organized groups. Different statuses and roles that the members assume are specified. Distinctions based on caste, colour, religion, class, language etc. are less rigid and there is greater tolerance towards other people or groups.

Limited Influence on Personality

Secondary groups are specialized in character. People involvement in them is also of limited significance. Members's attachment to them is also very much limited. Further people spend most of their time in primary groups than in secondary groups. Hence secondary groups have very limited influence on the personality of the members.

GROUP DYNAMICS

GROUP FORMATION

A group is able to share experiences, to provide feedback, to pool ideas, to generate insights, and provide an arena for analysis of experiences. The group provides a measure of support and reassurance. Moreover, as a group, learners may also plan collectively for change action. Group discussion is a very effective learning method.

Participation

Participation is a fundamental process within a group, because many of the other processes depend upon participation of the various members. Levels and degrees of participation vary. Some members are active participants while others are more withdrawn and passive. In essence, participation means involvement, concern for the task, and direct or indirect contribution to the group goal. If members do not participate, the group ceases to exist. Factors which affect members participation

- *The content or task of the group*: Is it of interest, importance and relevance?
- *The physical atmosphere*: Is it comfortable physically, socially and psychologically?
- *The psychological atmosphere*: Is it accepting, non-threatening?
- *Member's personal preoccupations*: Are there any distracting thoughts in their mind?
- *The level of interaction and discussions*: Is adequate information provided for everyone to understand?—is it at a level everyone understands?
- *Familiarity*: Between group members- do members know each other from before?

Communication

Communication within a group deals with the spoken and the unspoken, the verbal and the non-verbal, the explicit and the implied messages that are conveyed and exchanged relating to information and ideas, and feelings. Two-way communication implies a situation where not only the two parties talk to each other, but that they are listening to each other as well. It helps in

- Clarification of doubts, confusions and misconceptions
- Both parties understanding each other
- Receiving and giving of feedback

It indicates the degree of respect between the two parties.

Helpful hints for effective communication:

- Have a circular seating arrangement so that everyone can see and interact with everyone else
- If there are two facilitators, they should sit apart so that communication flow is not in one direction
- Respect individuals—let everyone call everyone else by name respectfully
- Encourage and support the quiet members to voice their opinions
- Try and persuade the people who speak too much to give others a chance
- Ensure that only one person speaks at a time or no one else will be heard
- Discourage sub groups from indulging in side talk

Problem Solving

Most groups find themselves unable to solve problems because they address the problem at a superficial level. After that they find themselves blocked because they cannot figure out why the problem occurred and how they can tackle it.

Therefore an effective problem solving procedure would be to:

- *Clearly define the problem*: Is it what appears on the surface or are there deep hidden aspects?
- Try to thoroughly explore and understand the causes behind the problem
- Collect additional information, from elsewhere if

necessary, and analyse it to understand the problem further

- The group should suspend criticism and judgment for a while and try to combine each other's ideas or add on improvements. The objectives should be to generate as many ideas and suggestions as possible. This is called "brainstorming" in a group, when individuals try lateral thinking.

Leadership

Leadership involves focussing the efforts of the people towards a common goal and to enable them to work together as one. In general we designate one individual as a leader. This individual may be chosen from within or appointed from outside.

Thus, one member may provide leadership with respect to achieving the goal while a different individual may be providing leadership in maintaining the group as a group. These roles can switch and change.

DEVELOPMENT OF GROUPS

The developmental process of small groups can be viewed in several ways. Firstly, it is useful to know the persons who compose a particular small group.

- People bring their past experiences
- People come with their personalities
- People also come with a particular set of expectations

The priorities and expectations of persons comprising a group can influence the manner in which the group develops over a period of time

Stages

Viewing the group as a whole we observe definite patterns of behaviour occurring within a group. These can be grouped into stages.

First Stage

The initial stage in the life of a group is concerned with

forming a group. This stage is characterized by members seeking safety and protection, tentativeness of response, seeking superficial contact with others, demonstrating dependency on existing authority figures. Members at this stage either engage in busy type of activity or show apathy.

Second Stage

The second stage in this group is marked by the formation of dyads and triads. Members seek out familiar or similar individuals and begin a deeper sharing of self. Continued attention to the subgroup creates a differentiation in the group and tensions across the dyads/triads may appear. Pairing is a common phenomenon.

Third Stage

The third developmental stage is marked by a more serious concern about task performance. The dyads/triads begin to open up and seek out other members in the group. Efforts are made to establish various norms for task performance. Members begin to take greater responsibility for their own group and relationship while the authority figure becomes relaxed.

Fourth Stage

This is a stage of a fully functional group where members see themselves as a group and get involved in the task. Each person makes a contribution and the authority figure is also seen as a part of the group. Group norms are followed and collective pressure is exerted to ensure the effectiveness of the group. The group redefines its goals in the light of information from the outside environment and shows an autonomous will to pursue those goals. The long-term viability of the group is established and nurtured.

FACILITATING A GROUP

A group cannot automatically function effectively, it needs to be facilitated. Facilitation can be described as a conscious process of assisting a group to successfully achieve its task while functioning as a group. Facilitation can be performed by members themselves, or with the help of an outsider.

To facilitate effectively the facilitator needs to:

- Understand what is happening within the group
- Be aware of his/her own personality
- And know how to facilitate

Group Diagnosis

The process of finding out what is going on in a group may be called diagnosing. It is an essential skill of a facilitator. Diagnosis involves understanding the causes after looking for clues within the group and outside the group. Some examples follow to show the point.

- *Problem*: Not everyone participates or shows interest and a few remain silent
- *Possible causes*: Perhaps the goal or task is not relevant to some of the participants. Some of the members may feel insecure or dominant on the basis of caste, class, education or gender.
- *Problem*: Some members ignore or disregard contributions from other members
- *Possible causes*: Members of the group may be nervous and unaware of others' needs.
- *Problem*: The group is not able to come to consensus or are unable to devise a plan to implement the decision.
- *Possible causes*: Perhaps the group lacks adequate information or skills to solve the problem. Perhaps the decision is threatening to some of the group members. Perhaps the group fears failure.

GROUP BEHAVIOUR

Group behaviour in sociology refers to the situations where people interact in large or small groups. The field of group dynamics deals with small groups that may reach consensus and act in a coordinated way. Groups of a large number of people in a given area may act simultaneously to achieve a goal that differs from what individuals would do acting alone. A large group is likely to show examples of group behaviour when people gathered in a given place and time act in a similar way-for example, joining a protest or march, participating in a fight or acting patriotically.

Special forms of large group behaviour are:

- Crowd "hysteria"
- Spectators—when a group of people gathered together on purpose to participate in an event like theatre play, cinema movie, football match, a concert, etc.
- Public—exception to the rule that the group must occupy the same physical place. People watching same channel on television may react in the same way, as they are occupying the same type of place—in front of television—although they may physically be doing this all over the world.

Group behaviour differs from mass actions which refers to people behaving similarly on a more global scale, while group behaviour refers usually to people in one place. If the group behaviour is coordinated, then it is called group action. Swarm intelligence is a special case of group behaviour, referring to the interaction between a group of agents in order to fulfil a given task. This type of group dynamics has received much attention by the soft computing community in the form of the particle swarm optimization family of algorithms.

THE IMPORTANCE OF GROUP SIZE

The distinction made earlier between small primary groups and larger secondary groups reflects the importance of group size for the functioning of a group, the nature of its members' attachments, and the group's stability. If you have ever taken a very small class, say fewer than 15 students, you probably noticed that the class atmosphere differed markedly from that of a large lecture class you may have been in.

In the small class, you got to know the professor better, and the students in the room got to know each other better. Attendance in the small class was probably more regular than in the large lecture class. Over the years, sociologists and other scholars have studied the effects of group size on group dynamics. One of the first to do so was German sociologist Georg Simmel who discussed the effects of groups of different sizes. The smallest group, of course, is the two-person group, or dyad, such as a married couple or two people engaged to be married or at least dating steadily. In this smallest of groups, Simmel noted, relationships can be very intense emotionally but also very unstable and short lived: if one person ends the relationship, the dyad ends as well. A triad, or three-person group, involves relationships that are still fairly intense, but it is also more stable than a dyad.

A major reason for this, said Simmel, is that if two people in a triad have a dispute, the third member can help them reach some compromise that will satisfy all the triad members. The downside of a triad is that two of its members may become very close and increasingly disregard the third member. As one example, some overcrowded college dorms are forced to house students in triples, or three to a room.

In such a situation, suppose that two of the roommates are night owls and like to stay up very late, while the third wants lights out by 11:00 p.m. If majority rules, as well it might, the third roommate will feel very dissatisfied and may decide to try to find other roommates. As groups become larger, the intensity of their interaction and bonding decreases, but their stability increases.

The major reason for this is the sheer number of relationships that can exist in a larger group. For example, in a dyad only one relationship exists, that between the two members of the dyad. In a triad, three relationships exist: A-B, A-C, and B-C. In a four-person group, the number of relationships rises to six: A-B, A-C, A-D, B-C, B-D, and C-D.

In a five-person group, 10 relationships exist, and in a six-person group, 15 exist. As the number of possible relationships rises, the amount of time a group member can spend with any other group member must decline, and with this decline comes less intense interaction and weaker emotional bonds. But as group size increases, the group also becomes more stable because it is large enough to survive any one member's departure from the group. When you graduate from your college or university, any clubs, organizations, or sports teams to which you belong will continue despite your exit, no matter how important you were to the group, as the remaining members of the group and new recruits will carry on in your absence.

Table. Number of Two-Person Relationships in Groups of Different Sizes

Number of Members	Number of Relationships
2 (A, B)	1 (A-B)
3 (A, B, C)	3 (A-B, A-C, B-C)
4 (A, B, C, D)	6 (A-B, A-C, A-D, B-C, B-D, C-D)
5 (A, B, C, D, E)	10 (A-B, A-C, A-D, A-E, B-C, B-D, B-E, C-D, C-E, D-E)
6 (A, B, C, D, E, F)	15 (A-B, A-C, A-D, A-E, A-F, B-C, B-D, B-E, B-F, C-D, C-E, C-F, D-E, D-F, E-F)

GROUP LEADERSHIP AND DECISION MAKING

Most groups have leaders. In the family, of course, the parents are the leaders, as much as their children sometimes might not like that. Even some close friendship groups have a leader or two who emerge over time. Virtually all secondary groups have leaders. These groups often have a charter, operations manual, or similar document that stipulates how leaders are appointed or elected and what their duties are. Sociologists commonly distinguish two types of leaders, instrumental and expressive.

An instrumental leader is a leader whose main focus is to achieve group goals and accomplish group tasks. Often instrumental leaders try to carry out their role even if they alienate other members of the group. The second type is the expressive leader, whose main focus is to maintain and improve the quality of relationships among group members and more generally to ensure group harmony. Some groups may have both types of leaders. Related to the leader types is leadership style. Three such styles are commonly distinguished. The first, authoritarian leadership, involves a primary focus on achieving group goals and on rigorous compliance with group rules and penalties for noncompliance. Authoritarian leaders typically make decisions on their own and tell other group members what to do and how to do it.

The second style, democratic leadership, involves extensive consultation with group members on decisions and less emphasis on rule compliance. Democratic leaders still make the final decision but do so only after carefully considering what other group members have said, and usually their decision will agree with the views of a majority of the members.

The final style is laissez-faire leadership. Here the leader more or less sits back and lets the group function on its own and really exerts no leadership role. When a decision must be reached, laissez-faire leadership is less effective than the other two in helping a group get things done. Whether authoritarian or democratic leadership is better for a group depends on the group's priorities.

If the group values task accomplishment more than anything else, including how well group members get along and how much they like their leader, then authoritarian leadership is preferable to democratic leadership, as it is better able to achieve group goals quickly and efficiently. But if group members place their highest priority on their satisfaction with decisions and decision making in the group, then they would want to have a lot of input in decisions.

In this case, democratic leadership is preferable to authoritarian leadership. Some small groups shun leadership and instead try to operate by consensus. In this model of decision making popularized by Quakers, no decision is made unless all group members agree with it. If even one member disagrees, the group keeps discussing the issue until it reaches a compromise that satisfies everyone.

If the person disagreeing does not feel very strongly about the issue or does not wish to prolong the discussion, she or he may agree to "stand aside" and let the group make the decision despite the lack of total consensus. But if this person refuses to stand aside, no decision may be possible. A major advantage of the consensus style of decision making is psychic. Because everyone has a chance to voice an opinion about a potential decision and no decisions are reached unless everyone agrees with them, group members will ordinarily feel good about the eventual decision and also about being in the group.

The major disadvantage has to do with time and efficiency. When groups operate by consensus, their discussions may become long and tedious, as no voting is allowed and discussion must continue until everyone is satisfied with the outcome. This means the group may well be unable to make decisions quickly and efficiently. One final issue in leadership has to do with gender differences in leadership styles.

Although the evidence indicates that women and men are equally capable of being good leaders, their leadership styles do tend to differ. Women are more likely to be democratic leaders, while men are more likely to be authoritarian leaders. Because of this difference, women leaders sometimes have trouble securing respect from their subordinates and are criticized for being too soft. Yet if they respond with a more masculine, or authoritarian, style, they may be charged with acting too much like a man and be criticized in ways a man would not be.

GROUPS, ROLES, AND CONFORMITY

We have seen in this and that groups are essential for social life, in large part because they play an important part in the socialization process and provide emotional and other support for their members. As sociologists have emphasized since the origins of the discipline during the 19th century, the influence of groups on individuals is essential for social stability.

This influence operates through many mechanisms, including the roles that group members are expected to play. Secondary groups such as business organizations are also fundamental to complex industrial societies such as our own. Social stability results because groups induce their members to conform to the norms, values, and attitudes of the groups themselves and of the larger society to which they belong. However, conformity to the group, or peer pressure, has a downside if it means that people might adopt group norms, attitudes, or values that are bad for some reason to hold and may even result in harm to others. Conformity is thus a double-edged sword. Unfortunately, bad conformity happens all too often, as several social-psychological experiments, to which we now turn, remind us.

SOLOMON ASCH AND PERCEPTIONS OF LINE LENGTHS

Several decades ago Solomon Asch conducted one of the first of these experiments. One of the lines on the right card is identical in length to the single line in the left card. Next, he had students meet in groups of at least six members and told them he was testing their visual ability. One by one he asked each member of the group to identify which of the three lines was the same length as the single line. One by one each student gave a wrong answer.

Finally, the last student had to answer, and about one-third of the time the final student in each group also gave the wrong answer that everyone else was giving. Unknown to these final students, all the other students were confederates or accomplices, to use some experimental jargon, as Asch had told them to give a wrong answer on purpose.

The final student in each group was thus a naive subject, and Asch's purpose was to see how often the naive subjects in all the groups would give the wrong answer that everyone else was giving, even though it was very clear it was a wrong answer.

After each group ended its deliberations, Asch asked the naive subjects who gave the wrong answers why they did so. Some replied that they knew the answer was wrong but they did not want to look different from the other people in the group, even though they were strangers before the experiment began. But other naive subjects said they had begun to doubt their own visual perception: they decided that if everyone else was giving a different answer, then somehow they were seeing the cards incorrectly. Asch's experiment indicated that groups induce conformity for at least two reasons. First, members feel pressured to conform so as not to alienate other members.

Second, members may decide their own perceptions or views are wrong because they see other group members perceiving things differently and begin to doubt their own perceptive abilities. For either or both reasons, then, groups can, for better or worse, affect our judgments and our actions.

STANLEY MILGRAM AND ELECTRIC SHOCK

Although the type of influence Asch's experiment involved was benign, other experiments indicate that individuals can conform in a very harmful way. One such very famous experiment was conducted by Yale University psychologist Stanley Milgram, who designed it to address an important question that arose after World War II and the revelation of the murders of millions of people during the Nazi Holocaust.

This question was, "How was the Holocaust possible?" Many people blamed the authoritarian nature of German culture and the so-called authoritarian personality that it inspired among German residents, who, it was thought, would be quite ready to obey rules and demands from authority figures.

Milgram wanted to see whether Germans would indeed be more likely than Americans to obey unjust authority. He devised a series of experiments and found that his American subjects were quite likely to give potentially lethal electric shocks to other people.

During the experiment, a subject, or "teacher" would come into a laboratory and be told by a man wearing a white lab coat to sit down at a table housing a machine that sent electric shocks to a "learner." Depending on the type of experiment, this was either a person whom the teacher never saw and heard only over a loudspeaker, a person sitting in an adjoining room whom the teacher could see through a window and hear over the loudspeaker, or a person sitting right next to the teacher. The teacher was then told to read the learner a list of word pairs, such as mother-father, cat-dog, and sun-moon. At the end of the list, the teacher was then asked to read the first word of the first word pair-for example, "mother" in our list-and to read several possible matches. If the learner got the right answer, the teacher would move on to the next word pair, but if the learner gave the wrong answer, the teacher was to administer an electric shock to the learner.

The initial shock was 15 volts, and each time a wrong answer was given, the shock would be increased, finally going up to 450 V, which was marked on the machine as "Danger: Severe Shock." The learners often gave wrong answers and would cry out in pain as the voltage increased. In the 200-V range, they would scream, and in the 400-V range, they would say nothing at all.

As far as the teachers knew, the learners had lapsed into unconsciousness from the electric shocks and even died. Before his study began, Milgram consulted several psychologists, who assured him that no sane person would be willing to administer lethal shock in his experiments. He thus was shocked to find that more than half the teachers went all the way to 450 V in the experiments, where they could only hear the learner over a loudspeaker and not see him.

Even in the experiments where the learner was sitting next to the teacher, some teachers still went to 450 V by forcing a hand of the screaming, resisting, but tied-down learner onto a metal plate that completed the electric circuit. It turned out that the learners were not actually being shocked. Instead the voice and screams heard through the loudspeaker were from a tape recorder, and the learner that some of the teachers saw was placed there by Milgram to pretend to be in agony.

Milgram concluded that people are quite willing, however reluctantly, to obey authority even if it means inflicting great harm on others. If that could happen in his artificial experiment situation, he thought, then perhaps the Holocaust was not so incomprehensible after all, and it would be too simplistic to blame the Holocaust just on the authoritarianism of German culture. Instead, perhaps its roots lay in the very conformity to roles and group norms that makes society possible in the first place. The same processes that make society possible may also make tragedies like the Holocaust possible.

THE THIRD WAVE

In 1969, concern about the Holocaust prompted Ron Jones, a high school teacher from Palo Alto, California, to conduct a real-life experiment that reinforced Milgram's findings by creating a Nazi-like environment in the school in just a few short days. He began by telling his sophomore history class about the importance of discipline and self-control. He had his students sit at attention and repeatedly stand up and sit down in quiet unison and saw their pride as they accomplished this task efficiently.

All of a sudden everyone in the class seemed to be paying rapt attention to what was going on. The next day, Jones began his class by talking about the importance of community and of being a member of a team or a cause. He had his class say over and over, "Strength through discipline, strength through community.

"Then he showed them a new class salute, made by bringing the right hand near the right shoulder in a curled position. He called it the Third Wave salute, because a hand in this position resembled a wave about to topple over. Jones then told the students they had to salute each other outside the classroom, which they did so during the next few days. As word of what was happening in Jones's class spread, students from other classes asked if they could come into his classroom.

On the third day of the experiment, Jones gave membership cards to every student in his class, which had now gained several new members. He told them they had to turn in the name of any student who was disobeying the class's rules. He then talked to them about the importance of action and hard work, both of which enhanced discipline and community.

Jones told his students to recruit new members and to prevent any student who was not a Third Wave member from entering the classroom. During the rest of the day, students came to him with reports of other students not saluting the right way or of some students criticizing the experiment. Meanwhile, more than 200 students had joined the Third Wave. On the fourth day of the experiment, more than 80 students squeezed into Jones's classroom.

Jones informed them that the Third Wave was in fact a new political movement in the United States that would bring discipline, order, and pride to the country and that his students were among the first in the movement. The next day, Jones said, the Third Wave's national leader, whose identity was still not public, would be announcing a grand plan for action on national television at noon. At noon the next day, more than 200 students crowded into the school auditorium to see the television speech. When Jones gave them the Third Wave salute, they saluted back. They chanted, "Strength through discipline, strength through community," over and over, and then sat in silent anticipation as Jones turned on a large television in front of the auditorium.

The television remained blank. Suddenly Jones turned on a movie projector and showed scenes from a Nazi rally and the Nazi death camps. As the crowd in the auditorium reacted with shocked silence, the teacher told them there was no Third Wave movement and that almost overnight they had developed a Nazi-like society by allowing their regard for discipline, community, and action to warp their better judgment. Many students in the auditorium sobbed as they heard his words.

The Third Wave experiment once again indicates that the normal group processes that make social life possible also can lead people to conform to standards-in this case fascism-that most of us would reject. It also helps us understand further how the Holocaust could have happened.

As Jones told his students in the auditorium, "You thought that you were the elect. That you were better than those outside this room. You bargained your freedom for the comfort of discipline and superiority. You chose to accept the group's will and the big lie over your own conviction.... Yes, we would all have made good Germans."

ZIMBARDO'S PRISON EXPERIMENT

In 1971, Stanford University psychologist Philip Zimbardo conducted an experiment to see what accounts for the extreme behaviours often seen in prisons: does this behaviour stem from abnormal personalities of guards and prisoners or, instead, from the social structure of prisons, including the roles their members are expected to play? His experiment remains a compelling illustration of how roles and group processes can prompt extreme behaviour.

Zimbardo advertised for male students to take part in a prison experiment and screened them out for histories of mental illness, violent behaviour, and drug use. He then assigned them randomly to be either guards or prisoners in the experiment to ensure that any behavioural differences later seen between the two groups would have to stem from their different roles and not from any preexisting personality differences had they been allowed to volunteer.

The guards were told that they needed to keep order. They carried no weapons but did dress in khaki uniforms and wore reflector sunglasses to make eye contact impossible. On the first day of the experiment, the guards had the prisoners, who wore gowns and stocking caps to remove their individuality, stand in front of their cells for the traditional prison "count." They made the prisoners stand for hours on end and verbally abused those who complained.

A day later the prisoners refused to come out for the count, prompting the guards to respond by forcibly removing them from their cells and sometimes spraying them with an ice-cold fire extinguisher to expedite the process. Some prisoners were put into solitary confinement. The guards also intensified their verbal abuse of the prisoners.

By the third day of the experiment, the prisoners had become very passive. The guards, several of whom indicated before the experiment that they would have trouble taking their role seriously, now were quite serious. They continued their verbal abuse of the prisoners and became quite hostile if their orders were not followed exactly. What had begun as somewhat of a lark for both guards and prisoners had now become, as far as they were concerned, a real prison. Shortly thereafter, first one prisoner and then a few more came down with symptoms of a nervous breakdown. Zimbardo and his assistants could not believe this was possible, as they had planned for the experiment to last for 2 weeks, but they allowed the prisoners to quit the experiment.

When the first one was being "released" the guards had the prisoners chant over and over that this prisoner was a bad prisoner and that they would be punished for his weakness. When this prisoner heard the chants, he refused to leave the area because he felt so humiliated. The researchers had to remind him that this was only an experiment and that he was not a real prisoner. Zimbardo had to shut down the experiment after only 6 days.

Zimbardo later observed that if psychologists had viewed the behaviours just described in a real prison, they would likely have attributed them to preexisting personality problems in both guards and prisoners. As already noted, however, his random assignment procedure invalidated this possibility. Zimbardo thus concluded that the guards' and prisoners' behavioural problems must have stemmed from the social structure of the prison experience and the roles each group was expected to play.

Zimbardo later wrote that these same processes help us understand "how good people turn evil," to cite the subtitle of his book, and thus help explain the torture and abuse committed by American forces at the Abu Ghraib prison in Iraq after the United States invaded and occupied that country in 2003.

Once again we see how two of the building blocks of social life-groups and roles-contain within them the seeds of regrettable behaviour and attitudes. As these examples suggest, sometimes people go along with the desires and views of a group against their better judgments, either because they do not want to appear different or because they have come to believe that the group's course of action may be the best one after all. Psychologist Irving Janis called this process groupthink and noted it has often affected national and foreign policy decisions in the United States and elsewhere. Group members often quickly agree on some course of action without thinking completely of alternatives. A well-known example here is the decision by President John F. Kennedy and his advisers in 1961 to take part in the invasion of the Bay of Pigs in Cuba. Although several advisers thought the plan ill advised, they kept quiet, and the invasion was an embarrassing failure.

After most Americans decided that the decision to invade Iraq in 2003 was misguided, many commentators said that the decision resulted from "collective groupthink" and regretted that they themselves had succumbed to it. Groupthink is also seen in jury decision making.

Because of the pressures to reach a verdict quickly, some jurors may go along with a verdict even if they believe otherwise. In juries and other small groups, groupthink is less likely to occur if at least one person expresses a dissenting view. Once that happens, other dissenters feel more comfortable voicing their own objections.

FORMAL ORGANIZATIONS

Modern societies are filled with formal organizations, or large secondary groups that follow explicit rules and procedures to achieve specific goals and tasks. Max Weber, one of the founders of sociology, recognized long ago that as societies become more complex, their procedures for accomplishing tasks rely less on traditional customs and beliefs and more on rational methods of decision making.

The development of formal organizations, he emphasized, allowed complex societies to accomplish their tasks in the most efficient way possible. Today we cannot imagine how any modern, complex society could run without formal organizations such as businesses and health-care institutions.

TYPES OF FORMAL ORGANIZATIONS

Sociologist Amitai Etzioni developed a popular typology of organizations based on how they induce people to join them and keep them as members once they do join. His three types are utilitarian, normative, and coercive organizations. Utilitarian organizations provide an income or some other personal benefit. Business organizations, ranging from large corporations to small Mom-and-Pop grocery stores, are familiar examples of utilitarian organizations. Colleges and universities are utilitarian organizations not only for the people who work at them but also for their students, who certainly see education and a diploma as important tangible benefits they can gain from higher education.

In contrast, normative organizations allow people to pursue their moral goals and commitments. Their members do not get paid and instead contribute their time or money because they like or admire what the organization does. The many examples of normative organizations include churches and synagogues, Boy and Girl Scouts, the Kiwanis Club and other civic groups, and groups with political objectives, such as the National Council of La Raza, the largest advocacy organization for Latino civil rights.

Alexis de Tocqueville observed some 175 years ago that the United States was a nation of joiners, and contemporary research finds that Americans indeed rank above average among democratic nations in membership in voluntary associations.

Some people end up in organizations involuntarily because they have violated the law or been judged to be mentally ill. Prisons and state mental institutions are examples of such coercive organizations, which, as total institutions seek to control all phases of their members' lives. Our chances of ending up in coercive organizations depend on various aspects of our social backgrounds.

For prisons one of these aspects is geographical. The distribution of imprisonment in the United States and shows the imprisonment rate for each of the four major census regions. This rate tends to be highest in the South and in the West. Do you think this pattern exists because crime rates are highest in these regions or instead because these regions are more likely than other parts of the United States to send convicted criminals to prisons?

BUREAUCRACIES: THE GOOD, THE BAD, AND THE UGLY

As discussed earlier, Max Weber emphasized that modern societies increasingly depend on formal organizations to accomplish key tasks. He particularly had in mind bureaucracies, or formal organizations with certain organizational features designed to achieve goals in the most efficient way possible.

He said that the ideal type of bureaucracy is characterized by several features that together maximize the efficiency and effectiveness of organizational decision making and goal accomplishment:

- *Specialization*: By specialization Weber meant a division of labour in which specific people have certain tasks-and only those tasks-to do. Presumably they are most skilled at these tasks and less skilled at others. With such specialization, the people who are best suited to do various tasks are the ones who work on them, maximizing the ability of the organization to have these tasks accomplished.
- *Hierarchy*: Equality does not exist in a bureaucracy. Instead its structure resembles a pyramid, with a few positions at the top and many more lower down. The chain of command runs from the top to the bottom, with the persons occupying the positions at the top supervising those below them. The higher you are in the hierarchy, the fewer people to whom you have to report. Weber thought a hierarchical structure maximizes efficiency because it reduces decision-making time and puts the authority to make the most important decisions in the hands of the people at the top of the pyramid who presumably are the best qualified to make them.
- *Written rules and regulations*: For an organization to work efficiently, everyone must know what to do and when to do it. This means their actions must be predictable. To ensure predictability, their roles and the organization's operating procedures must be

written in a manual with everyone in the organization expected to be familiar with its rules. Much of the communication among members of bureaucracies is written in the form of memos and e-mail rather than being verbal. This written communication leaves a paper trail so that accountability for individual behaviour can later be determined.

- *Impartiality and impersonality*: The head of a small, nonbureaucratic organization might prefer to hire people she or he knows and promote them on the same basis. Weber thought that impartiality in hiring, promotion, and firing would be much better for a large organization, as it guarantees people will advance through a firm based on their skills and knowledge, not on whom they know. Clients should also be treated impersonally, as an organization in the long run would be less effective if it gave favourable treatment to clients based on whom they know or on their nice personalities. As Weber recognized, the danger is that employees and clients alike become treated like numbers or cogs in a machine, with their individual needs and circumstances ignored in the name of organizational efficiency.
- *Record keeping*: As you probably know from personal experience, bureaucracies keep all kinds of records, especially in today's computer age. A small enterprise, say a Mom-and-Pop store, might keep track of its merchandise and the bills its customers owe with some notes scribbled here and there, even in the information technology age, but a large organization must have much more extensive record keeping to keep track of everything.

The Disadvantages of Bureaucracy

Taking all of these features into account, Weber thought bureaucracies were the most efficient and effective type of organization in a large, complex society. At the same time, he despaired over their impersonality, which he saw reflecting the growing dehumanization that accompanies growing societies.

As social scientists have found since his time, bureaucracies have other problems that undermine their efficiency and effectiveness:

- *Impersonality and alienation*: The first problem is the one just mentioned: bureaucracies can be very alienating experiences for their employees and clients alike. A worker without any sick leave left who needs to take some time off to care for a sick child might find a supervisor saying no, because the rules prohibit it. A client who stands in a long line might find herself turned away when she gets to the front because she forgot to fill out every single box in a form. We all have stories of impersonal, alienating experiences in today's large bureaucracies.
- *Red tape*: A second disadvantage of bureaucracy is "red tape," or, as sociologist Robert Merton called it, bureaucratic ritualism, a greater devotion to rules and regulations than to organizational goals. Bureaucracies often operate by slavish attention to even the pickiest of rules and regulations. If every "t" isn't crossed and every "i" isn't dotted, then someone gets into trouble, and perhaps a client is not served. Such bureaucratic ritualism contributes to the alienation already described.
- *Trained incapacity*: If an overabundance of rules and regulations and over attention to them lead to bureaucratic ritualism, they also lead to an inability of people in an organization to think creatively and to act independently. In the late 1800s, Thorstein Veblen called this problem trained incapacity. When unforeseen problems arise, trained incapacity may prevent organizational members from being able to handle them.
- *Bureaucratic incompetence*: Two popular writers have humorously pointed to special problems in

bureaucracies that undermine their effectiveness. The first of these, popularly known as Parkinson's law after its coiner, English historian C. Northcote Parkinson, says that work expands to fill the time available for it. To put it another way, the more time you have to do something, the longer it takes. The second problem is called the Peter Principle, also named after its founder, Canadian author Laurence J. Peter and says that people will eventually be promoted to their level of incompetence. In this way of thinking, someone who does a good job will get promoted and then get promoted again if she or he continues doing a good job. Eventually such people will be promoted to a job for which they are not well qualified, impeding organizational efficiency and effectiveness. Have you ever worked for someone who showed the Peter Principle?

- *Goal displacement and self-perpetuation*: Sometimes bureaucracies become so swollen with rules and personnel that they take on a life of their own and lose sight of the goals they were originally designed to achieve. People in the bureaucracy become more concerned with their job comfort and security than with helping the organization accomplish its objectives. To the extent this happens, the bureaucracy's efficiency and effectiveness are again weakened.

MICHELS'S IRON LAW OF OLIGARCHY

Several decades ago Robert Michels, a German activist and scholar, published his famous iron law of oligarchy, by which he meant that large organizations inevitably develop an oligarchy, or the undemocratic rule of many people by just a few people.

He said this happens as leaders increasingly monopolize knowledge because they have more access than do other organizational members to information and technology. They begin to think they are better suited than other people to lead their organizations, and they also do their best to stay in their positions of power, which they find very appealing. This latter goal becomes more important than helping the organization achieve its objectives and than serving the interests of the workers further down the organizational pyramid. Drawing on our earlier discussion of group size, it is also true that as an organization becomes larger, it becomes very difficult to continue to involve all group members in decision making, which almost inevitably becomes monopolized by the relatively few people at the top of the organization.

Michels thought oligarchization happens not only in bureaucracies but also in a society's political structures and said that the inevitable tendency to oligarchy threatens democracy by concentrating political decision-making power in the hands of a few.

As his use of the term iron law suggests, Michels thought the development of oligarchies was inevitable, and he was very pessimistic about democracy's future. Has our society as a whole lost some of its democracy in the ways Michels predicted? Some evidence supports his prediction. For example, many large organizations, including corporations, labour unions, political parties, and colleges and universities, do resemble the types of oligarchies over which Michels despaired.

In most of these, decision making is indeed concentrated in the hands of a few, who often do work, at least just as to their critics, for their own interests as least as much as they do for the interests of the organization and its members. On the other hand, organizational and political leaders do not work always for themselves and often have the interests of their organizations and the public in mind. Michels's law might not be so ironclad after all, but it does remind us to be on the alert for the undemocratic processes he predicted.

GENDER, RACE, AND FORMAL ORGANIZATIONS

Three types of organizations: utilitarian, normative, and coercive. What does the evidence indicate about the dynamics of gender and race in these organizations? We have already seen that women in utilitarian organizations such as businesses have made striking inroads but remain thwarted by a glass ceiling and the refusal of some subordinates to accept their authority. The workforce as a whole remains segregated by sex, as many women work in a relatively few occupations such as clerical and secretarial work.

This fact contributes heavily to the lower pay that women receive compared to men. Turning to race, effective federal and state laws against racial discrimination in the workplace arose in the aftermath of the Southern civil rights movement of the 1960s.

Although these laws have helped greatly, people of colour are still worse off than whites in hiring, promotion, and salaries, affirmative action efforts notwithstanding. Race and Ethnicity and Gender and Gender Inequality will further discuss the experiences of people of colour and of women, respectively, in the workplace. Much less research exists on gender and race in normative organizations.

But we do know that many women are involved in many types of these voluntary associations, especially those having to do with children and education and related matters. These associations allow them to contribute to society and are a source of self-esteem and, more practically, networking. Many people of colour have also been involved in normative organizations, especially those serving various needs of their communities.

One significant type of normative organization is the church, which has been extraordinarily important in the African-American community over the decades and was a key locus of civil rights activism in the South during the 1960s. Turning to coercive organizations, we know much about prisons and the race and gender composition of their inmates. Men, African Americans, and Latinos are overrepresented in prisons and jails.

This means that they constitute much higher percentages of all inmates than their numbers in the national population would suggest. Although men make up about 50% of the national population, for example, they account for more than

90% of all prisoners. Similarly, although African Americans are about 13% of the population, they account for more than 40% of all prisoners. The corresponding percentages for Latinos are about 15% and almost 20%, respectively. Why these patterns exist is unclear. Do they reflect discrimination against African Americans, Latinos, and men, or do they reflect higher offending rates by these groups?

GROUPS, ORGANIZATIONS, AND SOCIAL CHANGE

As we consider ways to try to improve our society, the role of groups and organizations becomes very important.

VEHICLES FOR SOCIAL CHANGE

One individual can certainly make a difference, but it is much more common for any difference to be made by individuals acting together-that is, by a group. In this regard, it is very clear that groups of many types have been and will continue to be vehicles for social reform and social change of many kinds. Many of the rights and freedoms Americans enjoy today were the result of committed efforts by social reform groups and social movements of years past: the abolitionist movement, the woman suffrage movement and contemporary women's movement, the labour movement, the civil rights movement, the gay rights movement, and the environmental movement, to name just a few.

Their experience reflects the wisdom of anthropologist Margaret Mead's famous quote that we should "never doubt that a small group of thoughtful, committed citizens can change the world. Indeed, it is the only thing that ever has." In today's world, there are innumerable social service and social advocacy groups that are attempting to bring about changes to benefit a particular constituency or the greater society, and you might well belong to one of these groups on your campus or in your home community.

All such groups, past, present, and future, are vehicles for social reform and social change, or at least have the potential for becoming such vehicles.

OBSTACLES TO SOCIAL CHANGE

Groups can bring about social reform and social change, but they can also thwart efforts to achieve a just society. For every social change and social reform effort that so many groups and organizations undertake, other groups and organizations try to block such efforts.

Groups may be the building blocks of social reform and social change, but they are also the building blocks for the status quo. If the study of sociology can be said to be the study of group life, as noted earlier, the study of social reform and social change can also be said to be the study of what groups and organizations do to try to bring about social reform or to maintain the status quo.

CHANGING GROUPS AND ORGANIZATIONS

Groups and organizations are typically set in their ways and do not often change their dynamics, goals, or other key aspects. This is especially true of the formal organizations we call bureaucracies, which, as we saw, are so committed and even "stuck" to certain procedures that they become inefficient and even alienating.

Groupthink can also set in and stifle creativity and keep group and organizational members from raising concerns about certain practices and/or goals. Whistle-blowing is now the common term for raising such concerns, especially when the concern involves illegal and/or potentially harmful behaviour.

It is not easy to be a whistle-blower, and several individuals who have "blown the whistle" have been harassed, fired, or sued for doing so. In response to such reprisals, various federal and state laws have been passed to protect whistle-blowers.

Still, it takes a certain amount of courage and no small amount of perseverance to be a whistle-blower. It is almost certain that some readers of this book will one day find themselves in a position where they, too, might have to decide whether to become a whistle-blower when they perceive some violation of the law and/or harmful behaviour to be occurring.

If so, they will have great potential for changing a group or an organization from within while performing a social good for the larger society.

IMPORTANT POINTS

- Social groups are the building blocks of social life, and it is virtually impossible to imagine a society without groups and difficult to imagine individuals not being involved with many types of groups. They are distinguished from social categories and social aggregates by the degree of interaction among their members and the identification of their members with the group.
- Primary groups are small and involve strong emotional attachments, while secondary groups are larger and more impersonal. Some groups become in-groups and vie, sometimes hostilely, with people they identify as belonging to out-groups. Reference groups provide standards by which we judge our attitudes and behaviour and can influence how we think and act.
- Social networks connect us through the people we know to other people they know. They are increasingly influential for successful employment but are also helpful for high-quality health care and other social advantages.
- The size of groups is a critical variable for their internal dynamics. Compared to large groups, small groups involve more intense emotional bonds but are also more unstable. These differences stem from the larger number of relationships that can exist in a larger group than in a smaller one.
- Instrumental and expressive leaders take different approaches in exercising leadership. Instrumental leaders focus more on solving tasks, even at the risk of alienating group members, while expressive leaders focus more on group relations. Of the three

major styles of leadership-authoritarian, democratic, and laissez-faire-laissez-faire leadership seems the least effective in helping a group achieve its goals.

- Women and men are equally effective as leaders but exhibit different leadership styles. Women tend to be expressive leaders, while men tend to be more authoritarian leaders. Women leaders still face problems in securing the respect of the group members they seek to lead.
- Processes of group conformity are essential for any society and for the well-being of its many individuals but also can lead to reprehensible norms and values. People can be influenced by their group membership and the roles they're expected to play to engage in behaviours most of us would condemn. Laboratory experiments by Asch, Milgram, and Zimbardo show how this can happen, while a real-life classroom experiment called the Third Wave dramatized how a fascist atmosphere could develop from everyday group processes.
- Formal organizations are commonly delineated just as to the motivations of the people who join them. Etzioni's popular typology, three types of formal organizations exist: utilitarian, normative, and coercive.
- Max Weber outlined several characteristics of bureaucracy that he felt make them the most efficient and effective type of large formal organization possible. At the same time, other scholars have pointed to several disadvantages of bureaucracies that limit their efficiency and effectiveness and thus thwart organizational goals.
- Robert Michels hypothesized that the development of oligarchies in formal organizations and political structures is inevitable. History shows that such "oligarchization" does occur but that society remains more democratic than Michels foresaw.
- Women and people of colour have long been

involved in normative organizations and continue to expand their numbers in utilitarian organizations, but in the latter they lag behind white men in rank and salary. In a major type of coercive organization, prisons, people of colour and men are over represented. The stage closes with the question of whether the reason for this over representation is the offending rates of these two groups or, instead, discrimination against them in criminal justice processing.

5

Deviance, Crime and Social Control

SOCIAL CONTROL AND THE RELATIVITY OF DEVIANCE

Deviance is behaviour that violates social norms and arouses negative social reactions. Some behaviour is considered so harmful that governments enact written laws that ban the behaviour. Crime is behaviour that violates these laws and is obviously an important type of deviance that concerns many Americans. The fact that both deviance and crime arouse negative social reactions reminds us that every society needs to ensure that its members generally obey social norms in their daily interaction. Social control refers to ways in which a society tries to prevent and sanction behaviour that violates norms. Just as a society like the United States has informal and formal norms so does it have informal and formal social control.

Generally, informal social control is used to control behaviour that violates informal norms, and formal social control is used to control behaviour that violates formal norms. We typically decline to violate informal norms, if we even think of violating them in the first place, because we fear risking the negative reactions of other people. These reactions, and thus examples of informal social control, include, but are not limited to, anger, disappointment, ostracism, and ridicule. Formal social control in the United States typically involves the legal system and also, for businesses, the many local, state, and federal regulatory agencies that constitute the regulatory system. Social control is never perfect, and so many norms and people exist that there are always some people who violate some norms.

In fact, Sociology and the Sociological Perspective, stressed that a society without deviance is impossible for at least two reasons. First, the collective conscience is never strong enough to prevent all rule breaking. Even in a "society of saints," such as a monastery, he said, rules will be broken and negative social reactions aroused. Second, because deviance serves several important functions for society any given society "invents" deviance by defining certain behaviours as deviant and the people who commit them as deviants. Because Durkheim thought deviance was inevitable for these reasons, he considered it a normal part of every healthy society. Although deviance is normal in this regard, it remains true that some people are more likely than others to commit it.

It is also true that some locations within a given society have higher rates of deviance than other locations; for example, U.S. cities have higher rates of violent crime than do rural areas. Still, Durkheim's monastery example raises an important point about the relativity of deviance: whether a behaviour is considered deviant depends on the circumstances in which the behaviour occurs and not on the behaviour itself. Although talking might be considered deviant in a monastery, it would certainly be considered very normal elsewhere. If an assailant, say a young male, murders someone, he faces arrest, prosecution, and, in many states, possible execution. Yet if a soldier kills someone in wartime, he may be considered a hero.

Killing occurs in either situation, but the context and reasons for the killing determine whether the killer is punished or given a medal. Deviance is also relative in two other ways. First, it is relative in space: a given behaviour may be considered deviant in one society but acceptable in another society. Culture and Society's discussion of sexual behaviour, where we saw that sexual acts condemned in some societies are often practiced in others. There we contrasted a small island off the coast of Ireland, where sex and nudity are considered disgusting, with another island in the South Pacific, where sexual activity is very common. We also saw that although many societies condemn homosexuality, in some societies homosexuality is actually fairly common. Second, deviance is relative in time: a behaviour in a given society may be considered deviant in one time period but acceptable many years later; conversely, a behaviour may be considered acceptable in one time period but deviant many years later.

In the late 1800s, many Americans used cocaine, marijuana, and opium, because they were common components of over-the-counter products for symptoms like depression, insomnia, menstrual cramps, migraines, and toothaches. Coca-Cola originally contained cocaine and, perhaps not surprisingly, became an instant hit when it went on sale in 1894. Today, of course, all three drugs are illegal.

The relativity of deviance in all of these ways is captured in a famous statement by sociologist Howard S. Becker who wrote several decades ago that deviance is not a quality of the act the person commits, but rather a consequence of the application by others of rules or sanctions to an "offender." The deviant is one to whom that label has been successfully applied; deviant behaviour is behaviour that people so label. This insight raises some provocative possibilities for society's response to deviance and crime.

First, harmful behaviour committed by corporations and wealthy individuals may not be considered deviant, perhaps because "respectable" people engage in them. Second, prostitution and other arguably less harmful behaviours may be considered very deviant because they are deemed immoral or because of bias against the kinds of people thought to be engaging in them. These considerations yield several questions that need to be answered in the study of deviance.

First, why are some individuals more likely than others to commit deviance? Second, why do rates of deviance differ within social categories such as gender, race, social class, and age? Third, why are some locations more likely than other locations to have higher rates of deviance? Fourth, why are some behaviours more likely than others to be considered deviant? Fifth, why are some individuals and those from certain social backgrounds more likely than other individuals to be considered deviant and punished for deviant behaviour? Sixth and last, but certainly not least, what can be done to reduce rates of violent crime and other serious forms of deviance? The sociological study of deviance and crime aims to answer all of these questions.

EXPLAINING DEVIANCE

If we want to reduce violent crime and other serious deviance, we must first understand why it occurs. Many theories of deviance exist, and together they offer a more complete explanation of deviance and the reactions to it than any one theory offers by itself. Before turning to them, we briefly discuss biological and psychological approaches, both of which stress factors lying inside the individual.

BIOLOGICAL AND PSYCHOLOGICAL APPROACHES

Although several biological and psychological explanations exist, they share a central proposition: deviants are different biologically or psychologically from nondeviants, and they have biological or psychological problems that predispose them to committing deviance. The implication is that deviants are biologically or psychologically abnormal. We have space here to discuss just a few of these explanations.

Early biological explanations focused on body size and shape. Towards the end of the 1800s, Italian physician Cesare Lombroso measured various body dimensions of Italian prisoners and decided their bodies resembled those of primitive men. He reasoned that criminals were evolutionary accidents, or atavists, whose brains were incapable of conforming to modern norms. Coming in the aftermath of Charles Darwin's theory of evolution, Lombroso's view gained instant popularity but was soon discredited for various methodological problems, including imprecise body measurements and the lack of adequate control groups. Nonetheless, his view that criminals are biologically different continues to guide today's biological research on crime and deviance. This research is much more sophisticated than the earlier work and has made important strides in understanding the possible biological bases of deviant behaviour.

One line of research focuses on heredity and violent crime. Studies of identical twins tend to find that if one twin has committed a crime, so has the other twin, and if one twin has not committed a crime, neither has the other one. Although this similarity suggests a genetic basis for criminality, identical twins are alike beyond their genes.

Usually they spend much time together, have the same friends, and are very close emotionally. These social similarities may explain why their activities, including criminal behaviour or the lack thereof, are so often alike. To avoid these possibilities, a few studies examine identical twins who were separated in infancy and reared by different families.

Some of these studies also find that if one twin has committed a crime, so has the other one. However, many of these twins were in fact raised by parents who were neighbours or relatives and even spent time with each other while they were growing up.

Because these "separated" twins were not so separated after all, the influence of their similar social environments on their similar behaviour cannot be ruled out. Because of these problems, many scholars say it is premature to conclude that a strong genetic basis for criminality exists. Other scholars, however, are convinced that such a basis does exist and argue that genes and the social environment have a joint influence on deviant behaviour.

The most popular contemporary psychological explanation of deviance focuses on various personality problems that are said to create deviant individuals. Several studies find that young children with behaviour problems and adolescents who commit delinquency are more likely than well-behaved youths to have personality problems such as impulsiveness and irritability.

These problems arise during early childhood and are thought to be caused by biological abnormalities or inadequate parenting. Several well-designed studies strongly suggest that early childhood programmes, including home visits to children at risk for antisocial behaviour may reduce these problems and thus reduce deviance, delinquency, and crime.

SOCIOLOGICAL EXPLANATIONS

Biological and psychological theories perhaps begin to explain why some individuals are more likely than others to commit deviance, but they have less to say about the other questions posed earlier: why rates of deviance differ within social categories and across locations, why some behaviours are more likely than others to be considered deviant, and why some kinds of people are more likely than others to be considered deviant and punished for deviant behaviour.

To answer these questions, sociological explanations are necessary. While biological and psychological theories suggest that deviants are different from nondeviants and are in that sense abnormal, sociological explanations suggest that deviants are normal people who have been influenced by the social environment to commit acts that violate social norms. Sociological explanations as a whole have important implications for successful programmes and policies to reduce deviance and crime. Consistent with this book's public sociology theme, a discussion of several such strategies. We now turn to the major sociological explanations of crime and deviance. A summary of these explanations appears in Table, "Theory Snapshot: Summary of Sociological Explanations of Deviance and Crime".

Table. Theory Snapshot: Summary of Sociological Explanations of Deviance and Crime

Major theory	Related explanation	Summary of explanation
Functionalist	Durkheim's views	Deviance has several functions: (a) it clarifies norms and increases conformity, (b) it strengthens social bonds among the people reacting to the deviant, and (c) it can help to lead to positive social change.

Social ecology	Certain social and physical characteristics of urban neighbourhoods contribute to high crime rates. These characteristics include poverty, dilapidation, population density, and population turnover.
Strain theory	Robert Merton, deviance among the poor results from a gap between the cultural emphasis on economic success and the inability to achieve such success through the legitimate means of working. Richard Cloward and Lloyd Ohlin, differential access to illegitimate means affects the type of deviance in which individuals experiencing strain engage.
Deviant subcultures	Poverty and other community conditions give rise to certain subcultures through which adolescents acquire values that promote deviant behaviour. Albert Cohen wrote that lack of success in school leads lower-class boys to join gangs whose value system promotes and rewards delinquency. Walter Miller wrote that delinquency stems from focal concerns, a taste for trouble, toughness, cleverness, and excitement. Marvin Wolfgang and Franco Ferracuti argued that a subculture of violence in inner-city areas promotes a violent response to insults and other problems.
Social control theory	Travis Hirschi wrote that delinquency results from weak bonds to conventional social institutions

		such as families and schools. These bonds include attachment, commitment, involvement, and belief.
Conflict		People with power pass laws and otherwise use the legal system to secure their position at the top of society and to keep the powerless on the bottom. The poor and minorities are more likely because of their poverty and race to be arrested, convicted, and imprisoned.
	Feminist perspectives	Inequality against women and antiquated views about relations between the sexes underlie rape, sexual assault, intimate partner violence, and other crimes against women. Sexual abuse prompts many girls and women to turn to drugs and alcohol use and other antisocial behaviour. Gender socialization is a key reason for large gender differences in crime rates.
Symbolic interactionism	Differential association theory	Edwin H. Sutherland argued that criminal behaviour is learned by interacting with close friends and family members who teach us how to commit various crimes and also about the values, motives, and rationalizations we need to adopt in order to justify breaking the law.
	Techniques of neutralization	Gresham M. Sykes and David Matza wrote that adolescents must neutralize potential guilt and shame by justifying their delinquency. Specific rationalizations include: (a) denial of responsibility, (b) denial

	of injury, (c) denial of the victim, (d) condemnation of the condemners, and (e) appeal to higher loyalties.
Labeling theory	Deviance results from being labeled a deviant; nonlegal factors such as appearance, race, and social class affect how often labeling occurs.

Functionalist Explanations

Several explanations may be grouped under the functionalist perspective in sociology, as they all share this perspective's central view on the importance of various aspects of society for social stability and other social needs.

Émile Durkheim: the Functions of Deviance

As noted earlier, Émile Durkheim said deviance is normal, but he did not stop there. In a surprising and still controversial twist, he also argued that deviance serves several important functions for society. First, Durkheim said, deviance clarifies social norms and increases conformity. This happens because the discovery and punishment of deviance reminds people of the norms and reinforces the consequences of violating them.

If your class were taking an exam and a student was caught cheating, the rest of the class would be instantly reminded of the rules about cheating and the punishment for it, and as a result they would be less likely to cheat. A second function of deviance is that it strengthens social bonds among the people reacting to the deviant.

An example comes from the classic story The Ox-Bow Incident, in which three innocent men are accused of cattle rustling and are eventually lynched. The mob that does the lynching is very united in its frenzy against the men, and, at least at that moment, the bonds among the individuals in the mob are extremely strong. A final function of deviance, said Durkheim, is that it can help to lead to positive social change. Although some of the greatest figures in history-Socrates, Jesus, Joan of Arc, Mahatma Gandhi, and Martin Luther King

Jr. to name just a few-were considered the worst kind of deviants in their time, we now honour them for their commitment and sacrifice. Sociologist Herbert Gans pointed to an additional function of deviance: deviance creates jobs for the segments of society-police, prison guards, criminology professors, and so forth-whose main focus is to deal with deviants in some manner.

If deviance and crime did not exist, hundreds of thousands of law-abiding people in the United States would be out of work! Although deviance can have all of these functions, many forms of it can obviously be quite harmful, as the story of the mugged voter that began this stage reminds us. Violent crime and property crime in the United States victimize millions of people and households each year, while crime by corporations has effects that are even more harmful, as we discuss later. Drug use, prostitution, and other "victimless" crimes may involve willing participants, but these participants often cause themselves and others much harm.

Although deviance just as to Durkheim is inevitable and normal and serves important functions, that certainly does not mean the United States and other nations should be happy to have high rates of serious deviance. The sociological theories we discuss point to certain aspects of the social environment, broadly defined, that contribute to deviance and crime and that should be the focus of efforts to reduce these behaviours.

Social Ecology: Neighbourhood and Community Characteristics

An important sociological approach, begun in the late 1800s and early 1900s by sociologists at the University of Chicago, stresses that certain social and physical characteristics of urban neighbourhoods raise the odds that people growing up and living in these neighbourhoods will commit deviance and crime.

This line of thought is now called the social ecology approach. Many criminogenic neighbourhood characteristics have been identified, including high rates of poverty, population density, dilapidated housing, residential mobility, and single-parent households. All of these problems are thought to contribute to social disorganization, or weakened social bonds and social institutions, that make it difficult to socialize children properly and to monitor suspicious behaviour.

Strain Theory

Failure to achieve the American dream lies at the heart of Robert Merton's famous strain theory. Sociology and the Sociological Perspective that Durkheim attributed high rates of suicide to anomie, or normlessness, that occurs in times when social norms are unclear or weak.

Adapting this concept, Merton wanted to explain why poor people have higher deviance rates than the nonpoor. He reasoned that the United States values economic success all else and also has norms that specify the approved means, working, for achieving economic success. Because the poor often cannot achieve the American dream of success through the conventional means of working, they experience a gap between the goal of economic success and the means of working.

This gap, which Merton likened to Durkheim's anomie because of the resulting lack of clarity over norms, leads to strain or frustration. To reduce their frustration, some poor people resort to several adaptations, including deviance, depending on whether they accept or reject the goal of economic success and the means of working.

Table, "Merton's Anomie Theory" presents the logical adaptations of the poor to the strain they experience. Let's review these briefly.

Table. Merton's Anomie Theory

	Adaptation Success	Goal of Economic Working	Means of
I.	Conformity		
II.	Innovation		-
III.	Ritualism	-	
IV.	Retreatism	-	-
V.	Rebellion	±	±

Despite their strain, most poor people continue to accept the goal of economic success and continue to believe they should work to make money. In other words, they continue to be good, law-abiding citizens. They conform to society's norms and values, and, not surprisingly, Merton calls their adaptation conformity. Faced with strain, some poor people continue to value economic success but come up with innovative means of achieving it.

They rob people or banks, commit fraud, or use other illegal means of acquiring money or property. Merton calls this adaptation innovation. Other poor people continue to work at a job while really giving up all hope of improving their lot in life. They go to work day after day as a habit. Merton calls this third adaptation ritualism. This adaptation does not involve deviant behaviour but is a logical response to the strain poor people experience.

In Merton's fourth adaptation, retreatism, some poor people withdraw from society by becoming hobos or vagrants or by becoming addicted to alcohol, heroin, or other drugs. Their response to the strain they feel is to reject both the goal of economic success and the means of working. Merton's fifth and final adaptation is rebellion.

Here poor people not only reject the goal of success and the means of working but work actively to bring about a new society with a new value system. These people are the radicals and revolutionaries of their time. Because Merton developed his strain theory in the aftermath of the Great Depression, in which the labour and socialist movements had been quite active, it is not surprising that he thought of rebellion as a logical adaptation of the poor to their lack of economic success. Although Merton's theory has been popular over the years, it has some limitations.

Perhaps most important, it overlooks deviance such as fraud by the middle and upper classes and also fails to explain murder, rape, and other crimes that usually are not done for economic reasons. It also does not explain why some poor people choose one adaptation over another. Merton's strain theory stimulated other explanations of deviance that built on his concept of strain. Differential opportunity theory, developed by Richard Cloward and Lloyd Ohlin, tried to explain why the poor choose one or the other of Merton's adaptations. Whereas Merton stressed that the poor have differential access to legitimate means, Cloward and Ohlin stressed that they have differential access to illegitimate means. For example, some live in neighbourhoods where organized crime is dominant and will get involved in such crime; others live in neighbourhoods rampant with drug use and will start using drugs themselves.

In a more recent formulation, two sociologists, Steven F. Messner and Richard Rosenfeld, expanded Merton's view by arguing that in the United States crime arises from several of our most important values, including an overemphasis on economic success, individualism, and competition. These values produce crime by making many Americans, rich or poor, feel they never have enough money and by prompting them to help themselves even at other people's expense.

Crime in the United States, then, arises ironically from the country's most basic values. In yet another extension of Merton's theory, Robert Agnew reasoned that adolescents experience various kinds of strain in addition to the economic type addressed by Merton. A romantic relationship may end, a family member may die, or students may be taunted or bullied at school. Repeated strain-inducing incidents such as these produce anger, frustration, and other negative emotions, and these emotions in turn prompt delinquency and drug use.

Deviant Subcultures

Some sociologists stress that poverty and other community conditions give rise to certain subcultures through which adolescents acquire values that promote deviant behaviour. One of the first to make this point was Albert K. Cohen, whose status frustration theory says that lower-class boys do poorly in school because schools emphasize middle-class values. School failure reduces their status and self-esteem, which the boys try to counter by joining juvenile gangs. In these groups, a different value system prevails, and boys can regain status and self-esteem by engaging in delinquency. Cohen had nothing to say about girls, as he assumed they cared little about how well they did in school, placing more importance on marriage and family instead, and hence would remain nondelinquent even if they did not do well.

Scholars later criticized his disregard for girls and assumptions about them. Another sociologist, Walter Miller, said poor boys become delinquent because they live amid a lower-class subculture that includes several focal concerns, or values, that help lead to delinquency. These focal concerns include a taste for trouble, toughness, cleverness, and excitement. If boys grow up in a subculture with these values, they are more likely to break the law. Their deviance is a result of their socialization. Critics said Miller exaggerated the differences between the value system in poor inner-city neighbourhoods and wealthier, middle-class communities. A very popular subcultural explanation is the so-called subculture of violence thesis, first advanced by Marvin Wolfgang and Franco Ferracuti.

In some inner-city areas, they said, a subculture of violence promotes a violent response to insults and other problems, which people in middle-class areas would probably ignore. The subculture of violence, they continued, arises partly from the need of lower-class males to "prove" their masculinity in view of their economic failure. Quantitative research to test their theory has failed to show that the urban poor are more likely than other groups to approve of violence.

On the other hand, recent ethnographic research suggests that large segments of the urban poor do adopt a "code" of toughness and violence to promote respect. As this conflicting evidence shows, the subculture of violence view remains controversial and merits further scrutiny.

Social Control Theory

Travis Hirschi argued that human nature is basically selfish and thus wondered why people do not commit deviance. His answer, which is now called social control theory was that their bonds to conventional social institutions such as the family and the school keep them from violating social norms. Hirschi's basic perspective reflects Durkheim's view that strong social norms reduce deviance such as suicide. Hirschi outlined four types of bonds to conventional social institutions. The first is attachment, which refers to how much we feel loyal to these institutions and care about the opinions of people in them, such as our parents and teachers. The more attached we are to our families and schools, the less likely we are to be deviant.

The second type is commitment, which refers to how much we value our participation in conventional activities such as getting a good education. The more committed we are to these activities and the more time and energy we have invested in them, the less deviant as suggested, be. The third dimension is involvement, or the amount of time we spend in conventional activities. The more time we spend, the less opportunity we have to be deviant. The final type of bond is belief, which refers to our acceptance of society's norms. The more we believe in these norms, the less we deviate. Hirschi's theory has been very popular. Many studies find that youths with weaker bonds to their parents and schools are more likely to be deviant. But the theory has its critics. One problem centres on the "chicken and egg" question of causal order. For example, many studies support social control theory by finding that delinquent youths often have worse relationships with their parents than do nondelinquent youths.

Is that because the bad relationships prompt the youths to be delinquent, as Hirschi thought? Or is it because the youths' delinquency worsens their relationship with their parents? Despite these questions, Hirschi's social control theory continues to influence our understanding of deviance. To the extent it is correct, it suggests several strategies for preventing crime, including programmes designed to improve parenting and relations between parents and children.

Conflict Explanations

Explanations of crime rooted in the conflict perspective reflect its general view that society is a struggle between the "haves" at the top of society with social, economic, and political power and the "have-nots" at the bottom. They assume that those with power pass laws and otherwise use the legal system to secure their position at the top of society and to keep the powerless on the bottom.

The poor and minorities are more likely because of their poverty and race to be arrested, convicted, and imprisoned. These explanations also blame street crime by the poor on the economic deprivation and inequality in which they live rather than on any moral failings of the poor. Some conflict explanations also say that capitalism helps create street crime by the poor.

An early proponent of this view was Dutch criminologist Willem Bonger who said that capitalism as an economic system involves competition for profit. This competition leads to an emphasis in a capitalist society's culture on egoism, or self-seeking behaviour, and greed. Because profit becomes so important, people in a capitalist society are more likely than those in noncapitalist ones to break the law for profit and other gains, even if their behaviour hurts others. Not surprisingly, conflict explanations have sparked much controversy.

Many scholars dismiss them for painting an overly critical picture of the United States and ignoring the excesses of noncapitalistic nations, while others say the theories overstate the degree of inequality in the legal system. In assessing the debate over conflict explanations, a fair conclusion is that their view on discrimination by the legal system applies more to victimless crime than to conventional crime, where it is difficult to argue that laws against such things as murder and robbery reflect the needs of the powerful.

However, much evidence supports the conflict assertion that the poor and minorities face disadvantages in the legal system. Simply put, the poor cannot afford good attorneys, private investigators, and the other advantages that money brings in court. As just one example, if someone much poorer than O. J. Simpson, the former football player and media celebrity, had been arrested, as he was in 1994, for viciously murdering two people, the defendant would almost certainly have been found guilty. Simpson was able to afford a defence costing hundreds of thousands of dollars and won a jury acquittal in his criminal trial.

Also in accordance with conflict theory's views, corporate executives, among the most powerful members of society, often break the law without fear of imprisonment, as we shall see in our discussion of white-collar. Finally, many studies support conflict theory's view that the roots of crimes by poor people lie in social inequality and economic deprivation.

Feminist Perspectives

Feminist perspectives on crime and criminal justice also fall into the broad rubric of conflict explanations and have burgeoned in the last two decades. Much of this work concerns rape and sexual assault, intimate partner violence, and other crimes against women that were largely neglected until feminists began writing about them in the 1970s. Their views have since influenced public and official attitudes about rape and domestic violence, which used to be thought as something that girls and women brought on themselves.

The feminist approach instead places the blame for these crimes squarely on society's inequality against women and antiquated views about relations between the sexes. Another focus of feminist work is gender and legal processing. Are women better or worse off than men when it comes to the chances of being arrested and punished? After many studies in the last two decades, the best answer is that we are not sure.

Women are treated a little more harshly than men for minor crimes and a little less harshly for serious crimes, but the gender effect in general is weak. A third focus of feminist work is the causes of female deviance and crime. Several studies find that the poverty, negative community conditions, and other factors that affect male criminality also affect female criminality. But they also find that the sexual abuse many girls suffer is a particular cause of many of their behaviour problems, including prostitution and drug and alcohol abuse. A final area concerns why females commit less crime than males. Most sociologists attribute this difference to gender socialization. Simply put, socialization into the male gender role, or masculinity, leads to values such as competitiveness and behavioural patterns such as spending more time away from home that all promote deviance.

Conversely, despite whatever disadvantages it may have, socialization into the female gender role, or femininity, promotes values such as gentleness and behaviour patterns such as spending more time at home that help limit deviance. Noting that males commit so much crime, Kathleen Daly and Meda Chesney-Lind wrote,

- A large price is paid for structures of male domination and for the very qualities that drive men to be successful, to control others, and to wield uncompromising power....Gender differences in crime suggest that crime may not be so normal after all. Such differences challenge us to see that in the lives of women, men have a great deal more to learn.

Symbolic Interactionist Explanations

Because symbolic interactionism focuses on the means people gain from their social interaction, symbolic interactionist explanations attribute deviance to various aspects of the social interaction and social processes that normal individuals experience. These explanations help us understand why some people are more likely than others living in the same kinds of social environments. Several such explanations exist.

Differential Association Theory

One popular set of explanations, often called learning theories, emphasizes that deviance is learned from interacting with other people who believe it is OK to commit deviance and who often commit deviance themselves. Deviance, then, arises from normal socialization processes. The most influential such explanation is Edwin H. Sutherland's differential association theory, which says that criminal behaviour is learned by interacting with close friends and family members. These individuals teach us not only how to commit various crimes but also the values, motives, and rationalizations that we need to adopt in order to justify breaking the law.

The earlier in our life that we associate with deviant individuals and the more often we do so, the more likely we become deviant ourselves. In this way, a normal social process, socialization, can lead normal people to commit deviance. Sutherland's theory of differential association was one of the most influential sociological theories ever.

Over the years much research has documented the importance of adolescents' peer relationships for their entrance into the world of drugs and delinquency. However, some critics say that not all deviance results from the influences of deviant peers. Still, differential association theory and the larger category of learning theories it represents remain a valuable approach to understanding deviance and crime.

Techniques of Neutralization

The view on deviant subcultures discussed earlier. Gresham M. Sykes and David Matza said this view ignores the fact that adolescents who commit delinquency often feel guilty or ashamed for doing so. They thus must come up with justifications for why it is OK to commit deviance. In short, they must "neutralize" their potential guilt or shame. Sykes and Matza said five such rationalizations, or techniques of neutralization, exist.

The first is denial of responsibility. Youths rationalize that because outside forces, such as the influence of deviant friends, are prompting them to break the law, they are not responsible for doing so. The second technique of neutralization is denial of injury. Here youths contemplating law breaking reason that no one will really be hurt by their actions.

The third rationalization is denial of the victim. Would-be delinquents reason that their potential victim deserves what is about to happen. A store's prices are far too high, so you decide to steal from it. The fourth is condemnation of the condemners. In this technique of neutralization, youths condemn police and other aspects of society as hopelessly corrupt and in no position to criticize the youths' own behaviour. The final technique of neutralization is appeal to higher loyalties. In this rationalization, potential lawbreakers reason that they need to break the law in order to help a friend, a family member, or another member of their primary groups. Sykes and Matza's theory has received mixed reviews.

On the one hand, many adolescents undoubtedly do feel guilty about breaking the law and must engage in techniques of neutralization before they can do so. On the other hand, some delinquents may not rationalize their behaviour until after they have already broken the law, which is not what Sykes and Matza thought. Critics also question Sykes and Matza's assumption that delinquents feel guilty about their behaviour.

Labeling Theory

If we arrest and imprison someone, we hope they will be "scared straight," or deterred from committing a crime again. Labeling theory assumes precisely the opposite: it says that labeling someone deviant increases the chances that the labeled person will continue to commit deviance. Labeling theory, this happens because the labeled person ends up with a deviant self-image that leads to even more deviance. Deviance is the result of being labeled.

This effect is reinforced by how society treats someone who has been labeled. Research shows that job applicants with a criminal record are much less likely than those without a record to be hired. Suppose you had a criminal record and had seen the error of your ways but were rejected by several potential employers.

Do you think you might be just a little frustrated? If your unemployment continues, might you think about committing a crime again? Meanwhile, you want to meet some law-abiding friends, so you go to a singles bar. You start talking with someone who interests you, and in response to this person's question, you say you are between jobs.

When your companion asks about your last job, you reply that you were in prison for armed robbery. How soon will it take for your companion to make an excuse like going to the bathroom, never to be seen again by you? As this scenario suggests, being labeled deviant can make it difficult to avoid a continued life of deviance. Although this consequence seems very plausible, the empirical evidence of the effects of being labeled is actually mixed.

Supporting labeling theory, some studies find that offenders treated more harshly by the criminal justice system are more apt to commit new offenses than those treated less harshly, but other studies find the opposite to be true. Still other studies find little effect of labeling one way or the other. Contrary to labeling theory, most studies also find that labeling does not worsen the self-image of those labeled.

Labeling theory also asks whether some people and behaviours are indeed more likely than others to acquire a deviant label. In particular, it asserts that nonlegal factors such as appearance, race, and social class affect how often official labeling occurs. William Chambliss's classic analysis of the "Saints" and the "Roughnecks" is an excellent example of this argument.

The Saints were eight male high-school students from middle-class backgrounds who were very delinquent, while the Roughnecks were six male students in the same high school who were also very delinquent but who came from poor, working-class families. Although the Saints' behaviour was arguably more harmful than the Roughnecks', their actions were considered harmless pranks, and they were never arrested.

After graduating from high school, they went on to college and graduate and professional school and ended up in respectable careers. In contrast, the Roughnecks were widely viewed as troublemakers and often got into trouble for their behaviour. As adults they either ended up in low-paying jobs or went to prison.

Although again labeling theory's view of this process sounds quite plausible, empirical support for this view is in fact mixed. Some studies find that extralegal factors such as appearance, race, class, and gender do affect the chances of arrest and other official labeling, but other studies find these factors do not matter very much. Despite the mixed evidence for labeling theory's two central assumptions on the effects of labeling and on possible biases in labeling, it has greatly influenced the study of deviance and crime in the last few decades and promises to do so for many years to come.

CRIME AND CRIMINALS

We now turn our attention from theoretical explanations of deviance and crime to certain aspects of crime and the people who commit it. What do we know about crime and criminals in the United States?

CRIME AND PUBLIC OPINION

One thing we know is that the American public is very concerned about crime. In a 2009 Gallup Poll, about 55% said crime is an "extremely" or "very" serious problem in the United States, and in other national surveys, about one-third of Americans said they would be afraid to walk alone in their neighbourhoods at night.

The sociological perspective, our social backgrounds affect our attitudes, behaviour, and life chances. Do gender and race affect our fear of crime? About 46% of women are afraid to walk alone at night, compared to only 17% of men. Because women are less likely than men to be victims of crime other than rape, their higher fear of crime reflects their heightened fear of rape and other types of sexual assault.

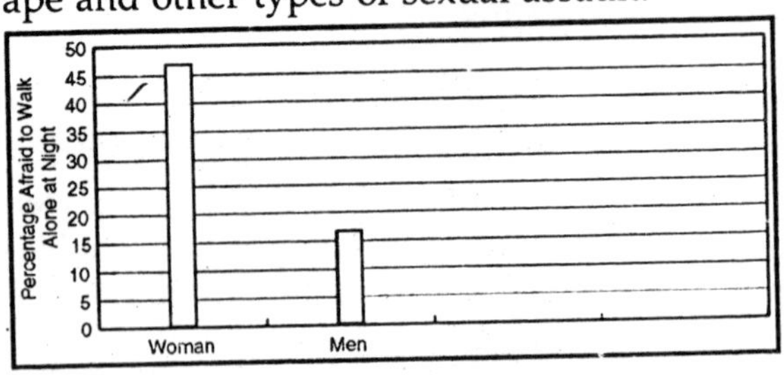

Fig. Gender and Fear of Crime

Race also makes a difference. African Americans are more afraid than whites of walking near their homes alone at night. This difference reflects the fact that African Americans are more likely than whites to live in large cities with high crime rates and to live in higher crime neighbourhoods within these cities.

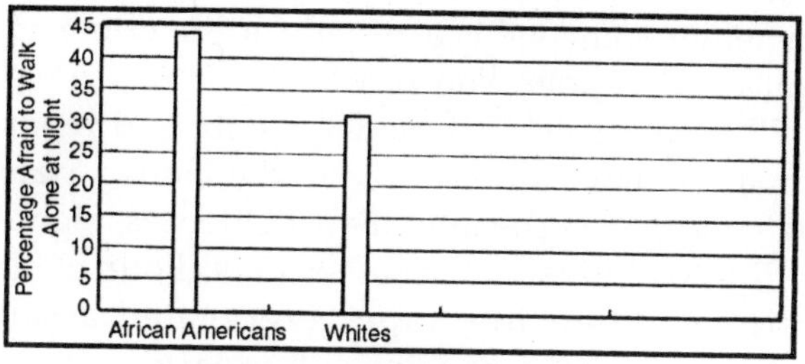

Fig. Race and Fear of Crime

Race also affects views about the criminal justice system. For example, African Americans are much less likely than whites to favour the death penalty in part because they perceive that the death penalty and criminal justice system in general are racially discriminatory.

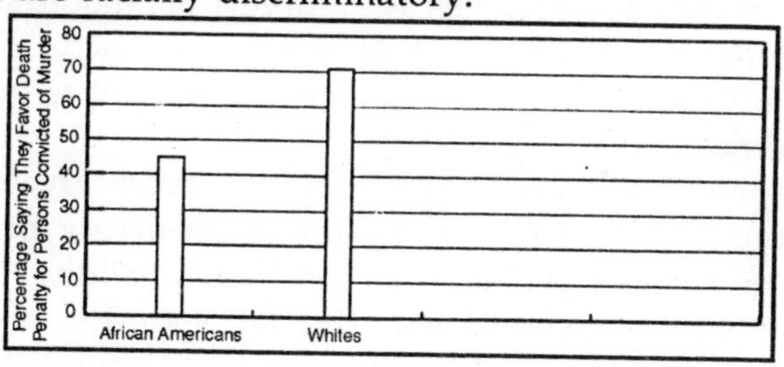

Fig. Race and Support for the Death Penalty

THE MEASUREMENT OF CRIME

It is surprisingly difficult to know how much crime occurs. Crime is not like the weather, when we all can see whether it is raining, snowing, or sunny. Usually when crime occurs, only the criminal and the victim, and sometimes an occasional witness, know about it. Although we have an incomplete picture of the crime problem, because of various data sources we still have a fairly good understanding of how much crime exists and of who is most likely to do it and be victimized by it. The government's primary source of crime data is the Uniform Crime Reports, published annually by the Federal

Bureau of Investigation. The FBI gathers its data from police departments around the country, who inform the FBI about crimes that have come to their attention. The police also tell the FBI whether someone is arrested for the crime and, if so, the person's age, gender, and race.

The FBI gathers all of these UCR data and reports them in an annual volume called Crime in the United States. Most UCR data concern the so-called Part I Offenses, eight felonies that the FBI considers the most serious. Four of these are violent crimes: homicide, rape, aggravated assault, and robbery; four are property crimes: burglary, larceny, motor vehicle theft, and arson.

The FBI, in 2008 almost 1.4 million violent crimes and 9.8 million property crimes occurred, for a total of almost 11.2 million serious crimes, or 3,667 for every 100,000 Americans. This is the nation's official crime rate, and by any standard it is a lot of crime. However, just as to surveys of random samples of crime victims, more than half of all crime victims do not report their crimes to the police, leaving the police unaware of the crimes.

The true crime problem is therefore much greater than suggested by the UCR. This under reporting of crime represents a major problem for the UCR's validity. Several other problems exist. First, the UCR omits crime by corporations and thus diverts attention away from their harm. Second, police practices affect the UCR. For example, the police do not record every report they hear from a citizen as a crime.

Sometimes they have little time to do so, sometimes they do not believe the citizen, and sometimes they deliberately fail to record a crime to make it seem that they are doing a good job of preventing crime. If they do not record the report, the FBI does not count it as a crime. If the police start recording every report, the official crime rate will rise, even though the actual number of crimes has not changed.

In a third problem, if crime victims become more likely to report their crimes to the police, which might have happened after the 911 emergency number became common, the official crime rate will again change, even if the actual number of crimes has not changed. To get a more accurate picture of crime, the federal government began in the early 1970s to administer a survey, now called the National Crime Victimization Survey, to tens of thousands of randomly selected U.S. households.

People in the households are asked whether they or their residence has been the victim of several different types of crimes in the past half year. Their responses are then extrapolated to the entire U.S. population to yield fairly accurate estimates of the actual number of crimes occurring in the nation. Still, the NCVS's estimates are not perfect.

Among other problems, some respondents decline to tell NCVS interviewers about victimizations they have suffered, and the NCVS's sample excludes some segments of the population, such as the homeless, whose victimizations therefore go uncounted. Table, "Number of Crimes: Uniform Crime Reports and National Crime Victimization Survey, 2008" lists the number of violent and property crimes as reported by the UCR and estimated by the NCVS. Note that these two crime sources do not measure exactly the same crimes.

For example, the NCVS excludes commercial crimes such as shoplifting, while the UCR includes them. The NCVS includes simple assaults while the UCR excludes them. These differences notwithstanding, we can still see that the NCVS estimates about twice as many crimes as the UCR reports to us.

Table. Number of Crimes: Uniform Crime Reports and National Crime Victimization Survey, 2008

Type of Crime	UCR	NCVS
Violent crime	1,382,012	4,856,510
Property crime	9,767,915	16,455,890
Total	11,149,927	21,312,400

A third source of crime information is the self-report survey. Here subjects, usually adolescents, are given an anonymous questionnaire and asked to indicate whether and how often they committed various offenses in a specific time period, usually the past year. They also answer questions about their family relationships, school performance, and other aspects of their backgrounds. Although these respondents do not always report every offense they committed, self-report studies yield valuable information about delinquency and explanations of crime. Like the NCVS, they underscore how much crime is committed that does not come to the attention of the police.

TYPES AND CORRELATES OF CRIME AND VICTIMIZATION

The three data sources just discussed give us a fairly good understanding of the types of crime, of who does them and who is victimized by them, and of why the crimes are committed. We have already looked at the "why"question when we reviewed the many theories of deviance. Let's look now at the various types of crime and highlight some important things about them.

Conventional Crime

By conventional crime we mean the violent and property offenses listed previously that worry average citizens more than any other type of crime. "Number of Crimes: Uniform Crime Reports and National Crime Victimization Survey, 2008" indicated, about 21 million violent and property victimizations occurred in the United States in 2008.

These offenses included some 16,300 murders, 204,000 rapes and sexual assaults, 552,000 robberies, and 840,000 aggravated assaults. Even more property crime occurs: 3.2 million burglaries, 12.3 million larcenies, and almost 800,000 motor vehicle thefts. The NCVS estimates that the crimes it measures cost their victims almost $20 billion each year in property losses, medical expenses, and time lost from work.

Generally, African Americans and other people of colour are more likely than whites to be victims of conventional crime, poor people more likely than wealthy people, men more likely than women and urban residents more likely than rural residents. To thesis these differences "Correlates of Violent Crime Victimization, 2008" presents some relevant comparisons for violent crime victimization. Violent crime is more common in urban areas than in rural areas. It varies geographically in at least one other respect, and that is among the regions of the United States. In general, violent crime is more common in the South and West than in the Midwest or Northeast. "U.S. Homicide Rates, 2008" depicts this variation for homicide rates. Louisiana has the highest homicide rate, 14.24 homicides per 100,000 residents, and New Hampshire has the lowest rate, 1.1 per 100,000 residents.

Although homicide is thankfully a rare occurrence, it is much more common in Louisiana than in New Hampshire, and it is generally more common in the South and West than in other regions. Scholars attribute the South's high rate of homicide and other violent crime to several factors, among them a subculture of violence, its history of slavery and racial violence, and its high levels of poverty.

When it comes to crime, we fear strangers much more than people we know, but NCVS data suggest our fear is somewhat misplaced. In cases of assault, rape, or robbery, the NCVS asks respondents whether they knew the offender. Strangers commit only about 36% of these offenses, meaning that almost two-thirds of the offenses are committed by someone the victim knows.

There is also a gender difference in this area: about 70% of women victims are attacked by someone they know compared to about half of male victims. Women have more to fear from men they know than from men they do not know. Another important fact about conventional crime is that most of it is intraracial, meaning that the offender and victim are usually of the same race.

For example, 83% of all single offender-single victim homicides in 2008 involved persons who were either both white or both African American. Who is most likely to commit conventional crime? As noted earlier, males are more likely than females to commit it because of gender differences in socialization. Opportunity may also matter, as during adolescence boys have more freedom than girls to be outside the home and to get into trouble.

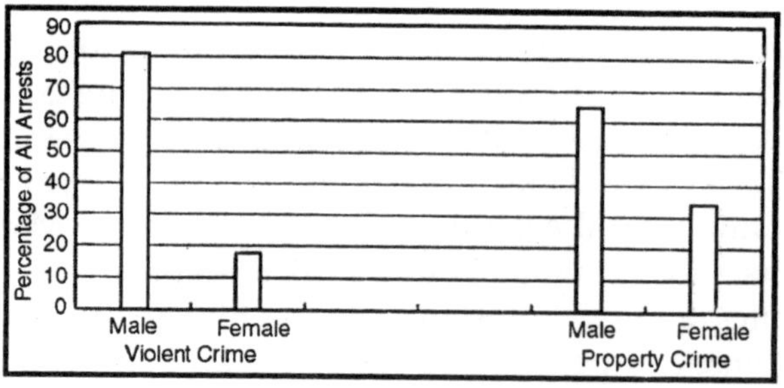

Fig. Gender and Arrest, 2008

Despite much controversy over what racial differences in arrest mean, African Americans have higher rates of arrest than whites for conventional crime. Criminologists generally agree that these rates indicate higher rates of offending. Although African Americans are about 13% of the U.S. population, they made up about 39% of all arrests for violent crime in 2008 and 30% of all arrests for property crime.

Much of these higher crime rates stem from the fact that African Americans are much poorer than whites on average and much more likely to live in the large cities with high crime rates and in the neighbourhoods in these cities with the highest crime rates. If whites lived under the same conditions, their crime rates would be much higher as well. Social class also makes a difference in conventional crime rates.

Most people arrested for conventional crime have low education and low incomes. Such class differences in arrest can be explained by several of the explanations of deviance already discussed, including strain theory. Note, however, that wealthier people commit most white-collar crimes. If the question is whether social class affects crime rates, the answer depends on what kind of crime we have in mind. One final factor affecting conventional crime rates is age.

The evidence is very clear that conventional crime is disproportionately committed by people 30 and under. For example, people in the 10-24 age group are about 22% of the U.S. population but account for about 45% of all arrests. During adolescence and young adulthood, peer influences are especially strong and "stakes in conventional activities," to use some sociological jargon, are weak. Once we start working full-time and get married, our stakes in society become stronger and our sense of responsibility grows. We soon realise that breaking the law might prove more costly than when we were 15.

White-Collar Crime

White-collar crime is crime committed as part of one's occupation. It ranges from fraudulent repairs by auto repair shops to corruption in the high-finance industry to unsafe products and workplaces in some of our largest corporations. It also includes employee theft of objects and cash. Have you ever taken something without permission from a place where you worked? Whether or not you have, many people steal from their employees, and the National Retail Federation estimates that employee theft involves some $20 billion annually.

White-collar crime also includes health-care fraud, which is estimated to cost some $100 billion a year as, for example, physicians and other health-care providers bill Medicaid for exams and tests that were never done or were unnecessary. And it also involves tax evasion: the IRS estimates that tax evasion costs the government some $300 billion annually, a figure many times greater than the cost of all robberies and burglaries.

One of the most serious recent examples of white-collar crime came to light in December 2008, when it was discovered that 70-year-old investment expert Bernard Madoff had engaged in a Ponzi scheme since the early 1990s in which he defrauded thousands of investors of an estimated $50 billion, the largest such scandal in U.S. history. Madoff pleaded guilty in February 2009 to 11 felonies, including securities fraud and money laundering, and was sentenced to 150 years in prison.

Some of the worst crime is committed by our major corporations. As just one example, price fixing in the corporate world costs the U.S. public about $60 billion a year. Even worse, an estimated 50,000 workers die each year from workplace-related illnesses and injuries that could have been prevented if companies had obeyed regulatory laws and followed known practices for safe workplaces. A tragic example of this problem occurred in April 2010, when an explosion in a mining cave in West Virginia killed 29 miners. It was widely thought that a buildup of deadly gases had caused the explosion, and the company that owned the mine had been cited many times during the prior year for safety violations related to proper gas ventilation. Corporations also make deadly products. In the 1930s the asbestos industry first realised their product was dangerous but hid the evidence of its danger, which was not discovered until 40 years later.

In the meantime thousands of asbestos workers came down with deadly asbestos-related disease, and the public was exposed to asbestos that was routinely put into buildings until its danger came to light. It is estimated that more than 200,000 people will eventually die from asbestos. Asbestos is not the only unsafe product.

The Consumer Product Safety Commission and the U.S. Centres for Disease Control and Prevention estimate that about 10,000 Americans die annually from dangerous products, including cars, drugs, and food. In perhaps the most notorious case, Ford Motor Company marketed the Pinto even though company officials knew the gas tank could catch fire and explode when hit from the rear end at low speeds.

Ford had determined it could fix each car's defect for $11 but that doing so would cost it more money than the amount of lawsuits it would eventually pay to the families of dead and burned Pinto victims if it did not fix the defect. Because Ford decided not to fix the defect, many people-estimates range from two dozen up to 500-people died in Pinto accidents. In a more recent example involving a motor vehicle company, Toyota was fined $16.4 million by the federal government in April 2010 for allegedly suppressing evidence that its vehicles were at risk for sudden acceleration.

The government's announcement asserted that Toyota "knowingly hid a dangerous defect for months from U.S. officials and did not take action to protect millions of drivers and their families". Corporations also damage the environment, as the BP oil spill that began in April 2010 reminds us. Because federal laws are lax or nonexistent, corporations can and do pollute the environment with little fear of serious consequences. One report, one-fifth of U.S. landfills and incinerators and one-half of wastewater treatment plants violate health regulations. It is estimated that between 50,000 and 100,000 Americans and 300,000 Europeans die every year from the side effects of air pollution; many of these deaths would not occur if corporations followed the law and otherwise did not engage in unnecessary pollution of the air, water, and land.

Critics also assert that laws against pollution are relatively weak and that government enforcement of these laws is often lax. Is white-collar crime worse than conventional crime? The evidence seems to say yes. A recent estimate put the number of deaths from white-collar crime annually at about 110,000, compared to "only"16,000 to 17,000 from homicide. The financial cost of white-collar crime to the public was also estimated at about $565 billion annually, compared to about $18 billion from conventional crime. Although we worry about conventional crime much more than white-collar crime, the latter harms the public more in terms of death and financial costs.

Victimless Crime

Victimless crime is illegal behaviour in which people willingly engage and in which there are no unwilling victims. The most common examples are drug use, prostitution, pornography, and gambling. Many observers say these crimes are not really victimless, even if people do engage in them voluntarily.

For example, many drug users hurt themselves and members of their family from their addiction and the physical effects of taking drugs. Prostitutes put themselves at risk for sexually transmitted disease and abuse by pimps and customers. Illegal gamblers can lose huge sums of money. Although none of these crimes is truly victimless, the fact that the people involved in them are not unwilling victims makes victimless crime different from conventional crime. Victimless crime raises controversial philosophical and sociological questions. The philosophical question is this: should people be allowed to engage in behaviour that hurts themselves? For example, our society lets adults smoke cigarettes, even though tobacco use kills several hundred thousand people every year. We also let adults gamble legally in state lotteries, at casinos and racetracks, and in other ways. We obviously let people of all ages eat "fat food" such as hamburgers, candy bars, and ice cream.

Few people would say we should prohibit these potentially harmful behaviours. Why, then, prohibit the behaviours we call victimless crime? Some scholars say that any attempt to decide which behaviours are so unsafe or immoral that they should be banned is bound to be arbitrary, and they call for these bans to be lifted. Others say that the state does indeed have a legitimate duty to ban behaviour the public considers unsafe or immoral and that the present laws reflect public opinion on which behaviours should be banned.

The sociological question is just as difficult to resolve: do laws against victimless crimes do more harm than good? Some scholars say these laws in fact do much more harm than good, and they call for the laws to be abolished or at least reconsidered for several reasons: the laws are ineffective even though they cost billions of dollars to enforce, and they lead to police and political corruption and greater profits for organized crime.

Laws against drugs further lead to extra violence, as youth gangs and other groups fight each other to corner the market for the distribution of drugs in various neighbourhoods. The opponents of victimless crime laws commonly cite the example of Prohibition during the 1920s, where the banning of alcohol led to all of these problems, which in turn forced an end to Prohibition by the early 1930s. If victimless crimes were made legal, opponents add, the government could tax the behaviours now banned and collect billions of additional tax dollars.

Those in favour of laws against victimless crimes cite the danger these behaviours pose for the people engaging in them and for the larger society. If we made drugs legal, they say, even more people would use them, and even more death and illness would occur. Removing the bans against behaviours such as drug use and prostitution, these proponents add, would imply that these behaviours are acceptable in a civil society.

The debate over victimless crimes and victimless crime laws will not end soon, as both sides have several good points to make. One thing that is clear is that our current law enforcement approach is not working. More than 1 million people are arrested annually for drug use and trafficking and other victimless crimes, but there is little evidence that using the law in this manner has lowered people's willingness to take part in victimless crime behaviour. Perhaps it is not too rash to say that a serious national debate needs to begin on the propriety of the laws against victimless crimes to determine what course of action makes the most sense for American society.

IMPORTANCE POINTS

- Deviance is behaviour that violates social norms and arouses negative reactions. What is considered deviant depends on the circumstances in which it occurs and varies by location and time period.
- Durkheim said deviance performs several important functions for society. It clarifies social norms, strengthens social bonds, and can lead to beneficial social change.
- Biological explanations of deviance assume that deviants differ biologically from nondeviants. Psychological explanations of deviance assume that deviants have a psychological problem that produces their deviance.
- Sociological theories emphasize different aspects of the social environment as contributors to deviance and crime.
- Crime in the United States remains a serious problem that concerns the public. Public opinion about crime does not always match reality and is related to individuals' gender and race among other social

characteristics. Women and African Americans are especially likely to be afraid of crime.

- Crime is difficult to measure, but the Uniform Crime Reports, National Crime Victimization Survey and self-report studies give us a fairly accurate picture of the amount of crime and of its correlates.
- Several types of crime exist. Conventional crime includes violent and property offenses and worries Americans more than any other type of crime. Such crime tends to be intraracial, and a surprising amount of violent crime is committed by people known by the victim. White-collar crim is more harmful than conventional crime in terms of personal harm and financial harm. Victimless crime is very controversial, as it involves behaviour by consenting adults. Scholars continue to debate whether the nation is better or worse off with laws against victimless crimes.
- To reduce crime, most criminologists say that a law-enforcement approach is not enough and that more efforts aimed at crime prevention are needed. These efforts include attempts to improve schools and living conditions in inner cities and programmes aimed at improving nutrition and parenting for the children who are at high risk for impairment to their cognitive and social development.

6

Gender and Gender Inequality

UNDERSTANDING SEX AND GENDER

Although the terms sex and gender are sometimes used interchangeably and do in fact complement each other, they nonetheless refer to different aspects of what it means to be a woman or man in any society.

Sex refers to the anatomical and other biological differences between females and males that are determined at the moment of conception and develop in the womb and throughout childhood and adolescence. Females, of course, have two X chromosomes, while males have one X chromosome and one Y chromosome. From this basic genetic difference spring other biological differences. The first to appear are the different genitals that boys and girls develop in the womb and that the doctor and parents look for when a baby is born so that the momentous announcement, "It's a boy!" or "It's a girl!" can be made.

The genitalia are called primary sex characteristics, while the other differences that develop during puberty are called secondary sex characteristics and stem from hormonal differences between the two sexes. In this difficult period of adolescents' lives, boys generally acquire deeper voices, more body hair, and more muscles from their flowing testosterone. Girls develop breasts and wider hips and begin menstruating as nature prepares them for possible pregnancy and childbirth. For better or worse, these basic biological differences between the sexes affect many people's perceptions of what it means to be female or male, as we shall soon discuss.

GENDER AS A SOCIAL CONSTRUCTION

Female sex is a biological concept, then gender is a social concept. It refers to the social and cultural differences a society assigns to people based on their sex. A related concept, gender roles, refers to a society's expectations of people's behaviour and attitudes based on whether they are females or males. Understood in this way, gender is a social construction.

How we think and behave as females and males is not etched in stone by our biology but rather is a result of how society expects us to think and behave based on what sex we are. As we grow up, we learn these expectations as we develop our gender identity, or our beliefs about ourselves as females or males. These expectations are called femininity and masculinity. Femininity refers to the cultural expectations we have of girls and women, while masculinity refers to the expectations we have of boys and men.

A familiar nursery rhyme nicely summarizes these two sets of traits:

- What are little boys made of?
- Snips and snails,
- And puppy dog tails,
- That's what little boys are made of.
- What are little girls made of?
- Sugar and spice,
- And everything nice,
- That's what little girls are made of.

As this nursery rhyme suggests, our traditional notions of femininity and masculinity indicate that we think females and males are fundamentally different from each other. In effect, we think of them as two sides of the same coin of being human. What we traditionally mean by femininity is captured in the adjectives, both positive and negative, we traditionally ascribe to women: gentle, sensitive, nurturing, delicate, graceful, cooperative, decorative, dependent, emotional, passive, and weak.

Thus, when we say that a girl or woman is very feminine, we have some combination of these traits, usually the positive ones, in mind: she is soft, dainty, pretty, even a bit flighty. What we traditionally mean by masculinity is captured in the adjectives, again both positive and negative, our society traditionally ascribes to men: strong, assertive, brave, active, independent, intelligent, competitive, insensitive, unemotional, and aggressive.

When we say that a boy or man is very masculine, we have some combination of these traits in mind: he is tough, strong, and assertive. These traits might sound like stereotypes of females and males in today's society, and to some extent they are, but differences between men and women in attitudes and behaviour do in fact exist. For example, women cry more often than men do. Men are more physically violent than women.

Women take care of children more than men do. Women smile more often than men. Men curse more often than women. When women talk with each other, they are more likely to talk about their personal lives than men are when they talk with each other. The two sexes even differ when they hold a cigarette. When a woman holds a cigarette, she usually has the palm of her cigarette-holding hand facing upward. When a man holds a cigarette, he usually has his palm facing downward.

SEXUAL ORIENTATION

Sexual orientation refers to a person's preference for sexual relationships with individuals of the other sex, one's own sex, or both sexes. The term also increasingly refers to transgendered individuals, those whose behaviour, appearance, and/or gender identity fails to conform to conventional norms. Transgendered individuals include transvestites and transsexuals. It is difficult to know precisely how many people are gay, lesbian, bisexual, or transgendered. One problem is conceptual.

For example, what does it mean to be gay or lesbian? Does one need to actually have sexual relations with a same-sex partner to be considered gay? What if someone is attracted to same-sex partners but does not actually engage in sex with such persons? What if someone identifies as heterosexual but engages in homosexual sex for money or for power and influence? These conceptual problems make it difficult to determine the extent of homosexuality. A second problem is empirical. Even if we can settle on a definition of homosexuality, how do we then determine how many people fit this definition?

For better or worse, our best evidence of the number of gays and lesbians in the United States comes from surveys of national samples of Americans in which they are asked various questions about their sexuality. Although these are anonymous surveys, obviously at least some individuals may be reluctant to disclose their sexual activity and thoughts to an interviewer.

Still, scholars think the estimates from these surveys are fairly accurate but that they probably underestimate by at least a small amount the number of gays and lesbians. A widely cited survey carried out by researchers at the University of Chicago found that 2.8% of men and 1.4% of women identified themselves as gay/lesbian or bisexual, with greater percentages reporting having had sexual relations with same-sex partners or being attracted to same-sex persons.

In the 2008 General Social Survey, 2.2% of men and 3.5% of women identified themselves as gay/lesbian or bisexual. Among individuals having had any sexual partners since turning 18, 2.2% of men reported having had at least some male partners, while 4.6% of women reported having had at least some female partners. Although precise numbers must remain unknown, it seems fair to say that between about 2% and 5% of Americans are gay/lesbian or bisexual.

Table. Prevalence of Homosexuality in the United States

Activity, Attraction, Oridentity	Men (%)	Women (%)
Find same-sex sexual relations appealing	4.5	5.6
Attracted to people of same sex	6.2	4.4
Identify as gay or bisexual	2.8	1.4
At least one sex partner of same sex during past year among those sexually active	2.7	1.3
At least one sex partner of same sex since turning 18	4.9	4.1

If it is difficult to determine the number of people who are gay/lesbian or bisexual, it is even more difficult to determine why some people have this sexual orientation while most do not have it. Scholars disagree on the "causes" of sexual orientation. Some scholars attribute it to unknown biological factor over which individuals have no control, just as individuals do not decide whether they are left-handed or right-handed.

Supporting this view, many gays say they realised they were gay during adolescence, just as straights would say they realised they were straight during their own adolescence. Other scholars say that sexual orientation is at least partly influenced by cultural norms, so that individuals are more likely to identify as gay or straight depending on the cultural views of sexual orientation into which they are socialized as they grow up. At best, perhaps all we can say is that sexual orientation stems from a complex mix of biological and cultural factors that remain to be determined.

THE DEVELOPMENT OF GENDER DIFFERENCES

What accounts for differences in female and male behaviour and attitudes? Do the biological differences between the sexes account for differences between these other differences? Or do these latter differences stem, as most sociologists think, from cultural expectations and from differences in the ways in which the sexes are socialized? These are critical questions, for they ask whether the differences between boys and girls and women and men stem more from biology or from society.

Biological explanations for human behaviour implicitly support the status quo. If we think behavioural and other differences between the sexes are due primarily to their respective biological makeups, we are saying that these differences are inevitable or nearly so and that any attempt to change them goes against biology and will likely fail.

As an example, consider the obvious biological fact that women bear and nurse children and men do not. Couple this with the common view that women are also more gentle and nurturing than men, and we end up with a "biological recipe" for women to be the primary caretakers of children. Many people think this means women are therefore much better suited than men to take care of children once they are born, and that the family might be harmed if mothers work outside the home or if fathers are the primary caretakers. That more than one-third of the public agrees that "it is much better for everyone involved if the man is the achiever outside the home and the woman takes care of the home and family."

To the extent this belief exists, women may not want to work outside the home or, if they choose to do so, they face difficulties from employers, family, and friends. Conversely, men may not even think about wanting to stay at home and may themselves face difficulties from employees, family, and friends if they want to do so. A belief in a strong biological basis for differences between women and men implies, then, that there is little we can or should do to change these differences. It implies that "anatomy is destiny," and destiny is, of course, by definition inevitable.

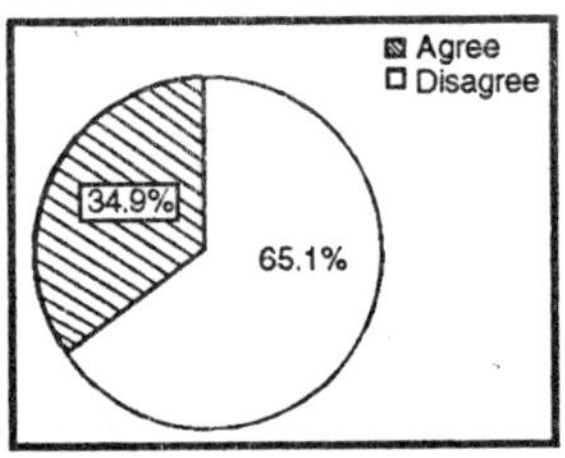

Fig. Belief That Women Should Stay at Home

Agreement or disagreement with statement that "it is much better for everyone involved if the man is the achiever outside the home and the woman takes care of the home and family."

This implication makes it essential to understand the extent to which gender differences do, in fact, stem from biological differences between the sexes or, instead, stem from cultural and social influences. If biology is paramount, then gender differences are perhaps inevitable and the status quo will remain. If culture and social influences matter much more than biology, then gender differences can change and the status quo may give way. With this backdrop in mind, let's turn to the biological evidence for behavioural and other differences between the sexes and then examine the evidence for their social and cultural roots.

BIOLOGY AND GENDER

Several biological explanations for gender roles exist, and we discuss two of the most important ones here. One explanation is from the related fields of sociobiology and evolutionary psychology and argues an evolutionary basis for traditional gender roles. Scholars advocating this view reason as follows. In prehistoric societies, few social roles existed. A major role centered on relieving hunger by hunting or gathering food.

The other major role centered on bearing and nursing children. Because only women could perform this role, they were also the primary caretakers for children for several years after birth. And because women were frequently pregnant, their roles as mothers confined them to the home for most of their adulthood. Meanwhile, men were better suited than women for hunting because they were stronger and quicker than women.

In prehistoric societies, then, biology was indeed destiny: for biological reasons, men in effect worked outside the home while women stayed at home with their children. Evolutionary reasons also explain why men are more violent than women. In prehistoric times, men who were more willing to commit violence against and even kill other men would "win out" in the competition for female mates.

They thus were more likely than less violent men to produce offspring, who would then carry these males' genetic violent tendencies. By the same token, men who were prone to rape women were more likely to produce offspring, who would then carry these males' "rape genes."

This early process guaranteed that rape tendencies would be biologically transmitted and thus provides a biological basis for the amount of rape that occurs today. If the human race evolved along these lines, sociobiologists and evolutionary psychologists continue, natural selection favoured those societies where men were stronger, braver, and more aggressive and where women were more fertile and nurturing.

Such traits over the millennia became fairly instinctual, meaning that men's and women's biological natures evolved differently. Men became, by nature, more assertive, daring, and violent than women, and women are, by nature, more gentle, nurturing, and maternal than men. To the extent this is true, these scholars add, traditional gender roles for women and men make sense from an evolutionary standpoint, and attempts to change them go against the sexes' biological natures.

This in turn implies that existing gender inequality must continue because it is rooted in biology. As the title of a book presenting the evolutionary psychology argument summarizes this implication, "biology at work: rethinking sexual equality". Critics challenge the evolutionary explanation on several grounds. First, much greater gender variation in behaviour and attitudes existed in prehistoric times than the evolutionary explanation assumes. Second, even if biological differences did influence gender roles in prehistoric times, these differences are largely irrelevant in today's world, in which, for example, physical strength is not necessary for survival.

Third, human environments throughout the millennia have simply been too diverse to permit the simple, straightforward biological development that the evolutionary explanation assumes. Fourth, evolutionary arguments implicitly justify existing gender inequality by implying the need to confine women and men to their traditional roles.

Recent anthropological evidence also challenges the evolutionary argument that men's tendency to commit violence, including rape, was biologically transmitted. This evidence instead finds that violent men have trouble finding female mates who would want them and that the female mates they find and the children they produce are often killed by rivals to the men. The recent evidence also finds those rapists' children are often abandoned and then die. As one anthropologist summarizes the rape evidence, "The likelihood that rape is an evolved adaptation extremely low. It just wouldn't have made sense for men in the to use rape as a reproductive strategy, so the argument that it's preprogrammed into us doesn't hold up".

A second biological explanation for traditional gender roles centres on hormones and specifically on testosterone, the so-called male hormone. One of the most important differences between boys and girls and men and women in the United States and many other societies is their level of aggression. Simply put, males are much more physically aggressive than females and in the United States commit about 85%-90% of all violent crimes.

Why is this so? This gender difference is often attributed to males' higher levels of testosterone. To see whether testosterone does indeed raise aggression, investigators typically assess whether males with higher testosterone levels are more aggressive than those with lower testosterone levels. Several studies find that this is indeed the case. For example, a widely cited study of Vietnam-era male veterans found that those with higher levels of testosterone had engaged in more violent behaviour.

However, this correlation does not necessarily mean that their testosterone increased their violence: as has been found in various animal species, it is also possible that their violence increased their testosterone. Because studies of human males can't for ethical and practical reasons manipulate their testosterone levels, the exact meaning of the results from these testosterone-aggression studies must remain unclear, just as to a review sponsored by the National Academy of Sciences.

Another line of research on the biological basis for sex differences in aggression involves children, including some as young as ages 1 or 2, in various situations. They might be playing with each other, interacting with adults, or writing down solutions to hypothetical scenarios given to them by a researcher. In most of these studies, boys are more physically aggressive in thought or deed than girls, even at a very young age. Other studies are more experimental in nature. In one type of study, a toddler will be playing with a toy, only to have it removed by an adult. Boys typically tend to look angry and to try to grab the toy back, while girls tend to just sit there and whimper. Because these gender differences in aggression are found at very young ages, researchers often say they must have some biological basis.

However, critics of this line of research counter that even young children have already been socialized along gender lines, a point to which we return later. To the extent this is true, gender differences in children's aggression may simply reflect socialization and not biology. In sum, biological evidence for gender differences certainly exists, but its interpretation remains very controversial. It must be weighed against the evidence, to which we next turn, of cultural variations in the experience of gender and of socialization differences by gender. One thing is clear: to the extent we accept biological explanations for gender, we imply that existing gender differences and gender inequality must continue to exist.

This implication prompts many social scientists to be quite critical of the biological viewpoint. As Linda L. Lindsey notes, "Biological arguments are consistently drawn upon to justify gender inequality and the continued oppression of women." In contrast, cultural and social explanations of gender differences and gender inequality promise some hope for change. Let's examine the evidence for these explanations.

CULTURE AND GENDER

Some of the most compelling evidence against a strong biological determination of gender roles comes from anthropologists, whose work on preindustrial societies demonstrates some striking gender variation from one culture to another. This variation underscores the impact of culture on how females and males think and behave. Margaret Mead was one of the first anthropologists to study cultural differences in gender.

In New Guinea she found three tribes-the Arapesh, the Mundugumor, and the Tchambuli-whose gender roles differed dramatically. In the Arapesh both sexes were gentle and nurturing. Both women and men spent much time with their children in a loving way and exhibited what we would normally call maternal behaviour. In the Arapesh, then, different gender roles did not exist, and in fact, both sexes conformed to what Americans would normally call the female gender role.

The situation was the reverse among the Mundugumor. Here both men and women were fierce, competitive, and violent. Both sexes seemed to almost dislike children and often physically punished them. In the Mundugumor society, then, different gender roles also did not exist, as both sexes conformed to what we Americans would normally call the male gender role. In the Tchambuli, Mead finally found a tribe where different gender roles did exist.

One sex was the dominant, efficient, assertive one and showed leadership in tribal affairs, while the other sex liked to dress up in frilly clothes, wear makeup, and even giggle a lot. Here, then, Mead found a society with gender roles similar to those found in the United States, but with a surprising twist. In the Tchambuli, women were the dominant, assertive sex that showed leadership in tribal affairs, while men were the ones wearing frilly clothes and makeup.

Mead's research caused a firestorm in scholarly circles, as it challenged the biological view on gender that was still very popular when she went to New Guinea. In recent years, Mead's findings have been challenged by other anthropologists. Among other things, they argue that she probably painted an overly simplistic picture of gender roles in her three societies.

Other anthropologists defend Mead's work and note that much subsequent research has found that gender-linked attitudes and behaviour do differ widely from one culture to another. If so, they say, the impact of culture on what it means to be a female or male cannot be ignored. Extensive evidence of this impact comes from anthropologist George Murdock, who created the Standard Cross-Cultural Sample of almost 200 preindustrial societies studied by anthropologists.

Murdock found that some tasks in these societies, such as hunting and trapping, are almost always done by men, while other tasks, such as cooking and fetching water, are almost always done by women. These patterns provide evidence for the evolutionary argument, as they probably stem from the biological differences between the sexes. Even so there were at least some societies in which women hunted and in which men cooked and fetched water.

More importantly, Murdock found much greater gender variation in several of the other tasks he studied, including planting crops, milking, and generating fires. Men primarily performed these tasks in some societies, women primarily performed them in other societies, and in still other societies both sexes performed them equally.

The gender responsibility for yet another task, weaving. Women are the primary weavers in about 61% of the societies that do weaving, men are the primary weavers in 32%, and both sexes do the weaving in 7% of the societies. Murdock's findings thesis how gender roles differ from one culture to another and imply they are not biologically determined.

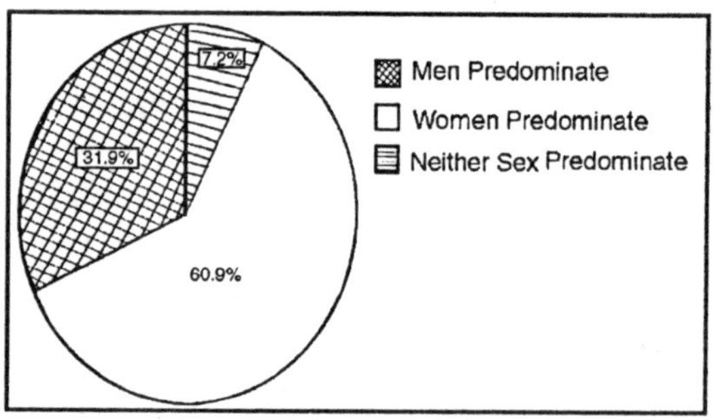

Fig. Gender Responsibility for Weaving

Anthropologists since Mead and Murdock have continued to investigate cultural differences in gender. Some of their most interesting findings concern gender and sexuality. Although all societies distinguish "femaleness" and "maleness," additional gender categories exist in some societies.

The Native Americans known as the Mohave, for example, recognize four genders: a woman, a woman who acts like a man, a man, and a man who acts like a woman. In some societies, a third, intermediary gender category is recognized.

Anthropologists call this category the berdache, who is usually a man who takes on a woman's role. This intermediary category combines aspects of both femininity and masculinity of the society in which it is found and is thus considered an androgynous gender.

Although some people in this category are born as intersexed individuals, meaning they have genitalia of both sexes, many are born biologically as one sex or the other but adopt an androgynous identity. An example of this intermediary gender category may be found in India, where the hirja role involves males who wear women's clothing and identify as women.

The hirja role is an important part of Hindu mythology, in which androgynous figures play key roles both as humans and as gods. Today people identified by themselves and others as hirjas continue to play an important role in Hindu practices and in Indian cultural life in general. Serena Nanda calls hirjas "human beings who are neither man nor woman" and says they are thought of as "special, sacred beings" even though they are sometimes ridiculed and abused.

Anthropologists have found another androgynous gender composed of women warriors in 33 Native American groups in North America. Walter L. Williams calls these women "amazons" and notes that they dress like men and sometimes even marry women. In some tribes girls exhibit such "masculine" characteristics from childhood, while in others they may be recruited into "amazonhood."

In the Kaska Indians, for example, a married couple with too many daughters would select one to "be like a man." When she was about 5 years of age, her parents would begin to dress her like a boy and have her do male tasks. Eventually she would grow up to become a hunter.

The androgynous genders found by anthropologists remind us that gender is a social construction and not just a biological fact. If culture does affect gender roles, socialization is the process through which culture has this effect. What we experience as girls and boys strongly influences how we develop as women and men in terms of behaviour and attitudes. To thesis this important dimension of gender, let's turn to the evidence on socialization.

SOCIALIZATION AND GENDER

The several agents of socialization, including the family, peers, schools, the mass media, and religion. Such socialization helps boys and girls develop their gender identity. Socialization into gender roles begins in infancy, as almost from the moment of birth parents begin to socialize their children as boys or girls without even knowing it.

Many studies document this process. Parents commonly describe their infant daughters as pretty, soft, and delicate and their infant sons as strong, active, and alert, even though neutral observers find no such gender differences among infants when they do not know the infants' sex. From infancy on, parents play with and otherwise interact with their daughters and sons differently.

They play more roughly with their sons-for example, by throwing them up in the air or by gently wrestling with them-and more quietly with their daughters. When their infant or toddler daughters cry, they warmly comfort them, but they tend to let their sons cry longer and to comfort them less.

They give their girls dolls to play with and their boys "action figures" and toy guns. While these gender differences in socialization are probably smaller now than a generation ago, they certainly continue to exist. Go into a large toy store and you will see pink aisles of dolls and cooking sets and blue aisles of action figures, toy guns, and related items.

Peers

Peer influences also encourage gender socialization. As they reach school age, children begin to play different games based on their gender. Boys tend to play sports and other competitive team games governed by inflexible rules and relatively large numbers of roles, while girls tend to play smaller, cooperative games such as hopscotch and jumping rope with fewer and more flexible rules. Although girls are much more involved in sports now than a generation ago, these gender differences in their play as youngsters persist and continue to reinforce gender roles. For example, they encourage competitiveness in boys and cooperation and trust among girls. Boys who are not competitive risk being called "sissy" or other words by their peers. The patterns we see in adult males and females thus have their roots in their play as young children.

Schools

School is yet another agent of gender socialization. First of all, school playgrounds provide a location for the gender-linked play activities just described to occur. Second, and perhaps more important, teachers at all levels treat their female and male students differently in subtle ways of which they are probably not aware. They tend to call on boys more often to answer questions in class and to praise them more when they give the right answer.

They also give boys more feedback about their assignments and other school work. At all grade levels, many and other books still portray people in gender-stereotyped ways. It is true that the newer books do less of this than older ones, but the newer books still contain some stereotypes, and the older books are still used in many schools, especially those that cannot afford to buy newer volumes.

Mass Media

Gender socialization also occurs through the mass media. On children's television shows, the major characters are male. On Nickelodeon, for example, the very popular Sponge Bob Square Pants is a male, as are his pet snail, Gary; his best friend, Patrick Star; their neighbour, Squidward Tentacles; and SpongeBob's employer, Eugene Crabs. Of the major characters in Bikini Bottom, only Sandy Cheeks is a female.

For all its virtues, Sesame Street features Bert, Ernie, Cookie Monster, and other male characters. Most of the Muppets are males, and the main female character, Miss Piggy, depicted as vain and jealous, is hardly an admirable female role model. As for adults' prime-time television, more men than women continue to fill more major roles in weekly shows, despite notable women's roles in shows such as The Good Wife and Grey's Anatomy. Women are also often portrayed as unintelligent or frivolous individuals who are there more for their looks than for anything else. Television commercials reinforce this image. Cosmetic ads abound, suggesting not only that a major task for women is to look good but also that their sense of self-worth stems from looking good.

Other commercials show women becoming ecstatic over achieving a clean floor or sparkling laundry. Judging from the world of television commercials, then, women's chief goals in life are to look good and to have a clean house. At the same time, men's chief goals, judging from many commercials, are to drink beer and drive cars. Women's and men's magazines reinforce these gender images.

Most of the magazines intended for teenage girls and adult women are filled with pictures of thin, beautiful models, advice on dieting, cosmetic ads, and substances on how to win. Conversely, the magazines intended for teenage boys and men are filled with ads and substances on cars and sports, advice on how to succeed in careers and other endeavors, and pictures of thin, beautiful women.

Religion

Another agent of socialization, religion, also contributes to traditional gender stereotypes. Many traditional interpretations of the Bible yield the message that women are subservient to men. This message begins in Genesis, where the first human is Adam, and Eve was made from one of his ribs. The major figures in the rest of the Bible are men, and women are for the most part depicted as wives, mothers, temptresses, and prostitutes; they are praised for their roles as wives and mothers and condemned for their other roles. More generally, women are constantly depicted as the property of men. The Ten Commandments includes a neighbour's wife with his house, ox, and other objects as things not to be coveted and many biblical passages say explicitly that women belong to men, such as this one from the New Testament:

- Wives be subject to your husbands, as to the Lord. For the husband is the head of the wife as Christ is the head of the Church. As the Church is subject to Christ, so let wives also be subject in everything to their husbands.

Several passages in the Old Testament justify the rape and murder of women and girls. The Koran, the sacred book of Islam, also contains passages asserting the subordinate role of women. This discussion suggests that religious people should believe in traditional gender views more than less religious people, and research confirms this relationship.

To thesis this shows the relationship in the General Social Survey between frequency of prayer and the view that "it is much better for everyone involved if the man is the achiever outside the home and the woman takes care of the home and family." People who pray more often are more likely to accept this traditional view of gender roles.

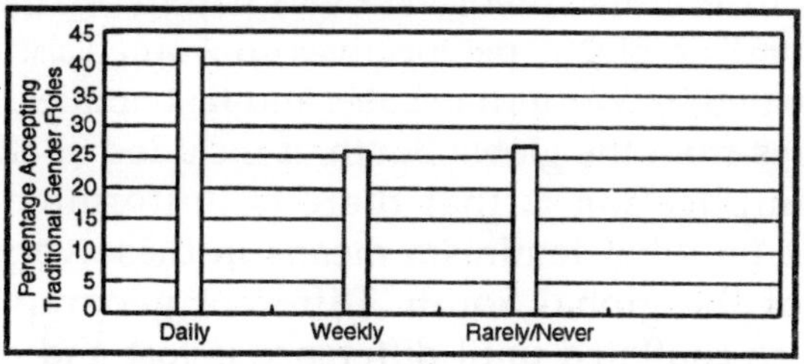

Fig. Frequency of Prayer and Acceptance of Traditional Gender Roles in the Family

Percentage agreeing that "it is much better for everyone involved if the man is the achiever outside the home and the woman takes care of the home and family."

A FINAL WORD ON THE SOURCES OF GENDER

Scholars in many fields continue to debate the relative importance of biology and of culture and socialization for how we behave and think as girls and boys and as women and men. The biological differences between females and males lead many scholars and no doubt much of the public to assume that masculinity and femininity are to a large degree biologically determined or at least influenced. In contrast, anthropologists, sociologists, and other social scientists tend to view gender as a social construction. Even if biology does matter for gender, they say, the significance of culture and socialization should not be underestimated. To the extent that gender is indeed shaped by society and culture, it is possible to change gender and to help bring about a society where both men and women have more opportunity to achieve their full potential.

FEMINISM AND SEXISM

While Western feminists and Western theoretical models of feminism have done a commendable job of deconstructing several age-old binaries that have characterised dominant philosophical and political thinking on gender, what is remarkable is the continued existence and even valorisation of the dichotomy of the West and 'the Rest' in their discourse. Readers on feminist theories, even if they claim to give 'multicultural' or 'global' perspectives on women's studies, are still dominated by Western debates and taxonomies. Feminist perspectives from the global South, if included at all.

The implication is that there is uniformity or even agreement on what feminism means in these very diverse cultures of the global South. Different geographies and histories are conflated until difference is lost and one 'third world feminism' becomes interchangeable with another, collapsing into one theoretical model the multiple struggles of very different women under very different conditions.

Even in collections that forefront non-Western feminisms, the incredible range, complexities and contested nature of 'feminisms' within different national histories is reduced to a singular unitary voice. Maitrayee Chaudhuri's collection Feminism in India challenges this reduction of local feminisms.

Tracing the history of the concept of feminism from colonial times to contemporary India, the anthology explores the infinite variety of Indian feminisms and their theoretical trajectories. As Chaudhuri says in her painstakingly thorough and methodical introduction if not one coherent framework, at least a dialogic body of work. The taxonomy of feminist theory usually deployed in the West delineates the categories of liberal, Marxist, socialist and black feminisms. Feminist writings in India can neither be pigeonholed into these categories nor be seen to follow the same developmental paths. Yet there has always been a continual engagement with Western theoretical positions not least because people in India have always lived in a world informed by Western reformist ideas such as liberalism and feminism.

Thus, Chaudhuri rejects claims that feminism in India has been a Western import. Rather, she says, ideas about women's rights and gender construction have always been debated in India, but differently. Though there has been a great degree of variance in this theorising both historically and within different women's social movements today, one aspect that runs through all the work is the fact that feminism in India has always had to negotiate around and distinguish itself from Western discourses.

As scholars and activists from different parts of the global South have argued, non- Western writers may choose to engage with non-Western thought and praxis. But no such choice exists for those working and writing in the peripheries given that, to use Arundhati Roy's felicitous phrase, we are all subjects of empire. Hence, Chaudhuri flatly states 'There is no turning away from our engagement with the West'.

This assertion is used by Chaudhuri to justify her inclusion in the anthology of writings from the late nineteenth-century onwards. Because feminism as we know it today, she argues, is a product of the modern entity of nation and nationhood, and because colonialism recast many of India's traditional hierarchies, she excludes any pre-colonial writing on gender from the text.

This is one of the few flaws in this otherwise significant anthology. As Tharu and Lalita's landmark collection of women writings in India has shown, there was a prolific exchange of ideas about gender construction and gender norms well before the late 1800s when Tarabai Shinde is supposed to have penned 'A Comparison of Men and Women.'

Shinde is remarkable for its discussions of the construction of gender norms as a radical critique of patriarchy. Seen as India's pioneering feminist literary critic, Shinde draws links between colonialism and the commodification of women's bodies.

In contrast to this polemical piece from an upper-caste Hindu woman is the position of the Oxford educated Parsi Christian reformer Cornelia Sorabji who saw education as the main means by which social transformation of women could be undertaken. Despite her legal training as a barrister in England, Sorabji argued that it was not law but education that could be the panacea sought by reformers attempting to end the practice of child marriage.

The Rokeya Sakhawat Hossain, a Bengali Muslim writer, very popular in her time. Her 'Sultana's Dream' is a feminist utopia which envisions a world where women are in charge of the public sphere. The double engagement with national identity and the woman question. It is through reading the selections included here that one can surmise the difficult choices facing women during the period of the nationalist struggles: whether or not to join the national movement; whether or not to support freedom of religion or freedom of women—issues seen as antithetical to one another.

Rather than give contemporary commentaries on nationalist texts, Chaudhuri lets historical documents speak for themselves. The 1931 'Karachi Resolution' on what 'swaraj' or 'self rule' in free India would entail, reads more impressively than the U.S. Bill of Rights. However, the gender issue is still marginalised as evidenced by the fact that only one of the resolutions expressly mentions protecting women's rights.

The 1947 report on 'Women's Role in a Planned Economy' is accompanied by a contextualised commentary by Leela Kasturi who lays out in great detail the lines along which a post-colonial India would dedicate itself to women's freedom and equality in a plural, multi-religious, multicultural society. Property rights, alimony, custody rights, and child maintenance were all detailed in this remarkable document. The largest and the most mainstream women's organisation in India at this time was the All India Women's Conference.

Founded in 1927, it was many-layered and always attempted to reflect the regional diversity of the movement. What would constitute the nation? What would be the role of women in independent India? What would the role of women be in the process of nation-building itself ? These discussions were fraught with divisions that spoke to religious, caste and other fissures within Indian society.

If feminist writing during twentieth century colonial India was characterised by societal hierarchies and a need to demarcate an Indian identity, feminist debates in post-colonial India dealt with ways in which feminist politics was practised. A part on 'Feminism in Independent India' includes some seminal thesiss that have interrogated both the connections and divergences within Left politics and feminist politics on issues such as agrarian land reform and workers' rights. Well known contemporary feminist thinkers and organisers like Gail Omvedt and Ilina Sen reiterate the need to re-theorise the fundamental causes of women's oppression in post-independent India.

The sometimes complete disenfranchisement of the rural poor raises fundamental questions about gendered power relations in society. Sen's also discusses some of the Indian women's movements much celebrated in the West such as the environmental movement called 'Chipko' and the labour and cooperative credit movement called SEWA. Both these and other struggles challenged the fundamental tenets of the national developmental policy which was predicated on rapid industrialisation at the expense of communities whose lives and livelihoods depended on land and forests.

These readings show that since independence much feminist activism and theorising has been geared at developing alternatives to existing state policy and redefining the enfranchisement and empowerment of women. But what about the poorest sessions of the society—the 'dalits'? The language of class cannot be ignored in any discussion of gender. Sharmila Rege concentrates on non-brahminical reconceptualisations of the feminist agenda in contemporary India. Her urging to reformulate the purely upper-caste historiographies could lead to more nuanced and dialectical understanding of gendered India. While this session is the thinnest, it is perhaps the richest for anyone wishing to learn about the key debates and concerns of grassroots feminist organising in contemporary India.

This session of the book alone provides an excellent overview of the multiplicity of voices that introductory texts on global feminism ignore. Surprisingly, 'Challenges to Feminism' dealing with the impact of the politics of the Hindu Right, the Hindutva movement and of globalisation, is the least nuanced and least satisfactory part of the anthology. Women's studies and economics volumes have documented well the ways in which financial institutions such as the International Monetary Fund and the World Bank have actively appropriated and exploited both the language and agenda of feminism to further their goals of privatisation and marketisation.

In reference to India, global economic policy documents have linked women's development and the nation's development in such a way that women are constructed as 'good' subjects because of their thrift and diligent labour. This, by contrast, pits them against those deemed 'bad' subjects by these international 'aid' agencies, namely their unruly men. This subject position created by discourses emanating from globalisation does not just interpellate rural women but also urban upper-class women, who are seen as liberated only if and when they entire the global market system as highly individualised conspicuous consumers.

Whether analysing the huge upsurge in public discourses selling the idea of beauty queens as liberated empowered femininity, print ads that co-opt the language of radical feminism or magazine editorials that equate modernity with conspicuous consumption, the selections all demonstrate the cooptation of the language of feminism by mainstream media and the coordinated backlash against genuine feminist positions. While the readings of popular vernacular press are useful in understanding how globalisation and its offer of a particular model of modernity are negotiated by women in contemporary India. In other words, the issue of globalisation of culture is not just a matter of academic interest. It has impacted in real terms the ways in which women construct a political identity using cultural icons.

How has the puncturing of cultural boundaries affected this process? How are hybrid identities disrupting the search for a peculiarly and specifically 'Indian' feminist identity? The impetus for the whole volume seems to be dictated by this search for the Indian roots of feminism and the possibilities of an 'authentic' or 'indigenous' feminism. The first and last parts of the book take up these concerns in innovative ways.

The extent of feminist commitments in India and the need for the orisation of sexuality within feminist formulations, they also provide an understanding of the 'anti-feminist' position and the reluctance of a vast number of Indians to use the 'F-word.' Madhu Kishwar 's' Why I Do Not Call Myself a Feminist' is just one voice in the struggle for an indigenous feminism that has raged on in India from the colonial times. The woman question in India historically has always been linked to anti-imperialist struggles whether for nationhood or an 'authentic' Indian identity. Much of theorising of Indian feminism has articulated the national question with the 'sanitised' image of Hindu upper-caste women.

The construction of a nationalist rhetoric that erased internal differences has been tantamount to emptying India's history of all its internal conflicts. 'It is at once a claim for a distinct non-Western identity and a brushing away of internal differences,' Chaudhuri asserts. In fact one of the most significant contributions of feminist theorising in the last two decades in India has been a sustained critique of essentialist notions of both the Indian nation and woman.

This quest for indigeneity has opened up political possibilities to engage with tradition and that are antithetical to fundamentalist assertions. Vidyut Bhagat explores the concept of tradition and she uses Marathi folklore to open up radical possibilities for the future of Indian feminism. Reminded me of Frantz Fanon's warning that a return to 'tradition' paradoxically might also limit efforts at liberation because it re-inscribes an essentialist, absolute and fixed notion of culture and tradition. This caution is perhaps also expressed by Rajeshwari Sunder Rajan on goddess-inspired Hindu feminism. As she says, this tradition has not only marginalised and alienated women in minority communities, but has also opened by possibilities of further exploitation of these very communities by the Hindu Right and the demarcation of more restrictive and repressive cultural lines. The end result is a nuanced conceptualisation of Indian feminisms.

As Oyeronke Oyewumi has written in the context of African feminisms, much critical writing by feminist scholars from the global South has been appropriated and tokenised in Western academia. She and many others have pointed out that this 'objectification' is predicated on the silencing of third world voices in the articulation of their own realities; this despite the proliferation of 'multicultural,' 'multiracial' and 'transnational' parts in women's studies and feminist anthologies.

Maitrayee Chaudhuri's collection deconstructs this objectification of 'third world' feminisms and reconstructs a plural, contradictory, complex notion of what feminist paradigms mean in India. The anthology demonstrates that the heterogeneity of Indian experience and the ever-changing gender relations has necessitated the articulation of multiple feminisms and multiple theoretical frameworks striated with common concerns.

These formulations have developed and transformed over time in response to the material realities of daily conditions of existence, ideological sensitivity to gender issues, the linguistic and political competencies, and historical events. Scholarly academics writing about India but, by activists and thinkers grounded in India and involved in its myriad feminist political battles, this book should be seen as a definitive work on gender scholarship in India.

GENDER INEQUALITY

We have said that the women's movement changed American life in many ways but that gender inequality persists. Let's look at examples of such inequality, much of it taking the form of institutional discrimination, which can occur even if it is not intended to happen. We start with gender inequality in income and the workplace and then move on to a few other spheres of life.

INCOME AND WORKPLACE INEQUALITY

In the last few decades, women have entered the workplace in increasing numbers, partly, and for many women mostly, out of economic necessity and partly out of desire for the sense of self-worth and other fulfillment that comes with work. This is true not only in the United States but also in other nations, including Japan, where views of women are more traditional than those in the United States.

In February 2010, 58.9% of U.S. women age 16 or older were in the labour force, compared to only 43.3% in 1970; comparable figures for men were 71.0% in 2010 and 79.7% in 1970. Thus while women's labour force participation continues to lag behind men's, they have narrowed the gap. The figures just cited include women of retirement age. When we just look at younger women, labour force participation is even higher. For example, 76.1% of women aged 35-44 were in the labour force in 2008, compared to only 46.8% in 1970.

Despite the gains women have made, problems persist. Perhaps the major problem is a gender gap in income. Women have earned less money than men ever since records started being kept. In the United States in the early 1800s, full-time women workers in agriculture and manufacturing earned less than 38% of what men earned. By 1885 they were earning about 50% of what men earned in manufacturing jobs.

As the 1980s began, full-time women workers' median weekly earnings were about 65% of men's. Women have narrowed the gender gap in earnings since then: their weekly earnings now are 80.2% of men's among full-time workers. Still, this means that for every $10,000 men earn, women earn only about $8,002. To turn that around, for every $10,000 women earn, men earn $12,469. This gap amounts to hundreds of thousands of dollars over a lifetime of working. Although such practices and requirements are now illegal, they still continue. The sex segregation they help create contributes to the continuing gender gap between female and male workers. Occupations dominated by women tend to have lower wages and salaries. Because women are concentrated in low-paying jobs, their earnings are much lower than men's.

As Table, "Median Annual Earnings of Year-Round, Full-Time Workers Aged 25 and Over, by Educational Attainment, 2007" shows, this gender gap exists for all levels of education and even increases with higher levels of education. On the average, college-educated women working full-time earn almost $17,700 less per year than their male counterparts.

Table. Median Annual Earnings of Year-Round, Full-Time Workers Aged 25 and Over, by Educational Attainment, 2007

	High School Dropout	High School Graduate	Some College or Associate's degree	Bachelor's Degree	Advanced Degree
Men	27,180	37,632	46,562	65,011	88,840
Women	20,341	27,477	34,745	47,333	61,228
Difference	6,839	10,155	11,817	17,678	27,612
Gender gap (%; women/men)	74.8	73.0	74.6	72.8	68.9

What accounts for the gender gap in earnings? A major reason is sex segregation in the workplace, which accounts for up to 45% of the gender gap. Although women have increased their labour force participation, the workplace remains segregated by gender. Almost half of all women work in a few low-paying clerical and service jobs, while men work in a much greater variety of jobs, including high-paying ones. Table "Gender Segregation in the Workplace for Selected Occupations, 2007" shows that many jobs are composed primarily of women or of men.

Part of the reason for this segregation is that socialization affects what jobs young men and women choose to pursue, and part of the reason is that women and men do not want to encounter difficulties they may experience if they took a job traditionally assigned to the other sex.

A third reason is that sex-segregated jobs discriminate against applicants who are not the "right" sex for that job. Employers may either consciously refuse to hire someone who is the "wrong" sex for the job or have job requirements and workplace rules that unintentionally make it more difficult for women to qualify for certain jobs.

Table. Gender Segregation in the Workplace for Selected Occupations, 2007

Occupation	Female Workers (%)	Male Workers (%)
Dental hygienists	99.2	0.8
Speech-language pathologists	98.0	2.0
Preschool and kindergarten teachers	97.3	2.7
Secretaries and administrative assistants	96.7	3.3
Registered nurses	91.7	9.3
Food servers (waiters/waitresses)	74.0	26.0
Lawyers	32.6	67.4
Physicians	30.0	70.0
Dentists	28.2	71.8
Computer software engineers	20.8	79.2
Carpenters	1.9	98.1
Electricians	1.7	98.3

This fact raises an important question: why do women's jobs pay less than men's jobs? Is it because their jobs are not important and require few skills? The evidence indicates otherwise: women's work is devalued precisely because it is women's work, and women's jobs thus pay less than men's jobs because they are women's jobs. Studies of comparable worth support this argument.

Researchers rate various jobs in terms of their requirements and attributes that logically should affect the salaries they offer: the importance of the job, the degree of skill it requires, the level of responsibility it requires, the degree to which the employee must exercise independent judgment, and so forth. They then use these dimensions to determine what salary a job should offer. Some jobs might be "better" on some dimensions and "worse" on others but still end up with the same predicted salary if everything evens out. When researchers make their calculations, they find that certain women's jobs pay less than men's even though their comparable worth is equal to or even higher than the men's jobs. For example, a social worker may earn less money than a probation officer, even though calculations based on comparable worth would predict that a social worker should earn at least as much.

The comparable worth research demonstrates that women's jobs pay less than men's jobs of comparable worth and that the average working family would earn several thousand dollars more annually if pay scales were reevaluated based on comparable worth and women paid more for their work. Even when women and men work in the same jobs, women often earn less than men and men are more likely than women to hold leadership positions in these occupations.

Census data provide ready evidence of the lower incomes women receive than men even in the same occupations. For example, female marketing and sales managers earn only 68% of what their male counterparts earn; female human resource managers earn only 68% of what their male counterparts earn; female claims adjusters earn only 83%; female accountants earn only 72%; female elementary and middle school teachers earn only 90%; and even female secretaries and clerical workers earn only 86%.

When variables like number of years on the job, number of hours worked per week, and size of firm are taken into account, these disparities diminish but do not disappear altogether, and it is very likely that sex discrimination by employers accounts for much of the remaining disparity. Litigation has suggested or revealed specific instances of sex discrimination in earnings and employment.

In July 2009, the Dell computer company, without admitting any wrongdoing, agreed to pay $9.1 million to settle a class action lawsuit, brought by former executives, that alleged sex discrimination in salaries and promotions. Earlier in the decade, a Florida jury found Outback Steakhouse liable for paying a woman site development assistant only half what it paid a man with the same title. After she trained him, Outback assigned him most of her duties, and when she complained, Outback transferred her to a clerical position. The jury awarded her $2.2 million in compensatory and punitive damages.

Some of the sex discrimination in employment reflects the existence of two related phenomena, the glass ceiling and the glass escalator. Women may be promoted in a job only to find they reach an invisible "glass ceiling" beyond which they cannot get promoted, or they may not get promoted in the first place.

In the largest U.S. corporations, women constitute only about 16% of the top executives, and women executives are paid much less than their male counterparts. Although these disparities stem partly from the fact that women joined the corporate ranks much more recently than men, they also reflect a glass ceiling in the corporate world that prevents qualified women from rising up above a certain level. Men, on the other hand, can often ride a "glass escalator" to the top, even in female occupations.

An example is seen in elementary school teaching, where principals typically rise from the ranks of teachers. Although men constitute only about 20% of all public elementary school teachers, they account for about 44% of all elementary school principals. Whatever the reasons for the gender gap in income, the fact that women make so much less than men means that female-headed families are especially likely to be poor.

In 2008, about 31% of these families lived in poverty, compared to only 6.7% of married-couple families. The term feminization of poverty refers to the fact that female-headed households are especially likely to be poor. The gendering of poverty in this manner is one of the most significant manifestations of gender inequality in the United States.

Sexual Harassment

Another workplace problem is sexual harassment, which, as defined by federal guidelines and legal rulings and statutes, consists of unwelcome sexual advances, requests for sexual favours, or physical conduct of a sexual nature used as a condition of employment or promotion or that interferes with an individual's job performance and creates an intimidating or hostile environment. Although men can be, and are, sexually harassed, women are more often the targets of sexual harassment, which is often considered a form of violence against women. This gender difference exists for at least two reasons, one cultural and one structural.

The cultural reason centres on the depiction of women and the socialization of men. As our discussion of the mass media and gender socialization indicated, women are still depicted in our culture as sexual objects who exist for men's pleasure. At the same time, our culture socializes men to be sexually assertive. These two cultural beliefs combine to make men believe that they have the right to make verbal and physical advances to women in the workplace. When these advances fall into the guidelines listed here, they become sexual harassment.

The second reason that most targets of sexual harassment are women is more structural. Reflecting the gendered nature of the workplace and of the educational system, typically the men doing the harassment are in a position of power over the women they harass. A male boss harasses a female employee, or a male professor harasses a female student or employee. These men realise that subordinate women may find it difficult to resist their advances for fear of reprisals: a female employee may be fired or not promoted, and a female student may receive a bad grade.

How common is sexual harassment? This is difficult to determine, as the men who do the sexual harassment are not about to shout it from the rooftops, and the women who suffer it often keep quiet because of the repercussions just listed. But anonymous surveys of women employees in corporate and other settings commonly find that 40%-65% of the respondents report being sexually harassed. In a survey of 4,501 women physicians, 36.9% reported being sexually harassed either in medical school or in their practice as physicians. Sexual harassment cases continue to make headlines. In one recent example, the University of Southern Mississippi paid $112,500 in September 2009 to settle a case brought by a women's tennis graduate assistant against the school's women's tennis coach; the coach then resigned for personal reasons. That same month, the CEO of a hospital in Washington State was reprimanded after a claim of sexual harassment was brought against him, and he was also fired for unspecified reasons.

WOMEN OF COLOUR: A TRIPLE BURDEN

Earlier we mentioned multicultural feminism, which stresses that women of colour face difficulties for three reasons: their gender, their race, and, often, their social class, which is frequently near the bottom of the socioeconomic ladder. They thus face a triple burden that manifests itself in many ways.

For example, women of colour experience "extra" income inequality. Earlier we discussed the gender gap in earnings, with women earning 79.4% of what men earn, but women of colour face both a gender gap and a racial/ethnic gap. Table, "The Race and Ethnicity and Gender Gap in Weekly Earnings for Full-Time Workers, 2007" depicts this double gap for full-time workers. We see a racial/ethnic gap among both women and men, as African Americans and Latinos of either gender earn less than whites, and we also see a gender gap between men and women, as women earn less than men within any race or ethnicity. These two gaps combine to produce an especially high gap between African American and Latina women and white men: African American women earn only 67.6% of what white men earn, and Latina women earn only 60% of what white men earn.

Table. The Race and Ethnicity and Gender Gap in Weekly Earnings for Full-Time Workers, 2007

	Median Weekly Earnings ($)	Percentage of White Male Earnings
Men		
White	788	—
Black	600	76.1
Latino	520	66.0

Women		
White	626	79.4
Black	533	67.6
Latina	473	60.0

These differences in income mean that African American and Latina women are poorer than white women. We noted earlier that about 31% of all female-headed families are poor. This masks race/ethnic differences among such families: 21.5% of families headed by non-Latina white women are poor, compared to 40.5% of families headed by African American women and also 40.5% of families headed by Latina women. While white women are poorer than white men, African American and Latina women are clearly poorer than white women.

SEXUAL ORIENTATION AND INEQUALITY

A recent report by a task force of the American Psychological Association stated that "same-sex sexual and romantic attractions, feelings, and behaviours are normal and positive variations of human sexuality". A majority of Americans do not share this opinion. In the 2008 General Social Survey, 52% of respondents said that "sexual relations between two adults of the same sex" is "always wrong."

Although, represents a substantial decline from the survey's 1973 finding of 74%, it is clear that many Americans remain sharply opposed to homosexuality. Not surprisingly, then, sexual orientation continues to be the source of much controversy and no small amount of abuse and discrimination directed towards members of the gay, lesbian, bisexual, and transgendered community.

These individuals experience various forms of abuse, mistreatment, and discrimination that their heterosexual counterparts do not experience. In this respect, their sexuality is the source of a good deal of inequality. For example, gay teenagers are very often the targets of taunting, bullying, physical assault, and other abuse in schools and elsewhere that sometimes drives them to suicide or at least to experience severe emotional distress. In 38 states, individuals can be denied employment or fired from a job because of their sexual orientation, even though federal and state laws prohibit employment discrimination for reasons related to race and ethnicity, gender, age, religious belief, and national origin. And in 45 states as of April 2010, same-sex couples are legally prohibited from marrying.

In most of these states, this prohibition means that same-sex couples lack hundreds of rights, responsibilities, and benefits that spouses enjoy, including certain income tax and inheritance benefits, spousal insurance coverage, and the right to make medical decisions for a partner who can no longer communicate because of disease or traumatic injury.

HOUSEHOLD INEQUALITY

Someone has to do housework, and that someone is usually a woman. It takes many hours a week to clean the bathrooms, cook, shop in the grocery store, vacuum, and do everything else that needs to be done. The best evidence indicates that women married to or living with men spend two to three times as many hours per work on housework as men spend.

This disparity holds true even when women work outside the home, leading sociologist Arlie Hochschild to observe in a widely cited book that women engage in a "second shift" of unpaid work when they come home from their paying job. The good news is that gender differences in housework time are smaller than a generation ago. The bad news is that a large gender difference remains.

As one study summarized the evidence on this issue, "women invest significantly more hours in household labour than do men despite the narrowing of gender differences in recent years". In the realm of household work, then, gender inequality persists.

VIOLENCE AGAINST WOMEN

Violence against women is a technical term used to collectively refer to violent acts that are primarily or exclusively committed against women. Similar to a hate crime, this type of violence targets a specific group with the victim's gender as a primary motive. The United Nations General Assembly defines "violence against women" as "any act of gender-based violence that results in, or is likely to result in, physical, sexual or mental harm or suffering to women, including threats of such acts, coercion or arbitrary deprivation of liberty, whether occurring in public or in private life."

The 1993 Declaration on the Elimination of Violence Against Women noted that this violence could be perpetrated by assailants of either gender, family members and even the "State" itself. Worldwide governments and organizations actively work to combat violence against women through a variety of programmes. A UN resolution designated November 25 as International Day for the Elimination of Violence against Women. Some historians believe that the history of violence against women is tied to the history of women being viewed as property and a gender role assigned to be subservient to men and also other women.

The UN Declaration on the Elimination of Violence against Women states that "violence against women is a manifestation of historically unequal power relations between men and women, which have led to domination over and discrimination against women by men and to the prevention of the full advancement of women, and that violence against women is one of the crucial social mechanisms by which women are forced into a subordinate position compared with men."

In the 1870s courts in the United States stopped recognizing the common-law principle that a husband had the right to "physically chastise an errant wife". In the UK the traditional right of a husband to inflict moderate corporal punishment on his wife in order to keep her "within the bounds of duty" was removed in 1891.

IMPACT ON SOCIETY

The World Health Organization reports that violence against women puts an undue burden on health care services with women who have suffered violence being more likely to need health services and at higher cost, compared to women who have not suffered violence. Several studies have shown a link between poor treatment of women and international violence. These studies show that one of the best predictors of inter- and intranational violence is the maltreatment of women in the society.

TYPES OF VIOLENCE

Domestic Violence

Women are more likely to be victimized by someone that they are intimate with, commonly called "Intimate Partner Violence" or. The impact of domestic violence in the sphere of total violence against women can be understood through the example that 40-70% of murders of women are committed by their husband or boyfriend.

Studies have shown that violence is not always perpetrated as a form of physical violence but can also be psychological and verbal. In unmarried relationships this is commonly called dating violence, whereas in the context of marriage it is called domestic violence.

Instances of IPV tend not to be reported to police and thus many experts believe that the true magnitude of the problem is hard to estimate. In the US, in 2005, 1181 women, in comparison with 329 men, were killed by their intimate partners.

Though this form of violence is often portrayed as an issue within the context of heterosexual relationships, it also occurs in lesbian relationships, daughter-mother relationships, roommate relationships and other domestic relationships involving two women. Violence against women in lesbian relationships is about as common as violence against women in heterosexual relationships.

Diagnosis Planning

The American Psychiatric Association planning and research committees for the forthcoming DSM-5 have canvassed a series of new Relational disorders which include Marital Conflict Disorder Without Violence or Marital Abuse

Disorder. Couples with marital disorders sometimes come to clinical attention because the couple recognize long-standing dissatisfaction with their marriage and come to the clinician on their own initiative or are referred by an astute health care professional. Secondly, there is serious violence in the marriage which is -"usually the husband battering the wife".

In these cases the emergency room or a legal authority often is the first to notify the clinician. Most importantly, marital violence" is a major risk factor for serious injury and even death and women in violent marriages are at much greater risk of being seriously injured or killed."

The authors of this study add that "There is current considerable controversy over whether male-to-female marital violence is best regarded as a reflection of male psychopathology and control or whether there is an empirical base and clinical utility for conceptualizing these patterns as relational.

"Recommendations for clinicians making a diagnosis of Marital Relational Disorder should include the assessment of actual or "potential" male violence as regularly as they assess the potential for suicide in depressed patients. Further, "clinicians should not relax their vigilance after a battered wife leaves her husband, because some data suggest that the period immediately following a marital separation is the period of greatest risk for the women.

Many men will stalk and batter their wives in an effort to get them to return or punish them for leaving. Initial assessments of the potential for violence in a marriage can be supplemented by standardized interviews and questionnaires, which have been reliable and valid aids in exploring marital violence more systematically.

"The authors conclude with what they call "very recent information" on the course of violent marriages which suggests that "over time a husband's battering may abate somewhat, but perhaps because he has successfully intimidated his wife. The risk of violence remains strong in a marriage in which it has been a feature in the past. Thus, treatment is essential here; the clinician cannot just wait and watch." The most urgent clinical priority is the protection of the wife because she is the one most frequently at risk, and clinicians must be aware that supporting assertiveness by a battered wife may lead to more beatings or even death.

State Violence

Labour Camps

Many women underwent extrajudicial punishment in labour camps of Nazi Germany and the Soviet Union. Their suffering was described in memories of former Gulag women prisoners Yevgenia Ginzburg, Eufrosinia Kersnovskaya and others.

War and Militarism

Militarism produces special environments that allow for increased violence against women. For example, during World War II, the Japanese military established brothels for soldiers, exploiting women for the purpose of creating access and entitlement for men.

Another example of violence against women incited by militarism during war took place in the Kovno Ghetto. Jewish male prisoners had access to Jewish women forced into camp brothels by the Nazis, who also used them. The 1998 United Nations International Criminal Tribunal for Rwanda recognized rape as a war crime.

Violence in Empowerment Systems

When police officers misuse their power as agents of the state to physically and sexually harass and assault women, the survivors feel much less able to report the violence. It is standard procedure for police to force entry into the victim's home even after the victim's numerous requests for them to go away.

Government agencies often disregard the victim's right to freedom of association with their perpetrator. Shelter workers are often reduced themselves to contributing to violence against women by exploiting their vulnerability in exchange for a paying job.

ACTIVISM

Many activists believe that working towards the elimination of domestic violence means working to eliminate a societal hierarchy enforced through sexism. INCITE! Women of Colour Against Violence cited racism within the anti-violence movement and suggest that violence against women will not end until the anti-violence movement redirects its goal from "ending violence against women "to "ending violence against women of colour." The same conclusion can be drawn for other systems of oppression.

RAPE

Susan Griffin began a classic thesis on rape in 1971 with this startling statement:

- I have never been free of the fear of rape. From a very early age I, like most women, have thought of rape as a part of my natural environment-something to be feared and prayed against like fire or lightning. I never asked why men raped; I simply thought it one of the many mysteries of human nature.

What do we know about rape? Why do men rape? Our knowledge about the extent and nature of rape and reasons for it comes from three sources: the FBI Uniform Crime Reports and the National Crime Victimization Survey and surveys of and interviews with women and men conducted by academic researchers.

From these sources we have a fairly good if not perfect idea of how much rape occurs, the context in which it occurs, and the reasons for it. What do we know?

The Extent and Context of Rape

The Uniform Crime Reports, about 89,000 reported rapes occurred in the United States in 2008, for a rate of about 58 for every 100,000 women age 12 or older. Because women often do not tell police they were raped, the NCVS probably yields a better estimate of rape. The NCVS, almost 204,000 rapes and sexual assaults occur annually, for a rate of 1.3 for every 1,000 women age 12 or older. Other research indicates that up to one-third of U.S. women will experience a rape or sexual assault, including attempts, at least once in their lives. A study of a random sample of 420 Toronto women involving intensive interviews yielded even higher figures: 56% said they had experienced at least one rape or attempted rape, and two-thirds said they had experienced at least one rape or sexual assault, including attempts.

The researchers, Melanie Randall and Lori Haskell, concluded that "it is more common than not for a woman to have an experience of sexual assault during their lifetime." These figures apply not just to the general public but also to college students.

About 20%-30% of women students in anonymous surveys report being raped or sexually assaulted, usually by a male student they knew beforehand. Thus at a campus of 10,000 students of whom 5,000 are women, about 1,000-1,500 will be raped or sexually assaulted over a period of 4 years, or about 10 per week in a 4-year academic calendar. The public image of rape is of the proverbial stranger attacking a woman in an alleyway.

While such rapes do occur, most rapes actually happen between people who know each other. A wide body of research finds that 60%-80% of all rapes and sexual assaults are committed by someone the woman knows, including husbands, ex- husbands, boyfriends, and ex-boyfriends, and only 20%-35% by strangers. A woman is thus two to four times more likely to be raped by someone she knows than by a stranger.

Explaining Rape

Sociological explanations of rape fall into cultural and structural categories similar to those for sexual harassment. Various "rape myths" in our culture support the absurd notion that women somehow enjoy being raped, want to be raped, or are "asking for it".

One of the most famous scenes in movie history occurs in the classic film Gone with the Wind, when Rhett Butler carries a struggling Scarlett O' Hara up the stairs. She is struggling because she does not want to have sex with him. The next scene shows Scarlett waking up the next morning with a satisfied, loving look on her face. The not-so-subtle message is that she enjoyed being raped. A related cultural belief is that women somehow ask or deserve to be raped by the way they dress or behave.

If she dresses attractively or walks into a bar by herself, she wants to have sex, and if a rape occurs, well, then, what did she expect? In the award-winning film The Accused, based on a true story, actress Jodie Foster plays a woman who was raped by several men on top of a pool table in a bar. The film recounts how members of the public questioned why she was in the bar by herself if she did not want to have sex and blamed her for being raped.

A third cultural belief is that a man who is sexually active with a lot of women is a stud. Although this belief is less common in this day of AIDS and other STDs, it is still with us. A man with multiple sex partners continues to be the source of envy among many of his peers. At a minimum, men are still the ones who have to "make the first move" and then continue making more moves.

There is a thin line between being sexually assertive and sexually aggressive. These three cultural beliefs-that women enjoy being forced to have sex, that they ask or deserve to be raped, and that men should be sexually assertive or even aggressive-combine to produce a cultural recipe for rape. Although most men do not rape, the cultural beliefs and myths just described help account for the rapes that do occur. Recognizing this, the contemporary women's movement began attacking these myths back in the 1970s, and the public is much more conscious of the true nature of rape than a generation ago.

That said, much of the public still accepts these cultural beliefs and myths, and prosecutors continue to find it difficult to win jury convictions in rape trials unless the woman who was raped had suffered visible injuries, had not known the man who raped her, and/or was not dressed attractively. Structural explanations for rape emphasize the power differences between women and men similar to those outlined earlier for sexual harassment. In societies that are male dominated, rape and other violence against women is a likely outcome, as they allow men to demonstrate and maintain their power over women. Supporting this view, studies of preindustrial societies and of the 50 states of the United States find that rape is more common in societies where women have less economic and political power.

Poverty is also a predictor of rape: although rape in the United States transcends social class boundaries, it does seem more common among poorer segments of the population than among wealthier segments, as is true for other types of violence. Scholars think the higher rape rates among the poor stem from poor men trying to prove their "masculinity" by taking out their economic frustration on women.

Reducing Rape

In sum, a sociological perspective tells us that cultural myths and economic and gender inequality help lead to rape, and that the rape problem goes far beyond a few psychopathic men who rape women. A sociological perspective thus tells us that our society cannot just stop at doing something about these men.

Instead it must make more far-reaching changes by changing people's beliefs about rape and by making every effort to reduce poverty and to empower women. This last task is especially important, for, as Randall and Haskell, the authors of the Toronto study cited earlier, observed, a sociological perspective on rape "means calling into question the organization of sexual inequality in our society." Aside from this fundamental change, other remedies such as additional and better funded rape-crisis centres would help women who experience rape and sexual assault.

Yet even here women of colour face an additional barrier. Because the anti-rape movement was begun by white, middle-class feminists, the rape-crisis centres they founded tended to be near where they live, such as college campuses, and not in the areas where women of colour live, such as inner cities and

Native American reservations. This meant that women of colour who experienced sexual violence lacked the kinds of help available to their white, middle-class counterparts, and, despite some progress, this is still true today.

PORNOGRAPHY

Back in the 1950s, young boys in the United States would through National Geographic magazine to peek at photos of native women who were partially nude. Those photos, of course, were not put there to excite boys across the country; instead they were there simply to depict native people in their natural habitat.

Another magazine began about the same time that also contained photos of nude women. Its name was Playboy, and its photos obviously had a much different purpose: to excite teenage boys and older men alike.

Other, more graphic magazines grew in its wake, and today television shows and PG-13 and R-rated movies show more nudity and sex than were ever imaginable in the days when National Geographic was a boy's secret pleasure. Beyond these movies and television shows, a powerful pornography industry now exists on the Internet, in porn stores, and elsewhere. Although Playboy quickly became very controversial, it is now considered tame compared to what else is available.

If things as different as National Geographic, Playboy, R-rated movies, and hard-core pornography show nudity and can be sexually arousing, what, then, should be considered pornography? Are at least some of the tamer pictures in Playboy really that different from the great paintings in art history that depict nude women? This question is not necessarily meant to defend Playboy; rather it is meant to stimulate your thinking over what exactly is and is not pornography and over what, if anything, our society can and should do about it.

Many people obviously oppose pornography, but two very different groups have been especially outspoken over the years. One of these groups, religious moralists, condemns pornography as a violation of religious values and as an offense to society's moral order. The other group, feminists, condemn pornography for its sexual objectification of women and especially condemns the hard-core pornography that glorifies horrible sexual violence against women.

Many feminists also charge that pornography promotes rape by reinforcing the cultural myths discussed earlier. As one writer put it in a famous phrase some 30 years ago, "Pornography is the theory, and rape the practice". This charge raises an important question: to what extent does pornography cause rape or other violence against women? The fairest answer might be that we do not really know. Many studies do conclude that pornography indeed causes rape. For example, male students who watch violent pornography in experiments later exhibit more hostile attitudes towards women than those watching consensual sex or nonsexual interaction.

However, it remains unclear whether viewing pornography has a longer-term effect that lasts beyond the laboratory setting, and scholars and other observers continue to disagree over pornography's effects on the rape rate. Even if pornography does cause rape, efforts to stop it run smack into the issue of censorship. In a free society, civil liberties advocates say, we must proceed very cautiously. Once we ban some forms of pornography, they ask, where do we stop? This issue aside, much of what we call pornography still degrades women by depicting them as objects that exist for men's sexual pleasure and by portraying them as legitimate targets of men's sexual violence. These images should be troubling for any society that values gender equality.

The extent of pornography in the United States may, for better or worse, reflect our historical commitment to freedom of speech, but it may also reflect our lack of commitment to full equality between women and men. Even if, as we have seen, the survey evidence shows growing disapproval of traditional gender roles, the persistence of pornography shows that our society has a long way to go towards viewing women as equally human as men.

THE BENEFITS AND COSTS OF BEING MALE

Most of the discussion so far has been about women, and with good reason: in a sexist society such as our own, women are the subordinate, unequal sex. But "gender" means more than "female," and a few comments about men are in order.

BENEFITS

We talked about "white privilege," the advantages that whites automatically have in a racist society whether or not they realise they have these advantages. Many scholars also talk about male privilege, or the advantages that males automatically have in a patriarchal society whether or not they realise they have these advantages.

A few examples thesis male privilege. Men can usually walk anywhere they want or go into any bar they want without having to worry about being raped or sexually harassed. Susan Griffin was able to write "I have never been free of the fear of rape" because she was a woman: it is no exaggeration to say that few men could write the same thing and mean it. Although some men are sexually harassed, most men can work at any job they want without having to worry about sexual harassment.

Men can walk down the street without having strangers make crude remarks about their looks, dress, and sexual behaviour. Men can apply for most jobs without worrying about being rejected or, if hired, not being promoted because of their gender. We could go on with many other examples, but the fact remains that in a patriarchal society, men automatically have advantages just because they are men, even if race, social class, and sexual orientation affect the degree to which they are able to enjoy these advantages.

COSTS

Yet it is also true that men pay a price for living in a patriarchy. Without trying to claim that men have it as bad as women, scholars are increasingly pointing to the problems men face in a society that promotes male domination and traditional standards of masculinity such as assertiveness, competitiveness, and toughness. Socialization into masculinity is thought to underlie many of the emotional problems men experience, which stem from a combination of their emotional inexpressiveness and reluctance to admit to, and seek help for, various personal problems. Sometimes these emotional problems build up and explode, as mass shootings by males at schools and elsewhere indicate, or express themselves in other ways.

Compared to girls, for example, boys are much more likely to be diagnosed with emotional disorders, learning disabilities, and attention deficit disorder, and they are also more likely to commit suicide and to drop out of high school. Men experience other problems that put themselves at a disadvantage compared to women. They commit much more violence than women do and, apart from rape, also suffer a much higher rate of violent victimization.

They die earlier than women and are injured more often. Because men are less involved than women in child-rearing, they also miss out on the joy of parenting that women are much more likely to experience. Growing recognition of the problems males experience because of their socialization into masculinity has led to increased concern over what is happening to American boys. Citing the strong linkage between masculinity and violence, some writers urge parents to raise their sons differently in order to help our society reduce its violent behaviour. In all of these respects, boys and men-and our nation as a whole-are paying a very real price for being male in a patriarchal society.

IMPORTANT POINTS

- Sex is a concept that refers to biological differences between females and males, while gender is a concept that refers to a society's expectations of how females and males should think and behave. To the extent that women and men and girls and boys are different, it's essential to determine how much of these differences stems from the biological differences between the sexes.

- In understanding gender differences, scholars continue to debate the value of biological explanations. Biological explanations centering on evolution, natural selection, and hormonal differences are provocative but ultimately imply that gender differences are inevitable and that the status quo must be maintained. In contrast, cultural and socialization explanations imply some hope for changing gender roles and for reducing gender inequality. Anthropologists find gender similarities across cultures that probably reflect the biological differences between the sexes, but they also find much cultural variation in gender roles that underscores the importance of culture and socialization for understanding gender.
- Many studies emphasize that socialization leads children in the United States to adopt the gender roles associated with femininity and masculinity. Parents view and interact with their daughters and sons differently, and children continue to learn their gender roles from their peers, schools, the mass media, and religion.
- Feminism refers to the belief that women should be equal to men. With feminism defined in this way, many more people hold feminist beliefs than might be willing to admit to it. The feminist movement began during the pre-Civil War abolitionist period and eventually won women the right to vote. Its reemergence in the late 1960s has changed many aspects of American life. Since then support for traditional gender roles has declined dramatically in national surveys. Several variables, including education, are associated with a feminist outlook, but, surprisingly, women are not consistently more likely than men to support feminist beliefs.
- Gender inequality in the workplace is manifested through the gender gap in earnings and through sexual harassment. Women earn less than 75% of

what men earn. Several reasons account for this gap, including sex segregation in the workplace, the devaluing of women's work, and outright sex discrimination by employers. Sexual harassment against women is quite common and stems from cultural beliefs about women's and men's roles and structural differences in the workplace in power between women and men.

- Gender inequality also exists in the household in the extent to which women and men perform housework. Women perform much more housework than men, even when they also work outside the home. Although some studies show that men perform more housework than they used to, recent evidence suggests that men are merely exaggerating the amount of housework they now perform by giving socially desirable responses to questions about their housework.
- Although women have made great gains in the world of politics in the United States, they still lag behind men in the extent to which they occupy legislative seats. This extent is higher in the United States than in many other countries, but lower than in many nations in Europe and elsewhere.
- Women of colour experience a triple burden based on their gender, race and ethnicity, and social class. Even though white women earn less money and are poorer than white men, women of colour earn less money and are poorer than white women.
- Violence against women is another manifestation of gender inequality. Research shows that up to one-third of U.S. women will be raped or sexually assaulted and that about 70%-80% of their assailants will be men they know. Cultural beliefs and structural differences in power explain why rape occurs. Pornography is often considered another type of violence against women, but questions continue over the definition of pornography and over whether

it does indeed promote rape and other forms of antiwoman violence. Efforts to combat pornography may run afoul of First Amendment protections for freedom of speech.

- In a patriarchal society men enjoy privileges just for being male, whether or not they recognize these privileges. At the same time, men also experience disadvantages, including violent behaviour and victimization and higher rates of certain emotional problems than those experienced by women.

7

Education and Religion

EDUCATION

With its plurality and paradoxes, India never ceases to fascinate. And education in India is only one among various other elements that have captured the attention of the world. While the United Nations is worried about the presence of a large number of illiterates, various other countries are amazed by the quality of some of the human resources that the Indian education system has produced.

The growth of the Indian economy in the recent past and the compulsion to sustain it is also forcing the Indian government to accelerate the process of developing all the branches of the Indian education system. Therefore, it would be very interesting to understand and analyse the various structures of education in India, its present condition and future developments.

INDIA EDUCATION HISTORICAL BACKGROUND

The Vedas, Puranas, Ayurveda, Yoga, Kautilya's Arthasahtra are only some of the milestones that the traditional Indian knowledge system boasts of. There are evidences of imparting formal education in ancient India under the Gurukul system.

Under the Gurukul system, young boys who were passing through the Brahmacharya stage of life had to stay at the Guru or the teacher's home and complete their education. Although the ancient system of education has produced many geniuses and still a major area of research, it was hardly egalitarian.

Women and people of lower castes gradually lost their right to educate themselves. The spread of Jainism, Buddhism, Bhakti and Sufi movements did have some liberating effects on the condition of the women, sudras and atisudras. But it is the English language and the reformation movements of the 19th century that had the most liberating effect in pre-independent India. Thus, the Britishers, although rightly criticized for devastating the Indian economy, can also be credited for bringing a revolution in the Indian education system.

INDIA EDUCATION PRESENT CONDITION

Soon after gaining independence in 1947, making education available to all had become a priority for the government. As discrimination on the basis of caste and gender has been a major impediment in the healthy development of the Indian society, they have been made unlawful by the Indian constitution. The 86th constitutional amendment has also made elementary education a fundamental right for the children between the age group- 6 to 14. The 2001 census, the total literacy rate in India is 65.38%. The female literacy rate is only 54.16%. The gap between rural and urban literacy rate is also very significant in India. This is evident from the fact that only 59.4% of rural population are literate as against 80. 3% urban population just as to the 2001 census.

In order to develop the higher education system, the government had established the University Grants Commission in 1953. The primary role of UGC has been to regulate the standard and spread of higher education in India. There has been a marked progress in the expansion of higher education if we look at the increase of higher educational institutes in India.

The higher education system in India comprise of more than 17,000 colleges, 20 central universities, 217 State Universities, 106 Deemed to Universities and 13 institutes of Natioanl importance. This number will soon inflate as the setting up of 30 more central universities, 8 new IITs, 7 IIMs and 5 new Indian Institutes of Science are now proposed.

EDUCATION SYSTEM IN INDIA

The present education system in India mainly comprises of primary education, secondary education, senior secondary education and higher education. Elementary education consists of eight years of education.

Each of secondary and senior secondary education consists of two years of education. Higher education in India starts after passing the higher secondary education or the 12th standard.

Depending on the stream, doing graduation in India can take three to five years. Post graduate courses are generally of two to three years of duration. After completing post graduation, scope for doing research in various educational institutes also remains open.

PROMINENT EDUCATIONAL INSTITUTES IN INDIA

There are quite a good number of educational institutes in India that can compete with the best educational institutes of the world. The Indian Institutes of Technology, Indian Institutes of Management, Indian Institutes of Science, National Law Schools, Jawaharlal Nehru University are some such institutes.

EDUCATION FOR THE MARGINALIZED IN INDIA

As education is the means for bringing socio- economic transformation in a society, various measures are being taken to enhance the access of education to the marginalized parts of the society. One such measure is the introduction of the reservation system in the institutes of higher education. Under the present law, 7.5% seats in the higher educational institutes are reserved for the scheduled tribes, 15% for scheduled castes and 27% for the non creamy layers of the Other Backward Classes.

Under the Indian constitution, various minority groups can also set up their own educational institutes. Efforts are also being taken to improve the access to higher education among the women of India by setting up various educational institutes exclusively for them or reserving seats in the already existing institutes. The growing acceptance of distance learning courses and expansion of the open university system is also contributing a lot in the democratization of higher education in India. Despite all the efforts to develop the education system in India, access, equity and quality of education in India continue to haunt the policy makers till this date. This has mainly been due to the widespread poverty and various prejudices. The inability to check the drop out rates among the marginalized sections of the population is another cause of worry. However, the renewed emphasis in the education sector in the 11th five year plan and increased expenditure in both primary and higher education can act as palliatives for the Indian education system.

ELEMENTARY EDUCATION IN INDIA

Education is important not only for the full development of one's personality, but also for the sustained growth of the nation. Elementary education in India, therefore, is the foundation on which the development of every citizen and the nation as a whole hinges. But making primary education available for all in India has also been one of the major challenges for the government.

Moreover, the quality of elementary education in India has also been a major cause of worry for the government. In fact, making elementary education in India accessible, universal and relevant has been a goal since the eighth five-year plan. Elementary education in India means eight years of schooling from the age of six. The government has made elementary education compulsory and free. But, the goal of universal elementary education in India has been very difficult to achieve till now.

Therefore it has introduced innovative ways of universalizing elementary education in India. After the District Primary Education Programme of 1994, the govt. has now launched the "Sarva Shiksha Abhiyan" or SSA. Sarva Shiksha Abhiyan was launched in 2001 to universalize and improve the quality of elementary education in India through community ownership of elementary education. In order to effectively decentralize the management, it has involved Panchayati Raj institutions, School Management Committees, Village and Urban Slum Level Education Committees, Parents 'Teachers'Associations, Mother Teacher Associations, Tribal Autonomous Councils and other grassroots level structures. SSA, apart from being a programme with clear time frame for Elementary Education, also offers opportunities to the states to develop their own vision of elementary education.

It has set 2007 as the deadline for providing primary education in India and 2010 as the deadline for providing useful and relevant elementary education to all children in the 6 to 14 age group. In order to improve the quality of elementary education in India, the SSA has emphasized on improving the student teacher ratio, teachers training, academic support, facilitating development of teaching learning material and providing to children from special focus groups etc. Despite all the efforts of the government of India, universalization of elementary education in India remains a distant dream. This is because of the persistent poverty and various prejudices prevailing in the Indian society. While the growth in female literacy is increasing at a faster rate than male literacy, the gap in the male female literacy has been a major hindrance in the universalization of elementary education in India.

While the total literacy rate is 65.38% just as to 2001 census, the female literacy rate is only 54.16%. Another area of concern is to reduce the gap between the rural and urban literacy rate. While 80. 3% urban people are literate, only 59.4% of the rural population is literate just as to 2001 census data. Thus reduction in poverty, promotion of female education, emphasis on rural education, providing incentives for retaining the children from weaker parts of the society would have to go together so that it can achieve the goal set by the Sarva Shiksha Abhiyan and also the Millennium Development goal by 2015 set by the UNESCO.

HIGHER EDUCATION IN INDIA

Higher Education in India is one of the most developed in the entire world. There has in fact been considerable improvement in the higher education scenario of India in both quantitative and qualitative terms. In technical education, the IITs, and in management, the IIMs have already marked their names among the top higher educational institutes of the world.

Moreover the Jawaharlal University and Delhi University are also regarded as good higher educational institutes for doing postgraduates courses and research in science, humanities and social sciences. As a result, students from various parts of the world are coming today for higher education in India.

HIGHER EDUCATION SYSTEM IN INDIA

Higher education in India starts after the higher Secondary or 12th standard. While it takes 3 years for completing a B.A., B.Sc or B.Com pass or honours degree from a college in India, pursuing an engineering course would take four years and five years for completing a bachelor of medicine or bachelor of law degree. Postgraduate courses generally are of two years duration. But there are some courses like Master of Computer Application that are of three years duration. For those who cannot afford to attend regular classes for various preoccupations can pursue correspondence courses from various Open Universities and distance learning institutes in India.

HIGHER EDUCATION INSTITUTES IN INDIA

Universities and its constituent colleges are the main institutes of higher education in India. There are at present 227 government-recognized Universities in India. Out of them 20 are central universities, 109 are deemed universities and 11 are Open Universities and rest are state universities.

Most of these universities in India have affiliating colleges where undergraduate courses are being taught. However Jawaharlal University is a remarkable exception to this rule. Apart from these higher education institutes there are several private institutes in India that offer various professional courses in India. The Department of higher Education, government of India, there are 16,885 colleges, 99.54 lakh students and 4.57 lakh teachers in various higher education institutes in India.

KEY PLAYERS IN THE HIGHER EDUCATION SYSTEM IN INDIA

The University Grant Commission of India is not only the lone grant giving agency in the country, but also responsible for coordinating, determining and maintaining the standards in institutions of higher education. Apart from the UGC here are various professional councils that are responsible for recognizing courses, promoting professional institutes and providing grants to undergraduate programmes.

All India Council for Technical Education, Distance Education Council, Indian Council for Agriculture Research, Bar Council of India, and National Council for Teacher Education Rehabilitation Council of India, Medical Council of India, Pharmacy Council of India, Indian Nursing Council, Dentist Council of India, Central Council of Homeopathy and the Central Council of Indian Medicine are the statutory professional councils of India.

THE CURRENT SCENE

India is today one of the fastest developing countries of the world with the annual growth rate going above 9%. In order to sustain that rate of growth, there is need to increase the number of institutes and also the quality of higher education in India. Therefore the Prime Minister of India has announced the establishment of 8 IITs, seven Indian Institutes of Management and five Indian Institutes of Science, Education and Research and 30 Central Universities in his speech to the nation on the 60th Independence Day. The outlay for education during the 11th Five Year Plan, which runs from the current fiscal to 2012-13, represents a four-fold increase over the previous plan and stands at Rs 2500 billion.

WOMEN'S EDUCATION IN INDIA

Women constitute almost half of the population in the world. But the hegemonic masculine ideology made them suffer a lot as they were denied equal opportunities in different parts of the world. The rise of feminist ideas have, however, led to the tremendous improvement of women's condition through out the world in recent times. Access to education has been one of the most pressing demands of theses women's rights movements. Women's education in India has also been a major preoccupation of both the government and civil society as educated women can play a very important role in the development of the country.

HISTORY OF WOMEN'S EDUCATION IN INDIA

Although in the Vedic period women had access to education in India, they had gradually lost this right. However, in the British period there was revival of interest in women's education in India. During this period, various socio religious movements led by eminent persons like Raja Ram Mohan Roy, Iswar Chandra Vidyasagar emphasized on women's education in India. Mahatma Jyotiba Phule, Periyar and Baba Saheb Ambedkar were leaders of the lower castes in India who took various initiatives to make education available to the women of India.

However women's education got a fillip after the country got independence in 1947 and the government has taken various measures to provide education to all Indian women. As a result women's literacy rate has grown over the three decades and the growth of female literacy has in fact been higher than that of male literacy rate. While in 1971 only 22% of Indian women were literate, by the end of 2001 54.16% female were literate. The growth of female literacy rate is 14.87% as compared to 11.72% of that of male literacy rate.

IMPORTANCE OF WOMEN'S EDUCATION IN INDIA

Women's education in India plays a very important role in the overall development of the country. It not only helps in the development of half of the human resources, but in improving the quality of life at home and outside. Educated women not only tend to promote education of their girl children, but also can provide better guidance to all their children. Moreover educated women can also help in the reduction of infant mortality rate and growth of the population.

OBSTACLES

Gender discrimination still persists in India and lot more needs to be done in the field of women's education in India. The gap in the male-female literacy rate is just a simple indicator. While the male literary rate is more than 75% just as to the 2001 census, the female literacy rate is just 54.16%. Prevailing prejudices, low enrollment of girl child in the schools, engagements of girl children in domestic works and high drop out rate are major obstacles in the path of making all Indian women educated.

MONTESSORI EDUCATION IN INDIA

The Montessori method of education in India is today accepted as one of the most effective ways of developing the cognitive capabilities of the children. From a very modest beginning in the early 20th century, the Montessori system of education has come a long way in influencing child pedagogy. The philosophy of Montessori education is that a child can learn most from its experiences and not from mugging up or listening only to the teacher.

The role of the teacher under this system of education is that of an enabler. As Maria Montessori, the person behind the innovation of this fantastic method of education herself says in her Education for a New World, "The task of the teacher becomes that of preparing a series of motives of cultural activity, spread over a specially prepared environment, and then refraining from obtrusive interference".

Maria Montessori was born in 1870 in Italy and went to become the first women in the country to earn a medical degree. Her ideas were first implemented in Rome in 1913 when an international course was started. During the World War II, Maria was forced into exile from Italy and she had come to India. It was during her stay in India that Maria had developed most of her ideas and gave some concrete shape to them. Montessori's views are today accepted not only for elementary education but also for infancy education and middle and high school education. Montessori had firmly believed that the children and adolescents should be given an opportunity to learn from the environment and nature rather than coercing them in classrooms.

MONTESSORI METHOD OF EDUCATION

The schools that follow the Montessori method in India allow the children to do anything that interest them and the role of the teacher is to help them accomplish their tasks whenever approached. Children of different ages may be allowed to work in the same room.

The primary aim of all the Montessori schools in India has been to develop the child physically, mentally and socially so that they can eventually become responsible persons. Montessori Preschools all over the world use identical equipments with which the children work. This system of education today has attained maturity and the Montessori education in India is now quite developed.

The number of schools following the Montessori method is continuously increasing through the length and breath of the country. The Indian Montessori Centre has also started providing Indian Montessori Training Courses and the online Montessori Training Courses to train the adults in the Montessori method of education in India.

TECHNICAL EDUCATION IN INDIA

The history of imparting formal technical education in India can be traced back to mid 19th century, although it got momentum in 20th century with the set up of Constitution of Technical Education Committee of the Central University Board of Education in 1943; Preparation of Sergeant Report in 1944 and Formation of All India Council of technical Education in 1945. With the country gaining independence in 1947, the development of technical education had become a major concern for the government of India to face the new challenges and move the country forward. The set up of Indian Institutes of Technology, Indian Institutes of Management and Indian Institutes of Science was a major step in the development of technical education in the country. The quality of education of these institutes have managed to change the outlook of India so much that this ancient country which was earlier known for yoga and mediation is now known for computer engineers.

However, it does not mean that the challenge of making technical education accessible to the rural populace and other under developed parts of the society has been overcome. In order to maintain the standard of technical education, a statutory authority- The All India Council for Technical Education -was set up in 1945.

AICTE is responsible for planning, formulation and maintenance of norms and standards, quality assurance through accreditation, funding in priority areas, monitoring and evaluation, maintaining parity of certification and awards and ensuring coordinated and integrated development and management of technical education in the country.

TECHNICAL EDUCATION COURSES IN INDIA

The courses, which are known as 'technical' in India and therefore come under the purview of All India Council of Technical Education are—degree and diploma courses in Engineering, Master degree Courses in Engineering, Master of Computer Application, Master of Business Administration, Pharmacy Courses, Courses in Architecture and Applied Arts and Hotel Management and Catering Technology Courses.

INSTITUTES OFFERING TECHNICAL EDUCATION IN INDIA

As the technical education courses in India are quite diverse, the number of institutes providing technical courses in India is also huge. The number of AICTE approved institutes that offer engineering degree courses in India is—4,39,689. There are around 1244 institutes in India that offer diploma courses in engineering, 415 institutes offer diploma courses in Pharmacy, 63 institutes offer diploma courses in Hotel Management and Catering Technology Courses and 25 AICTE approved institutes that offer diploma courses in Architecture. The number of AICTE approved institutes that offer master of Computer Application courses in India is 1012. Likewise the AICTE also approves institutes from time to time institutes that offer MBA courses, M.E./M.Tech, Architecture and Applied Arts Courses, Hotel Management and Catering Technology Courses.

Given the importance of technical education in the further development of the nation, the Government of India is keen on developing some more institutes in the line of IITs, IIMs and IISCs. The Prime Minister of India has unleashed a plan to establish 8 IITs, 7 IIMs and 5 IISCs to improve the spread and quality of technical education in the country. These institutes along with various private institutes and foreign technical colleges have the potential of making technical education accessible to all parts of society in India without compromising on the quality of education.

FACILITIES FOR INTERNATIONAL STUDENTS IN INDIA

Surprises are always waiting as you enter any new place. One may take time adjusting him/ her in the new environment. It is normal to feel excited, confused and even overwhelmed. These problems are mainly faced by the international students when they arrive in India.

They may face problems like language problem, accommodation problem and food problem and so on. But international student's offices at most of the institutes provide facilities for International Students in India that can ease their woes. Moreover the Government of India has also set up the Education Consultants of India to cater to the needs of the growing number of International Students in India. Colleges and institutes The international students are required to carry the necessary documents along with them such as admission letter, passport, residence permit etc. The international students can avail the residential permit after registering themselves at the Foreigner's Registration Office within a period of seven days from their arrival. All over the country offer different courses for the international students. International students can apply for medical courses, engineering courses, applied arts courses etc. The government has reserved some seats for foreign students and students from other developing countries. International students can get admission through this reserved quota.

For more information related to these admissions, the students can contact the Indian High Commission located in their countries. Self-financing international students looking for admission to postgraduate courses can also choose from the various courses that are offered by the Indian universities. Apart from the Government of India, there are some private educational institutes that provide various facilities for international students in India.

The Government of India offers various scholarships annually to international students. These scholarships are offered to those who are interested in pursuing their studies in India. Some of the scholarships offered by the government are Cultural Exchange Programme, Commonwealth Scheme, SAARC Scholarship Scheme and ICCR Scholarship Scheme.

MADRASSA EDUCATION IN INDIA

Madrassa education in India aims at educating Muslim children living in this country. Madrassas were originally established to spread the message of Islam and impart religious teaching on its followers. The Ulamas, a group of religious specialists used to perform the role of teachers in Madrassa to spread Islam outside the Arabian Peninsula.

A Madrassa was as treated as a high school or college earlier. In the Islamic era, there were thousands of Madrassas which were as big as some universities today. They were full with exhibit museums, libraries and visiting scholar programmes. Great scholars and professors dedicated their lives in the Madrassas for learning the philosophy of Islam, the Farsi language, and more significantly, to broaden knowledge among ordinary public. Monarchs as well as masses were educated in the Madrassas in the yesteryears. And even today Madrassa education in India has played a vital role in educating thousands of Muslim children. The importance of Madrassas lies in its potential to make education available to the poorer part of the society. The central as well as the state government of India provide various facilities to make easy the Madrassa education in India. To help Muslim students get higher education, the Central government is trying to permit Madrassa students to join conventional courses in various colleges and universities.

Institutes such as Aligarh Muslim University, Jamia Milia Islamia and Jamia Hamdard grant equality of qualifications from Madrassas. Aligarh Muslim University and Jamia have a correspondence commission that evaluates the degrees of students from Madrassas. The Madrassas apply to the committee regarding their courses and the committee recommends the levels of formal education systems comparing to the Madrassa education.

The government thinks that the equality system may help conquer the educational backwardness of Muslims. The equality system would help them to offer better job chances. Most of the Madrassa students face the lack of knowledge of science and mathematics. The only option for the Madrassa students is to learn subjects like Urdu, Arabic, Persian and Islamic studies along with Yunani medicine. Some Madrassas teach subjects such as information technology and journalism.

The aim of the government is to bring all Madrassas under the roof of the Central Madrassa Board to increase the quality of education provided. However the need of the hour is to impart education that are relevant and help the Muslim children in building up capabilities so that they can compete on an equal footing with other students of the country.

SPECIAL EDUCATION IN INDIA

Providing access to basic education is a duty the Indian state that has taken upon itself. Therefore the government has taken various measures to provide access to education to all categories of students. Thus the differently able children are provided special education in India so that they can seriously engage in improving the quality of their life. With the advancement of technology, Special education in India for physically disabled or mentally challenged is also fast improving. But some recent research has thrown fresh insights on Special education in India was present since the pre independence time, with very few schools or NGOs helping intellectually impaired children.

Today India has come a long way and made a good progress in the field of disability rehabilitation. Presently India has four national institutes for effective implementation of this special education through various government schemes. The popular national level institutes for disabled persons are the National institute for Hearing Handicapped, National Institute for the Mentally Handicapped, National Institute of the Visually Handicapped and National Institute for orthopedically handicapped.

National Institute of Rehabilitation, Training and Research and The Institute for Physically Handicapped are other two national level institutes run by government. Moreover, government has initiated District Rehabilitation Centre scheme in ten states to make all-inclusive rehabilitation. Moreover, four Regional Rehabilitation Training Centres are there to train the staff and teachers who work with these institutes. Today due to global competitiveness, education scenario in India is fast changing. Along with that, special education is also catching importance and various government agencies are working hard to make it available to masses.

There are almost 37 diploma courses in the field of special education in India some of the institutes offer courses like B.Ed as well. All these courses are regulated and governed by the Rehabilitation Council of India -a legislative body under the Ministry of Social Justice and Empowerment. However over the years many scholars have questioned the importance of special education in India as they feel that it leads to segregation and isolation of the differently abled children. They argue that by segregating the children at young age the very purpose bringing all children to the mainstream of, the purpose of special education is defeated. Therefore, to keep the special education at par with regular education, vocational courses are also initiated. Also, there has been a National Policy of Education, in which government has declared that education of children with gentle disabilities will be in regular schools. Due to such reforms and regulations, the quality and reach of special education in India has increased over the years giving new hopes and bright future for disabled.

DISTANCE EDUCATION COUNCIL

In a huge country like India where fruits of development are not equally distributed, the importance of distance education is tremendous. It can significantly improve the quality of life of the people by making technology-mediated education accessible to the remotest corner of the country and all those who cannot afford to attend regular classes. But maintaining the quality of distance education is a hilarious task.

Therefore the Distance Education Council or DEC, as it is now popularly known, was established under the Indira Gandhi National Open University Act, 1985 primarily to determine the standards of distance education in India. It is also responsible for promotion and co-ordination of the distance education system. Approval of the Distance Education Council is mandatory for all the degrees awarded through distance education in India.

Therefore it would be good for the students to pursue distance-learning courses from institutes that are recognized by the Distance Education Council. Distance education council provides the guiding principles of education to support excellence, promotes use of modern technology, and permits a union of all educational systems. The council allocates funds through a joint networking for access of education, by providing training to all.

The council works for the harmonization, resolves the standards of teaching, valuation, and investigation in such systems. This council encourages a mixture of accessibility and novelty in education at the University level. To fulfill this purpose the council makes use of the current scientific knowledge and new technology. It tries to make more collaboration among the various Universities across India. The distance education council also encourages state government to open more universities and some distance education courses to make an association of such institutions. The council offers support and grants with educational guidelines about open and distance education.

The distance education council creates rules and measures in reverence of admission, certification and valuation. The distance education council consults with the state governments and other agencies to find out primary areas in which the distance education programmes could be arranged. To support such programmes is an important duty of the council. The council finds out the specific customer groups and various programmes that can be arranged for them. The council promotes some novel education systems of University level education that are stretchy and open. The distance education council decides the eligibility criteria for enrolment, age level for admission and manner of exam. The distance education council promotes the arrangement of programmes of human resource development for the distance education system.

The council collects and distributes information concerning to the different programmes provided by various open universities. One of the major responsibilities of the council is to assign Review Committees at the proper time to study and evaluate the performance of distance education institutes.

MEDICAL COUNCIL OF INDIA

Medical Council of India, which is responsible for maintaining uniform standards of both undergraduate and postgraduate studies of medicine in India, was established under the Indian Medical Council Act, 1933 in the year 1934. However, in order to meet the new challenges of medical education in India, the earlier act was repealed and a new Indian medical Council Act 1956 was enacted.

It has been modified in 1964, 1993 and 2001 since then. Thus the primary responsibilities of the Medical Council of India are to maintain the uniform standards of undergraduate and postgraduate medical education, recognition of the medical institutions in our country or abroad, permanent or provisional registration of the qualified doctors and reciprocality with foreign countries in case of mutual recognition of medical qualifications.

CONSTITUTION OF MEDICAL COUNCIL OF INDIA

Under Section 3(1) of Indian Medical Council Act, 1956, Medical Council of India contains following members- one member from every state having the nomination by the Central Government, one member elected by the Senate of University who is one of the members of University's medical faculty, one member from every state of India where the State Medical Register is maintained.

The members should be elected by persons inscribed in the medical register. They should have the medical qualifications included in Part-II of the Third Schedule or in the First and Second Schedule. There are 7 members having the medical qualifications included in Part I of the Third Schedule.

There are 8 members that are nominated by the Central Government. The President and Vice-President are elected by the members of Council from amongst themselves.

FUNCTIONS OF MEDICAL COUNCIL OF INDIA

The Medical Council of India performs various important functions including maintenance of standards of medical education in India, offering permission to start new medical colleges, some new courses and increasing number of seats in the colleges, recognition and de-recognition of Indian and Foreign qualifications, maintenance of All India Medical Register, permanent and provisional registration of qualified doctors, registration of additional qualifications etc.

RELIGION IN INDIA

Religions in India are an integral part of the Indian tradition and culture. It is a way of life and it dominates day to day life. The force of religion can be felt from education to politics and the major religions that are followed in secular India are Hinduism, Buddhism, Christianity, Jainism, Islam and Sikhism. India is well-known to be the land of philosophy and spirituality. Hinduism is the oldest religions and is believed to have originated 6000 years ago.

Hinduism relates to a colourful religion comprising of numerous Gods and goddesses. Buddhism and Jainism are the other two religions in India that developed around 500 BC. Earlier, Buddhism and Jainism were quite popular. Speaking about religions in India, Hinduism, Jainism and Buddhism are viewed as the ancient religions and the Indian philosophy molders.

The dominant religion is the Hindu religion and India is the place of birth for Hinduism. Hinduism tenets follow on righteousness, wealth, desire and liberation. Islam is the next religion largest to Hinduism. Islam came to India by the invaders and Arab traders in the 8th century spreading the message of tolerance and peace and their festivals include Muharram, Eid-ul-fitr, Shabe-barat and Eid-ul-azha. Christianity follows the Islamic religion and is one of the significant parts of the Indian society.

Christians also celebrate all the important festivals. Buddhism and Jainism are also the major religions and form a part of the Indian society and culture. Jainism holds a significant place and focuses right conduct, right knowledge and right faith. Jainism strictly believes in non-violence and owing to this they cover their nose and mouth using a mask or cloth while breathing. Sikhism is also followed and has large number of followers. Besides, the main religions there are other separate religions as well.

The religion in India though diverse is followed without any barriers. In fact, all the religions celebrate their occasions and festivals in a pomp and grand manner. The religions developed in India as well belong to the non-Indian religions. The biggest non-Indian religion represents the Islam religion who constitute to nearly 12% of the population. The Indian population includes Christians representing 2%. Apart from them there are Zoroastrians as well making below 0.01%. There are Jews as well. Christianity and Judaism also have equal place in India. The religions in India are given equal respect and all the festivals and practices are observed with sincerity. Nothing is being compared or criticized. Every religion has all the rights to observe their function on their own accord and this is the opulence of India.

8

Health and Medicine

UNDERSTANDING HEALTH, MEDICINE, AND SOCIETY

Health refers to the extent of a person's physical, mental, and social well-being. This definition, taken from the World Health Organization's treatment of health, emphasizes that health is a complex concept that involves not just the soundness of a person's body but also the state of a person's mind and the quality of the social environment in which she or he lives. The quality of the social environment in turn can affect a person's physical and mental health, underscoring the importance of social factors for these twin aspects of our overall well-being. Medicine is the social institution that seeks both to prevent, diagnose, and treat illness and to promote health as just defined. Dissatisfaction with the medical establishment has been growing.

Part of this dissatisfaction stems from soaring health-care costs and what many perceive as insensitive stinginess by the health insurance industry, as the 2009 battle over health-care reform showed. Some of the dissatisfaction also reflects a growing view that the social and even spiritual realms of human existence play a key role in health and illness. This view has fueled renewed interest in alternative medicine. We return later to these many issues for the social institution of medicine.

THE SOCIOLOGICAL APPROACH TO HEALTH AND MEDICINE

We usually think of health, illness, and medicine in

individual terms. When a person becomes ill, we view the illness as a medical problem with biological causes, and a physician treats the individual accordingly. A sociological approach takes a different view. Unlike physicians, sociologists and other public health scholars do not try to understand why any one person becomes ill.

Instead, they typically examine rates of illness to explain why people from certain social backgrounds are more likely than those from others to become sick. Here, our social location in society-our social class, race and ethnicity, and gender-makes a critical difference. The fact that our social backgrounds affect our health may be difficult for many of us to accept. We all know someone, and often someone we love, who has died from a serious illness or currently suffers from one.

There is always a "medical" cause of this person's illness, and physicians do their best to try to cure it and prevent it from recurring. Sometimes they succeed; sometimes they fail. Whether someone suffers a serious illness is often simply a matter of bad luck or bad genes: we can do everything right and still become ill. In saying that our social backgrounds affect our health, sociologists do not deny any of these possibilities.

They simply remind us that our social backgrounds also play an important role. A sociological approach also emphasizes that a society's culture shapes its understanding of health and illness and practice of medicine. In particular, culture shapes a society's perceptions of what it means to be healthy or ill, the reasons to which it attributes illness, and the ways in which it tries to keep its members healthy and to cure those who are sick.

Knowing about a society's culture, then, helps us to understand how it perceives health and healing. By the same token, knowing about a society's health and medicine helps us to understand important aspects of its culture. An interesting example of culture in this regard is seen in Japan's aversion to organ transplants, which are much less common in that nation than in other wealthy nations.

Japanese families dislike disfiguring the bodies of the dead, even for autopsies, which are also much less common in Japan than other nations. This cultural view often prompts them to refuse permission for organ transplants when a family member dies, and it leads many Japanese to refuse to designate themselves as potential organ donors.

As culture changes over time, it is also true that perceptions of health and medicine may also change. Sociology and the Sociological Perspective that physicians in top medical schools a century ago advised women not to go to college because the stress of higher education would disrupt their menstrual cycles. This nonsensical advice reflected the sexism of the times, and we no longer accept it now, but it also shows that what it means to be healthy or ill can change as a society's culture changes.

A society's culture matters in these various ways, but so does its social structure, in particular its level of economic development and extent of government involvement in health-care delivery. Poor societies have much worse health than richer societies. At the same time, richer societies have certain health risks and health problems, such as pollution and liver disease, that poor societies avoid.

The degree of government involvement in health-care delivery also matters: the United States lags behind many Western European nations in several health indicators, in part because the latter nations provide much more national health care than does the United States. Although illness is often a matter of bad luck or bad genes, then, the society we live in can nonetheless affect our chances of becoming and staying ill.

SOCIOLOGICAL PERSPECTIVES ON HEALTH AND MEDICINE

The major sociological perspectives on health and medicine all recognize these points but offer different ways of understanding health and medicine that fall into the functional, conflict, and symbolic interactionist approaches. Together they provide us with a more comprehensive understanding of health, medicine, and society than any one approach can do by itself. Table, "Theory Snapshot" summarizes what they say.

Table. Theory Snapshot

Theoretical Perspective	Major Assumptions
Functionalism	Good health and effective medical care are essential for the smooth functioning of society. Patients must perform the "sick role" in order to be perceived as legitimately ill and to be exempt from their normal obligations. The physician-patient relationship is hierarchical: the physician provides instructions, and the patient needs to follow them.
Conflict theory	Social inequality characterizes the quality of health and the quality of health care. People from disadvantaged social backgrounds are more likely to become ill and to receive inadequate health care. Partly to increase their incomes, physicians have tried to control the practice of medicine and to define social problems as medical problems.
Symbolic interactionism	Health and illness are social constructions: Physical and mental conditions have little or no objective reality but instead are considered healthy or ill conditions only if they are defined as such by a society. Physicians "manage the situation"to display their authority and medical knowledge.

The Functionalist Approach

As conceived by Talcott Parsons, the functionalist perspective on health and medicine emphasizes that good health and effective medical care are essential for a society's ability to function. Ill health obviously impairs our ability to perform our roles in society, and if too many people are unhealthy, society's functioning and stability suffer. This was especially true for premature death, said Parsons, because it prevents individuals from fully carrying out all their social roles and thus represents a "poor return" to society for the various costs of pregnancy, birth, child care, and socialization of the individual who ends up dying early. Poor medical care is likewise dysfunctional for society, as people who are ill face greater difficulty in becoming healthy and people who are healthy are more likely to become ill.

For a person to be considered legitimately sick, said Parsons, several expectations must be met. He referred to these expectations as the sick role. First, sick people should not be perceived as having caused their own health problem. If we eat high-fat food, become obese, and have a heart attack, we evoke less sympathy than if we had practiced good nutrition and maintained a proper weight. If someone is driving drunk and smashes into a tree, there is much less sympathy than if the driver had been sobre and skidded off the road in icy weather.

Second, sick people must want to get well. If they do not want to get well or, worse yet, are perceived as faking their illness or malingering after becoming healthier, they are no longer considered legitimately ill by the people who know them or, more generally, by society itself. Third, sick people are expected to have their illness confirmed by a physician or other health-care professional and to follow the professional's advice and instructions in order to become well.

If a sick person fails to do so, she or he again loses the right to perform the sick role. If all of these expectations are met, said Parsons, sick people are treated as sick by their family, their friends, and other people they know, and they become exempt from their normal obligations to all of these people. Sometimes they are even told to stay in bed when they want to remain active. Physicians also have a role to perform, said Parsons. First and foremost, they have to diagnose the person's illness, decide how to treat it, and help the person become well. To do so, they need the cooperation of the patient, who must answer the physician's questions accurately and follow the physician's instructions. Parsons thus viewed the physician-patient relationship as hierarchical: the physician gives the orders and the patient follows them.

Parsons was certainly right in emphasizing the importance of individuals'good health for society's health, but his perspective has been criticized for several reasons. First, his idea of the sick role applies more to acute illness than to chronic illness. Although much of his discussion implies a person temporarily enters a sick role and leaves it soon after following adequate medical care, people with chronic illnesses can be locked into a sick role for a very long time or even permanently.

Second, Parsons's discussion ignores the fact that our social location in society in the form of social class, race and ethnicity, and gender affects both the likelihood of becoming ill and the quality of medical care we receive. Third, Parsons wrote approvingly of the hierarchy implicit in the physician-patient relationship. Many experts say today that patients need to reduce this hierarchy by asking more questions of their physicians and by taking a more active role in maintaining their health. To the extent that physicians do not always provide the best medical care, the hierarchy that Parsons favoured is at least partly to blame.

The Conflict Approach

The conflict approach emphasizes inequality in the quality of health and of health-care delivery. As noted earlier, the quality of health and health care differ greatly around the world and within the United States. Society's inequities along social class, race and ethnicity, and gender lines are reproduced in our health and health care. People from disadvantaged social backgrounds are more likely to become ill, and once they do become ill, inadequate health care makes it more difficult for them to become well.

The evidence of inequities in health and health care is vast and dramatic. The conflict approach also critiques the degree to which physicians over the decades have tried to control the practice of medicine and to define various social problems as medical ones. Their motivation for doing so has been both good and bad. On the good side, they have believed that they are the most qualified professionals to diagnose problems and treat people who have these problems.

On the negative side, they have also recognized that their financial status will improve if they succeed in characterizing social problems as medical problems and in monopolizing the treatment of these problems. Once these problems become "medicalized," their possible social roots and thus potential solutions are neglected. Several examples thesis conflict theory's criticism. Alternative medicine is becoming increasingly popular but so has criticism of it by the medical establishment.

Physicians may honestly feel that medical alternatives are inadequate, ineffective, or even dangerous, but they also recognize that the use of these alternatives is financially harmful to their own practices. Eating disorders also thesis conflict theory's criticism. Many of the women and girls who have eating disorders receive help from a physician, a psychiatrist, a psychologist, or another health-care professional.

Although this care is often very helpful, the definition of eating disorders as a medical problem nonetheless provides a good source of income for the professionals who treat it and obscures its cultural roots in society's standard of beauty for women. Obstetrical care provides another example. In most of human history, midwives or their equivalent were the people who helped pregnant women deliver their babies.

In the 19th century, physicians claimed they were better trained than midwives and won legislation giving them authority to deliver babies. They may have honestly felt that midwives were inadequately trained, but they also fully recognized that obstetrical care would be quite lucrative. In a final example, many hyperactive children are now diagnosed with ADHD, or attention-deficit/hyperactivity disorder. A generation or more ago, they would have been considered merely as overly active. After Ritalin, a drug that reduces hyperactivity, was developed, their behaviour came to be considered a medical problem and the ADHD diagnosis was increasingly applied, and tens of thousands of children went to physicians' offices and were given Ritalin or similar drugs.

The definition of their behaviour as a medical problem was very lucrative for physicians and for the company that developed Ritalin, and it also obscured the possible roots of their behaviour in inadequate parenting, stultifying schools, or even gender socialization, as most hyperactive kids are boys.

Critics of the conflict approach say that its assessment of health and medicine is overly harsh and its criticism of physicians' motivation far too cynical. Scientific medicine has greatly improved the health of people in the industrial world; even in the poorer nations, moreover, health has improved from a century ago, however inadequate it remains today.

Although physicians are certainly motivated, as many people are, by economic considerations, their efforts to extend their scope into previously nonmedical areas also stem from honest beliefs that people's health and lives will improve if these efforts succeed. Certainly there is some truth in this criticism of the conflict approach, but the evidence of inequality in health and medicine and of the negative aspects of the medical establishment's motivation for extending its reach remains compelling.

The Interactionist Approach

The interactionist approach emphasizes that health and illness are social constructions. This means that various physical and mental conditions have little or no objective reality but instead are considered healthy or ill conditions only if they are defined as such by a society and its members.

The ADHD example just discussed also thesiss interactionist theory's concerns, as a behaviour that was not previously considered an illness came to be defined as one after the development of Ritalin. In another example, in the late 1800s opium use was quite common in the United States, as opium derivatives were included in all sorts of over-the-counter products. Opium use was considered neither a major health nor legal problem. That changed by the end of the century, as prejudice against Chinese Americans led to the banning of the opium dens they frequented, and calls for the banning of opium led to federal legislation early in the 20th century that banned most opium products except by prescription. In a more current example, an attempt to redefine obesity is now under way in the United States.

Obesity is a known health risk, but a "fat pride" movement composed mainly of heavy individuals is arguing that obesity's health risks are exaggerated and calling attention to society's discrimination against overweight people. Although such discrimination is certainly unfortunate, critics say the movement is going too far in trying to minimize obesity's risks.

The symbolic interactionist approach has also provided important studies of the interaction between patients and health-care professionals. Consciously or not, physicians "manage the situation" to display their authority and medical knowledge. Patients usually have to wait a long time for the physician to show up, and the physician is often in a white lab coat; the physician is also often addressed as "Doctor," while patients are often called by their first name.

Physicians typically use complex medical terms to describe a patient's illness instead of the more simple terms used by laypeople and the patients themselves. Management of the situation is perhaps especially important during a gynecological exam. When the physician is a man, this situation is fraught with potential embarrassment and uneasiness because a man is examining and touching a woman's genital area.

Under these circumstances, the physician must act in a purely professional manner. He must indicate no personal interest in the woman's body and must instead treat the exam no differently from any other type of exam. To further "desex" the situation and reduce any potential uneasiness, a female nurse is often present during the exam. Critics fault the symbolic interactionist approach for implying that no illnesses have objective reality.

Many serious health conditions do exist and put people at risk for their health regardless of what they or their society thinks. Critics also say the approach neglects the effects of social inequality for health and illness. Despite these possible faults, the symbolic interactionist approach reminds us that health and illness do have a subjective as well as an objective reality.

HEALTH AND MEDICINE IN INTERNATIONAL PERSPECTIVE

As with many topics in sociology, understanding what happens in other societies and cultures helps us to understand what happens in our own society. This part's discussion of health and health care across the globe, then, helps shed some light on what is good and bad about U.S. health and medicine.

INTERNATIONAL DISPARITIES IN HEALTH AND ILLNESS

The nations of the world differ dramatically in the quality of their health and health care. The poorest nations suffer terribly. Their people suffer from poor nutrition, unsafe water, inadequate sanitation, a plethora of diseases, and inadequate health care. One disease they suffer from is AIDS. Some 33 million people worldwide have HIV/AIDS, and two-thirds of these live in sub-Saharan Africa.

Two million people, most of them from this region, died in 2008 from HIV/AIDS. All of these problems produce high rates of infant mortality and maternal mortality and high death rates. For all of these reasons, people in the poorest nations have shorter life spans than those in the richest nations. A few health indicators should indicate the depth of the problem. An important indicator, infant mortality for nations grouped into four income categories.

The striking contrast between the two groups provides dramatic evidence of the health problems poor nations face. 80 children in the poorest nations die before their first birthday for every 1,000 live births, the poor nations have serious problems indeed. The world differs in access to adequate sanitation facilities. Whereas this percentage is at least 98% in the wealthy nations of North America, Western Europe, and Australia and New Zealand, it is less than 33% in many poor nations in Africa and Asia.

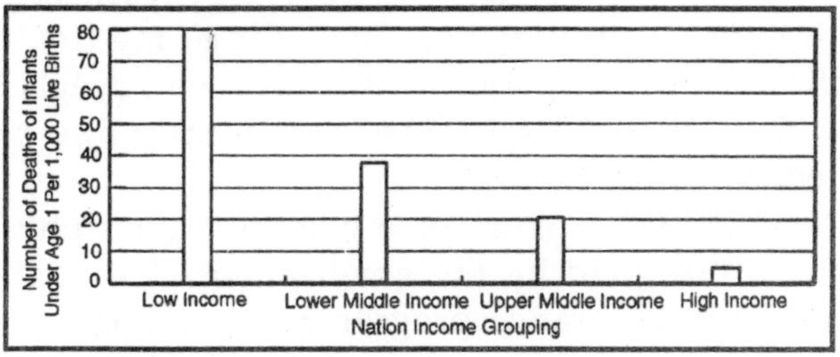

Fig. Infant Mortality for Low Income, Lower Middle Income, Higher Middle Income, and High Income Nations, 2008

Aging and the Elderly, an international map on life expectancy. That map was certainly relevant for understanding aging around the globe but is also relevant for understanding worldwide disparities in health and health care. We reproduce this map here.

Not surprisingly, the global differences in this map are similar to those for adequate sanitation, "Percentage of Population With Access to Adequate Sanitation Facilities, 2008". North America, Western Europe, and Australia and New Zealand have much longer life expectancies than Africa and Asia, where some nations have expectancies below 50 years. The society we live in can affect our life span by more than a quarter of a century.

HEALTH CARE IN INDUSTRIAL NATIONS

Industrial nations throughout the world, with the notable exception of the United States, provide their citizens with some form of national health care and national health insurance. Although their health-care systems differ in several respects, their governments pay all or most of the costs for health care, drugs, and other health needs.

In Denmark, for example, the government provides free medical care and hospitalization for the entire population and pays for some medications and some dental care. In France, the government pays for some of the medical, hospitalization, and medication costs for most people and all of these expenses for the poor, unemployed, and children under the age of 10. In Great Britain, the National Health Service pays most medical costs for the population, including medical care, hospitalization, prescriptions, dental care, and eyeglasses. In Canada, the National Health Insurance system also pays for most medical costs.

Patients do not even receive bills from their physicians, who instead are paid by the government. Although these national health insurance programmes are not perfect-for example, people sometimes must wait for elective surgery and some other procedures-they are commonly credited with reducing infant mortality, extending life expectancy, and more generally for enabling their citizenries to have relatively good health. In all of these respects, these systems offer several advantages over the health-care model found in the United States.

THEORIES OF HEALTH AND ILLNESS IN INDIA

Theories about health and illness deal with the ideas people use to explain how to maintain a healthy state and why they become ill. Ideas about illness causation may include such ideas as breach of taboo, soul loss, germs, upset in the hot-cold balance of the body, or a weakening of the body's immune system. Theories of illness causation derive from the underlying cognitive orientation of a cultural group, and therapeutic practice usually follows the same cultural logic.

Anthropologists often divide theories of illness into two broad categories: personalistic and naturalistic. In a personalistic system, illness is believed to be caused by the intervention of a sensate agent who may be a supernatural being or a human being with special powers. The sick person's illness is considered to be a direct result of the malign influence of these agents. In naturalistic causation, illness is explained in impersonal terms. When the body is in balance with the natural environment, a state of health prevails. However, when that balance is disturbed, illness results.

Often, people invoke both types of causation in explaining an episode of illness, and treatment may entail two corresponding types of therapy. Personalistic theories of illness, illness may be linked to transgressions of a moral and spiritual nature. If someone has violated a social norm or breached a religious taboo, he or she may invoke the wrath of a deity, and sickness-as a form of divine punishment-may result. Possession by evil spirits is also thought to be a cause of illness in many cultures.

This may be due to inappropriate behaviour on the part of the patient-failure to carry out the proper rituals of respect for a dead ancestor, for example-or it may be simply due to bad luck. Sometimes, one person's envy of another's good fortune is believed to exert a malign influence through the "evil eye," which can result in illness or other calamities. Witches and sorcerers are malevolent human beings who manipulate secret rituals and charms to bring calamity upon their enemies.

Recovery from an illness arising from personalistic causes usually involves the use of ritual and symbolism, most often by practitioners who are specially trained in these arts. Naturalistic theories of disease causation tend to view health as a state of harmony between a human being and his or her environment; when this balance is upset, illness will result. The humoural system is a naturalistic approach to illness whose roots are over two thousand years old. Humoural concepts of health and illness are widely found in India, southeast Asia, China, and, in a somewhat different form, in Latin and South America. Maintaining humoural balance involves attention to appropriate diet and activity, including regulating one's diet just as to the seasons.

Illnesses may be categorized into those due to excess heat and those due to excess cold. Treatment of an illness of overheat would involve measures such as giving cooling foods and application of cool compresses. In India, the ancient system of Ayurveda is based on naturalistic ideas of illness causation. Therapy in Ayurveda includes a vast pharmacopeia of preparations made from herbs and minerals, and dietary advice also forms part of every prescription.

Ayurveda is actively practised in India today and has shaped the way Indians think about their bodies in health and in illness. An important set of theories about health and illness, often called "vitalist"theories, is widespread in China, South Asia, and Southeast Asia. When vital forces within the body flow in a harmonious pattern, a positive state of health is maintained. Illness results when this smooth flow of energy is disrupted, and therapeutic measures are aimed at restoring a normal flow of energy in the body.

In China this vital force is known as "chi"; in India it is called "prana." In China the ancient art of acupuncture is based on this understanding of the body. Acupuncture needles are inserted at various points along the "meridians," or energy orientations, of the body. The stimulation of the needles helps to restore a proper flow of energy within the body. In India, yoga is used therapeutically to restore a balanced energy flow through body and mind. Biomedicine is founded on a naturalistic set of theories about the body, and these theories are continually evolving.

One of the core theories of contemporary biomedicine, the germ theory of disease, is of relatively recent origin. An older biomedical concept, the miasma theory of disease, poisonous emanations from rotting vegetation or carcasses were believed to cause disease. By the mid-1800s, controversy still raged as to whether miasma or a waterborne pathogen was the cause for cholera.

The "body-as-machine" metaphor has been a powerful way of conceptualizing the body within biomedicine, and a core assumption of the value system of biomedicine is that diagnosis and treatment should be based on scientific data. However, treatment approaches are often not rigorously analysed scientifically before being employed therapeutically. For example, angina pectoris has been treated in a variety of ways, including with the use of xanthines, khellin, vitamin E ligation of the internal mammary artery, and implantation of this artery. These treatments were used for many years before controlled trials finally showed that the efficacy of these treatments were no better than placebo alone. Ritual and symbolism play important roles in the healing process in biomedicine, as they do in other healing systems. Taking a prescribed medication, for example, has a symbolic as well as a pharmacological effect. Symbolically, taking the medication may indicate to others that the person is unwell and is deserving of concern and sympathy. Surgical treatments such as coronary bypass surgery employ complex equipment and are performed in specialized settings.

These settings and equipment all have powerful symbolic associations as well as technical functions. Rituals are patterned forms of behaviour that have symbolic significance, that often help to provide a context of meaning in a strange or frightening situation. Both patients who undergo the surgery and surgeons who perform the surgery are involved in rituals that serve to order a life-changing event.

The processes of obtaining informed consent, getting a patient prepped for surgery, and complex stages of post-operative care all have ritual as well as technical functions. Alternative therapies have been rapidly gaining in popularity worldwide. These therapies are diverse, ranging from traditional treatments adapted from their lands of origin, such as acupuncture and shiatsu, to newly developed forms of therapy such as therapeutic touch.

Many alternative therapies have underlying theories of illness causation that are quite different from that of biomedicine. In therapies such as acupuncture, reiki, and shiatsu the concept of vital energy, or chi, is the basis for the practice. Successful therapy is that which regulates and harmonizes energy flows. In iridology, particular areas on the iris of the eye are thought to correspond to specific body organs, and a diagnosis of malfunction of the organs can be made by an examination of the iris.

Conceptually, this theory of illness links to an ancient philosophical system of "homologies" that makes connections between the cosmic and the terrestrial; between the outer environment and the inner; and between the external body and the internal body. All theories of health and illness serve to create a context of meaning within which the patient can make sense of his or her bodily experience. A meaningful context for illness usually reflects core cultural values, and allows the patient to bring order to the chaotic world of serious illness and to regain some sense of control in a frightening situation.

MEDICINE AND HEALTH CARE IN INDIA

Healthcare in India features a universal health care system run by the constituent states and territories of India. The Constitution charges every state with "raising of the level of nutrition and the standard of living of its people and the improvement of public health as among its primary duties". The National Health Policy was endorsed by the Parliament of India in 1983 and updated in 2002.

However, the government sector is understaffed and under financed; poor services at state-run hospitals force many people to visit private medical practitioners. Government hospitals, some of which are among the best hospitals in India, provide treatment at taxpayer expense. Most essential drugs are offered free of charge in these hospitals. Government hospitals provide treatment either free or at minimal charges. For example, an outpatient card at AIIMS costs a one time fee of rupees 10 and thereafter outpatient medical advice is free. In-hospital treatment costs depend on financial condition of the patient and facilities utilized by him but are usually much less than the private sector.

For instance, a patient is waived treatment costs if he is below poverty line. Another patient may seek for an air-conditioned room if he is willing to pay extra for it. The charges for basic in-hospital treatment and investigations are much less compared to the private sector. The cost for these subsidies comes from annual allocations from the central and state governments. Primary health care is provided by city and district hospitals and rural primary health centres. These hospitals provide treatment free of cost.

Primary care is focused on immunization, prevention of malnutrition, pregnancy, child birth, postnatal care, and treatment of common illnesses. Patients who receive specialized care or have complicated illnesses are referred to secondary and tertiary care hospitals. In recent times, India has eradicated mass famines, however the country still suffers from high levels of malnutrition and disease especially in rural areas. Water supply and sanitation in India is also a major issue in the country and many Indians in rural areas lack access to proper sanitation facilities and safe drinking water.

However, at the same time, India's health care system also includes entities that meet or exceed international quality standards. The medical tourism business in India has been growing in recent years and as such India is a popular destination for medical tourists who receive effective medical treatment at lower costs than in developed countries.

HEALTHCARE INFRASTRUCTURE

The Indian healthcare industry is seen to be growing at a rapid pace and is expected to become a US$280 billion industry by 2020. The Indian healthcare market was estimated at US$35 billion in 2007 and is expected to reach over US$70 billion by 2012 and US$145 billion by 2017. The Investment Commission of India the healthcare sector has experienced phenomenal growth of 12 per cent per annum in the last 4 years. Rising income levels and a growing elderly population are all factors that are driving this growth. In addition, changing demographics, disease profiles and the shift from chronic to life-style diseases in the country has led to increased spending on healthcare delivery.

Even so, the vast majority of the country suffers from a poor standard of healthcare infrastructure which has not kept up with the growing economy. Despite having centres of excellence in healthcare delivery, these facilities are limited and are inadequate in meeting the current healthcare demands. Nearly one million Indians die every year due to inadequate healthcare facilities and 700 million people have no access to specialist care and 80% of specialists live in urban areas. In order to meet manpower shortages and reach world standards India would require investments of up to $20 billion over the next 5 years. Forty per cent of the primary health centres in India are understaffed. WHO statistics there are over 250 medical colleges in the modern system of medicine and over 400 in the Indian system of medicine and homeopathy. India produces over 250,000 doctors annually in the modern system of medicine and a similar number of ISM&H practitioners, nurses and para professionals. Better policy regulations and the establishment of public private partnerships are possible solutions to the problem of manpower shortage.

India faces a huge need gap in terms of availability of number of hospital beds per 1000 population. With a world average of 3.96 hospital beds per 1000 population India stands just a little over 0.7 hospital beds per 1000 population.. Moreover, India faces a shortage of doctors, nurses and paramedics that are needed to propel the growing healthcare industry.

India is now looking at establishing academic medical centres for the delivery of higher quality care with leading examples of The Manipal Group and All India Institute of Medical Sciences already in place. As incomes rise and the number of available financing options in terms of health insurance policies increase, consumers become more and more engaged in making informed decisions about their health and are well aware of the costs associated with those decisions.

In order to remain competitive, healthcare providers are now not only looking at improving operational efficiency but are also looking at ways of enhancing patient experience overall. India has approximately 600,000 allopathic doctors registered to practice medicine. This number however, is higher than the actual number practicing because it includes doctors who have emigrated to other countries as well as doctors who have died. India licenses 18,000 new doctors a year..

CENTRAL GOVERNMENT'S ROLE

Critics say that the national policy lacks specific measures to achieve broad stated goals. Particular problems include the failure to integrate health services with wider economic and social development, the lack of nutritional support and sanitation, and the poor participatory involvement at the local level. Central government efforts at influencing public health have focused on the five-year plans, on coordinated planning with the states, and on sponsoring major health programmes.

Government expenditures are jointly shared by the central and state governments. Goals and strategies are set through central-state government consultations of the Central Council of Health and Family Welfare. Central government efforts are administered by the Ministry of Health and Family Welfare, which provides both administrative and technical services and manages medical education. States provide public services and health education. The 1983 National Health Policy is committed to providing health services to all by 2000. In 1983 health care expenditures varied greatly among the states and union territories, from Rs 13 per capita in Bihar to Rs 60 per capita in Himachal Pradesh, and Indian per capita expenditure was low when compared with other Asian countries outside of South Asia.

Although government health care spending progressively grew throughout the 1980s, such spending as a percentage of the gross national product remained fairly constant. In the meantime, health care spending as a share of total government spending decreased. During the same period, private-sector spending on health care was about 1.5 times as much as government spending.

EXPENDITURE

In the mid-1990s, health spending amounted to 6% of GDP, one of the highest levels among developing nations. The established per capita spending is around Rs 320 per year with the major input from private households. State governments contribute 15.2%, the central government 5.2%, third-party insurance and employers 3.3%, and municipal government and foreign donors about 1.3, just as to a 1995 World Bank study.

Of these proportions, 58.7% goes towards primary health care and 38.8% is spent on secondary and tertiary inpatient care. The rest goes for nonservice costs. The fifth and sixth five-year plans included programmes to assist delivery of preventive medicine and improve the health status of the rural population. Supplemental nutrition programmes and increasing the supply of safe drinking water were high priorities. The sixth plan aimed at training more community health workers and increasing efforts to control communicable diseases. There were also efforts to improve regional imbalances in the distribution of health care resources.

The Seventh Five-Year Plan budgeted Rs 33.9 billion for health, an amount roughly double the outlay of the sixth plan. Health spending as a portion of total plan outlays, however, had declined over the years since the first plan in 1951, from a high of 3.3% of the total plan spending in FY 1951-55 to 1.9% of the total for the seventh plan. Mid-way through the Eighth Five-Year Plan, however, health and family welfare was budgeted at Rs 20 billion, or 4.3% of the total plan spending for FY 1994, with an additional Rs 3.6 billion in the nonplan budget.

PRIMARY SERVICES

Health care facilities and personnel increased substantially between the early 1950s and early 1980s, but because of fast population growth, the number of licensed medical practitioners per 10,000 individuals had fallen by the late 1980s to three per 10,000 from the 1981 level of four per 10,000. In 1991 there were approximately ten hospital beds per 10,000 individuals.

For comparison, in China there are 1.4 doctors per 1000 people. Primary health centres are the cornerstone of the rural health care system. By 1991, India had about 22,400 primary health centres, 11,200 hospitals, and 27,400 clinics. These facilities are part of a tiered health care system that funnels more difficult cases into urban hospitals while attempting to provide routine medical care to the vast majority in the countryside. Primary health centres and subcenters rely on trained paramedics to meet most of their needs.

The main problems affecting the success of primary health centres are the predominance of clinical and curative concerns over the intended emphasis on preventive work and the reluctance of staff to work in rural areas. In addition, the integration of health services with family planning programmes often causes the local population to perceive the primary health centres as hostile to their traditional preference for large families.

Therefore, primary health centres often play an adversarial role in local efforts to implement national health policies. In 1989 by the Ministry of Health and Family Welfare, the total number of civilian hospitals for all states and union territories combined was 10,157. In 1991 there was a total of 811,000 hospital and health care facilities beds. The geographical distribution of hospitals varied just as to local socio-economic conditions. In India's most populous state, Uttar Pradesh, with a 1991 population of more than 139 million, there were 735 hospitals as of 1990.

In Kerala, with a 1991 population of 29 million occupying an area only one-seventh the size of Uttar Pradesh, there were 2,053 hospitals. Although central government has set a goal of health care for all by 2000, hospitals are distributed unevenly. Private studies of India's total number of hospitals in the early 1990s were more conservative than official Indian data, estimating that in 1992 there were 7,300 hospitals. Of this total, nearly 4,000 were owned and managed by central, state, or local governments. Another 2,000, owned and managed by charitable trusts, received partial support from the government, and the remaining 1,300 hospitals, many of which were relatively small facilities, were owned and managed by the private sector. The use of state-of-the-art medical equipment was primarily limited to urban centres in the early 1990s.

A network of regional cancer diagnostic and treatment facilities was being established in the early 1990s in major hospitals that were part of government medical colleges. By 1992 twenty-two such centres were in operation. Most of the 1,300 private hospitals lacked sophisticated medical facilities, although in 1992 approximately 12% possessed state-of-the-art equipment for diagnosis and treatment of all major diseases, including cancer. The fast pace of development of the private medical sector and the burgeoning middle class in the 1990s have led to the emergence of the new concept in India of establishing hospitals and health care facilities on a for-profit basis. By the late 1980s, there were approximately 128 medical colleges—roughly three times more than in 1950.

These medical colleges in 1987 accepted a combined annual class of 14,166 students. Data for 1987 show that there were 320,000 registered medical practitioners and 219,300 registered nurses. Various studies have shown that in both urban and rural areas people preferred to pay and seek the more sophisticated services provided by private physicians rather than use free treatment at public health centres.

TRADITIONAL PRACTICES

Indigenous or traditional medical practitioners continue to practice throughout the country. The two main forms of traditional medicine practised are the ayurvedic system, which deals with mental and spiritual as well as physical well-being, and the unani herbal medical practice. A vaidya is a practitioner of the ayurvedic tradition, and a hakim is a practitioner of the unani or Greek tradition. These professions are frequently hereditary.

A variety of institutions offer training in indigenous medical practice. Only in the late 1970s did official health policy refer to any form of integration between European-trained medical personnel and indigenous medical practitioners. In the early 1990s, there were ninety-eight ayurvedic colleges and seventeen unani colleges operating in both the governmental and non-governmental sectors.

HEALTH INSURANCE

The majority of the Indian population is unable to access high quality healthcare provided by private players as a result of high costs. Many are now looking towards insurance companies for providing alternative financing options so that they too may seek better quality healthcare. The opportunity remains huge for insurance providers entering into the Indian healthcare market since 75% of expenditure on healthcare in

India is still being met by 'out-of-pocket' consumers. Even though only 10% of the Indian population today has health insurance coverage, this industry is expected to face tremendous growth over the next few years as a result of several private players that have entered into the market. Health insurance coverage among urban, middle- and upper-class Indians, however, is significantly higher and stands at approximately 50%.

The Insurance Regulatory and Development Authority is the governing body responsible for promoting insurance business and introducing insurance regulations in India. The share of public sector companies in health insurance premiums was 76% and that of private sector companies was 24% for the period 2005-06. Health insurance premiums collected over 2005-06 registered a growth of 35% over the previous year.

In 2001 the IRDA introduced provisions for Third Party Administrators to support the administration and management of health insurance products offered by insurance companies. TPAs are facilitators in the coordination process between the health insurance provider and the hospital. Currently there are 27 TPAs registered under the IRDA.

Health insurance has a way of increasing accessibility to quality healthcare delivery especially for private healthcare providers for whom high cost remains a barrier. In order to encourage foreign health insurers to enter the Indian market the government has recently proposed to raise the foreign direct investment limit in insurance from 26% to 49%. Increasing health insurance penetration and ensuring affordable premium rates are necessary to drive the health insurance market in India.

ISSUES

Disease

India suffers from high levels of disease including Malaria, and Tuberculosis where one third of the world's tuberculosis cases are in India. In addition, India along with Nigeria, Pakistan and Afghanistan is one of the four countries worldwide where polio has not as yet been eradicated.

Ongoing government of India education about HIV has led to decreases in the spread of HIV in recent years. The number of people living with AIDS in India is estimated to be between 2 and 3 million. However in terms of the total population this is a small number. The country has had a sharp decrease in the estimated number of HIV infections; 2005 reports had claimed that there were 5.2 million to 5.7 million people afflicted with the virus.

Pollution

The World Health Organization 900,000 Indians die each year from drinking contaminated water and breathing in polluted air. As India grapples with these basic issues, new challenges are emerging for example there is a rise in chronic adult diseases such as cardiovascular illnesses and diabetes as a consequence of changing lifestyles.

Malnutrition

Half of children in India are underweight, one of the highest rates in the world and nearly same as Sub-Saharan Africa. India contributes to about 5.6 million child deaths every year, more than half the world's total.

Water and Sanitation

Water supply and sanitation in India is a matter of concern. As of 2003, it was estimated that only 30% of India's wastewater was being treated, with the remainder flowing into rivers or groundwater. The lack of toilet facilities in many areas also presents a major health risk; open defecation is widespread even in urban areas of India, and it was estimated in 2002 by the World Health Organisation that around 700,000 Indians die each year from diarrhoea. No city in India has full-day water supply. Most cities supply water only a few hours a day. In towns and rural areas the situation is even worse.

MEDICAL TOURISM

India is quickly becoming a hub for medical tourists seeking quality healthcare at an affordable cost. Nearly 450,000 foreigners sought medical treatment in India last year with Singapore not too far behind and Thailand in the lead with over a million medical tourists. As the Indian healthcare delivery system strives to match international standards the Indian healthcare industry will be able to tap into a substantial portion of the medical tourism market.

Already 13 Indian hospitals have been accredited by the Joint Commission International. Accreditation and compliance with quality expectations are important since they provide tourists with confidence that the services are meeting international standards. Reduced costs, access to the latest medical technology, growing compliance to international quality standards and ease of communication all work towards India's advantage. It is not uncommon to see citizens of other nations seek high quality medical care in the US over the past several decades; however in recent times the pattern seems to be reversing. As healthcare costs in the US are rising, price sensitivity is soaring and people are looking at medical value travel as a viable alternative option.

In the past the growth potential of the medical travel industry in India has been hindered by capacity and infrastructure constraints but that situation is now changing with strong economic progress in India as well as in other developing nations. With more and more hospitals receiving JCI accreditations outside the US, concerns on safety and quality of care are becoming less of an issue for those choosing to travel for medical treatment at an affordable cost.

The combined cost of travel and treatment in India is still a fraction of the amount spent on just medical treatment alone in western countries. In order to attract foreign patients many Indian hospitals are promoting their international quality of healthcare delivery by turning to international accreditation agencies to standardize their protocols and obtain the required approvals on safety and quality of care.

IMPORTANT POINTS

- A sociological approach emphasizes the relationship between health, medicine, and society. Our social backgrounds influence our health and access to health care, while the culture and social structure of a society influences its perceptions of health and illness and ways of healing.

- Sociological perspectives on health and illness fall into the functional, conflict, and interactionist approaches encountered. The functional view emphasizes the importance of health for a society's stability and the roles that people play when they are sick. The conflict view stresses inequality in the quality of health and health-care delivery and efforts by physicians to monopolize the practice of medicine to increase their profits. The interactionist view, health and illness are social constructions subject to people's and society's interpretations. The interactionist view also studies how medical professionals and patients interact and the way professionals manage understandings of such interaction.
- Health and the quality of health care differ widely around the world and reflect global stratification. The earth's poorest nations have extremely high rates of infant mortality and life-threatening diseases such as AIDS and very low life expectancy. Despite efforts of organizations like the World Health Organization, the poor health of the poor nations'residents remains a serious problem.
- The United States ranks ahead of most of the world's nations in most health indicators, and health in the United States has greatly improved in the last century. At the same time, the United States lags behind most other industrial nations in important health indicators such as infant mortality and life expectancy. Moreover, serious disparities exist within the United States in the social distribution of health, as evidenced by the study of social epidemiology.
- Social class, race and ethnicity, and gender all affect the quality of health. Poor people lack health

insurance and access to health, face high amounts of stress, live in unhealthy social and physical environments, and are more apt to engage in unhealthy lifestyles. For all of these reasons, their health is worse than that of the nonpoor. African Americans, Hispanics, and Native Americans all fare worse than whites on many health indicators, in large part because of their poverty and history of discrimination. Women fare worse than men on several heath indicators, but men have lower life expectancies because of their higher rates of certain life-threatening illnesses. These rates are thought to be due to men's biology, unhealthy lifestyles brought on by their masculine socialization, and unwillingness to seek medical treatment.

- Social factors also help explain different rates of mental illness. The poor have higher rates of mental disorders than the nonpoor because of the stress of poverty and other negative life conditions. Women are more likely than men to be depressed and to suffer from some other disorders, but men are more likely to have antisocial personality disorders with symptoms that make them a threat to others. Clear racial and ethnic differences in mental disorders have not been found, perhaps because the strong family bonds and religious faith of many minorities help protect them from disorders that would otherwise be expected from their poverty and discrimination. In looking at Mexican-Americans, there's some evidence that living in American society raises the risks of mental disorders.
- The history of medicine reflects a move from religious and spiritual approaches to healing to scientific approaches. In prehistoric societies priests tried to appease the angry gods or chase away the evil spirits who were thought to cause physical and mental illness. Ancient civilizations made great advances in our understanding of health and illness,

and the rise of scientific medicine beginning in the 1600s helped pave the path for today's scientific approach.

- Despite these medical advances, health care in the United States today faces several problems. The United States is alone in not offering universal national health insurance; its absence is thought to help account for the country's low ranking in the industrial world on major health indicators, as significant numbers of our poor and minorities lack health insurance. Managed care has also come under criticism for restricting coverage of important medical procedures and prescription medicines. Racial and gender bias in health care is another problem that has adverse effects on the nation's health. Other quality-of-care problems include tired physicians, a lack of emergency-room physicians, and numerous mistakes made in hospitals. Disagreement over alternative medicine reflects the historic battle between the medical establishment and other healers, while self-referral and other issues raise important questions for medical ethics. Meanwhile, health-care fraud costs the nation some $100 billion annually and remains an important problem for the nation to address.

9

Population, Urbanization, and Social Movements

POPULATION

We have commented that population growth is an important source of other changes in society. A generation ago, population growth was a major issue in the United States and some other nations. Zero population growth, or ZPG, was a slogan often heard.

There was much concern over the rapidly growing population in the United States and, especially, around the world, and there was fear that our "small planet" could not support massive increases in the number of people. Some of the most dire predictions of the time warned of serious food shortages by the end of the century.

Those predictions did not come to pass, and concern over population growth has faded as the world's resources seem to be standing up to population growth. Widespread hunger in Africa and other regions does exist, with hundreds of millions of people suffering from hunger and malnutrition, but many experts attribute this problem not to overpopulation and lack of food but rather to problems in distributing the sufficient amount of food that actually does exist to people in poor nations.

Concern over population growth also decreased because of criticism by people of colour that ZPG was directed largely at their ranks and smacked of racism. The call for population control, they said, was a disguised call for controlling the growth of their own populations and thus reducing their influence. Still another reason for the reduced concern over population growth is that birth rates in many industrial nations have slowed considerably. Some nations are even experiencing population declines, while several more are projected to have population declines by 2050.

For a country to maintain its population, the average woman needs to have 2.1 children, the replacement level for population stability. But several industrial nations, not including the United States, are far below this level. Increased birth control is one reason for their lower fertility rates, but so are the decisions by women to stay in school longer and then to go to work right after their schooling ends and not having their first child until somewhat later.

Ironically, these nations' population declines have begun to concern demographers and policy makers. Because people in many industrial nations are living longer while the birth rate drops, these nations are increasingly having a greater proportion of older people and a smaller proportion of younger people. In several European nations, there are more people 61 or older than 19 or younger.

As this trend continues, it will become increasingly difficult to take care of the health and income needs of so many older persons, and there may be too few younger people to fill the many jobs and provide the many services that an industrial society demands.

The smaller labour force may also mean that governments will have fewer income tax dollars to provide these services. To deal with these problems, several governments have initiated pronatalist policies aimed at encouraging women to have more children.

In particular, they provide generous child-care subsidies, tax incentives, and flexible work schedules designed to make it easier to bear and raise children, and some even provide couples outright cash payments when they have an additional child. Russia in some cases provides the equivalent of about $9,000 for each child beyond the first, while Spain provides 2,500 euros.

DEMOGRAPHY AND DEMOGRAPHIC CONCEPTS

As all of these issues indicate, changes in the size and composition of population have important implications for other social changes. The study of population is so significant that it occupies a special subfield within sociology called demography. To be more precise, demography is the study of changes in the size and composition of population. It encompasses several concepts: fertility and birth rates, mortality and death rates, and migration.

Fertility and Birth Rates

Fertility refers to the number of live births. Demographers use several measures of fertility. One measure is the crude birth rate, or the number of live births for every 1,000 people in a population in a given year. To determine the crude birth rate, the number of live births in a year is divided by the population size, and this result is then multiplied by 1,000. For example, in 2008 the United States had a population of about 304 million and 4,251,095 births. Dividing the latter figure by the former figure gives us 0.0140 rounded off. We then multiply this quotient by 1,000 to yield a crude birth rate of 14.0 births per 1,000 population. We call this a "crude" birth rate because the denominator, population size, consists of the total population, not just the number of women or even the number of women of childbearing age.

A second measure is the general fertility rate or the number of live births per 1,000 women aged 15-44. This is calculated in a manner similar to that for the crude fertility rate, but in this case the number of births is divided by the number of women aged 15-44 before multiplying by 1,000. The U.S. general fertility rate for 2007 was about 69.5. A third measure is the total fertility rate, or the number of children an average woman is expected to have in her lifetime.

This measure often appears in the news media and is more easily understood by the public than either of the first two measures. In 2007, the U.S. total fertility rate was 2.1. Sometimes the total fertility rate is expressed as the average number of births that an average group of 1,000 women would be expected to have. In this case, the average number of children that one woman is expected to have is simply multiplied by 1,000. Using th:s latter calculation, the U.S. total fertility rate in 2007 was 2,100.

The U.S. general fe-tility rate has changed a lot since 1920, dropping from 101 in 1920 to 70 in 1935, during the Great Depression, before rising afterward until 1955. The fertility rate then fell steadily after 1960 until the 1970s but has remained rather steady since then, fluctuating only slightly between 65 and 70 per 1,000 women aged 15-44.

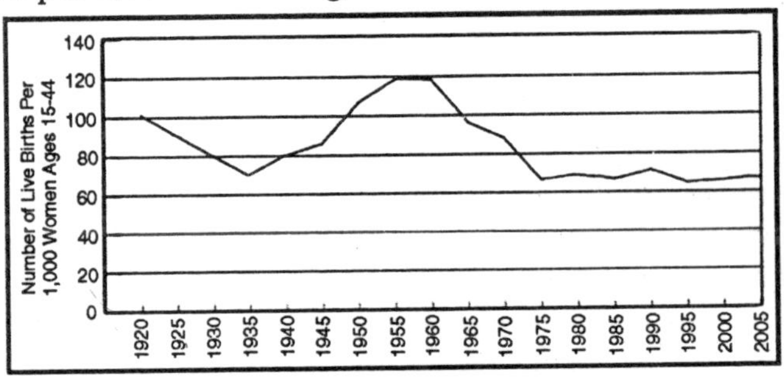

Fig. General Fertility Rate, 1920-2005

The fertility rate varies by race and ethnicity. It is lowest for non-Latina white women and the highest for Latina women. Along with immigration, the high fertility rate of Latina women has fueled the large growth of the Latino population. Latinos now account for about 16% of the U.S. population, and their proportion is expected to reach more than 30% by 2050.

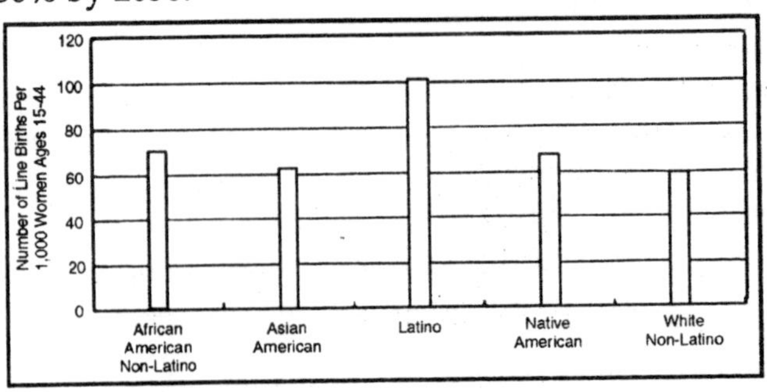

Fig. Race, Ethnicity, and Fertility Rates, 2006

The fertility rate of teenagers is a special concern because of their age. Although it is still a rate that most people wish were lower, it dropped steadily through the 1990s, before leveling off after 2002 and rising slightly by 2007. Although most experts attribute this drop to public education campaigns and increased contraception, the United States still has the highest rate of teenage pregnancy and fertility of any industrial nation. Teenage fertility again varies by race and ethnicity, with Latina teenagers having the highest fertility rates and Asian American teenagers the lowest.

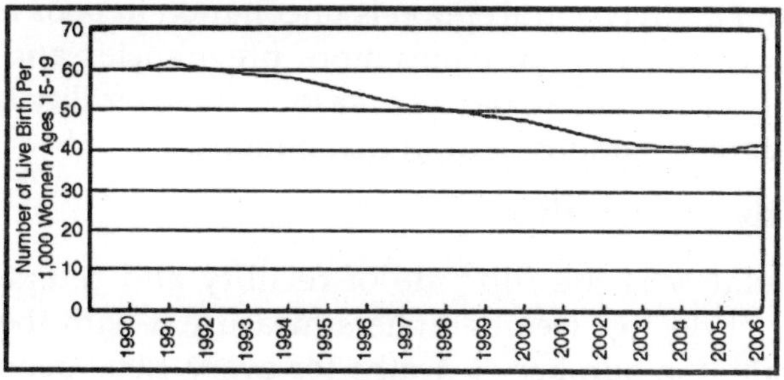

Fig. Teenage Fertility Rate, 1990-2006

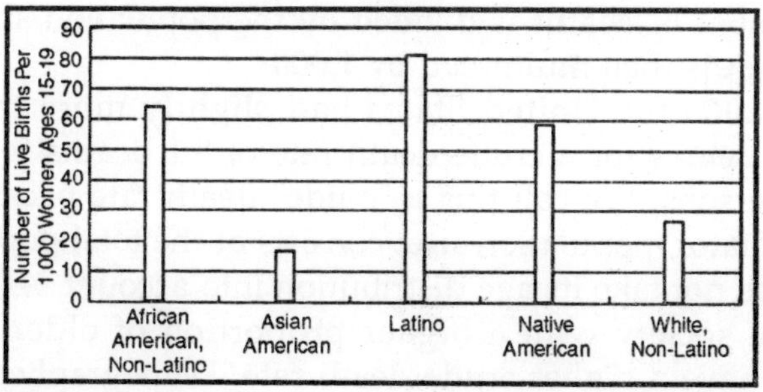

Fig. Race, Ethnicity, and Teenage Fertility Rates, 2007

Fertility rates also differ around the world and are especially high in poor nations. Demographers identify several reasons for these high rates. First, poor nations are usually agricultural ones. In agricultural societies, children are an important economic resource, as a family will be more productive if it has more children.

This means that families will ordinarily try to have as many children as possible. Second, infant and child mortality rates are high in these nations. Because parents realise that one or more of their children may die before adulthood, they have more children to "make up" for the anticipated deaths. A third reason is that many parents in low-income nations prefer sons to daughters, and, if a daughter is born, they "try again" for a son.

Fourth, traditional gender roles are often very strong in poor nations, and these roles include the belief that women should be wives and mothers above all. With this ideology in place, it is not surprising that women will have several children. Finally, contraception is uncommon in poor nations. Without contraception, many more pregnancies and births obviously occur. For all of these reasons, then, fertility is much higher in poor nations than in rich nations.

Mortality and Death Rates

Mortality is the flip side of fertility and refers to the number of deaths. Demographers measure it with the crude death rate, the number of deaths for every 1,000 people in a population in a given year. To determine the crude death rate, the number of deaths is divided by the population size, and this result is then multiplied by 1,000.

In 2006 the United States had slightly more than 2.4 million deaths for a crude death rate of 8.1 deaths for every 1,000 persons. We call this a "crude" death rate because the denominator, population size, consists of the total population and does not take its age distribution into account. All things equal, a society with a higher proportion of older people should have a higher crude death rate. Demographers often calculate age-adjusted death rates that adjust for a population's age distribution.

Migration

Another demographic concept is migration, the movement of people into and out of specific regions. Since the dawn of human history, people have migrated in search of a better life, and many have been forced to migrate by ethnic conflict or the slave trade. Several classifications of migration exist. When people move into a region, we call it in-migration, or immigration; when they move out of a region, we call it out-migration, or emigration. The in-migration rate is the number of people moving into a region for every 1,000 people in the region, while the out-migration rate is the number of people moving from the region for every 1,000 people. The difference between the two is the net migration rate. Migration can also be either domestic or international in scope.

Domestic migration happens within a country's national borders, as when retired people from the northeastern United States move to Florida or the Southwest. International migration happens across national borders. When international immigration is heavy, as it has been into the United States and Western Europe in the last few decades, the effect on population growth and other aspects of national life can be significant. Domestic migration can also have a large impact.

The great migration of African Americans from the South into northern cities during the first half of the 20th century changed many aspects of those cities' lives. Meanwhile, the movement during the past few decades of northerners into the South and Southwest also had quite an impact: the housing market initially exploded, for example, and traffic increased.

POPULATION GROWTH

Three of the factors just discussed determine population growth: fertility, mortality, and net migration. The natural growth rate is simply the difference between the crude birth rate and the crude death rate. The U.S. natural growth rate is about 0.6% per year. When immigration is also taken into account, the total population growth rate has been almost 1.0% per year.

The annual population growth rate of all the nations in the world. Note that many African nations are growing by at least 3% per year or more, while most European nations are growing by much less than 1% or are even losing population, as discussed earlier. Overall, the world population is growing by about 80 million people annually. To determine how long it takes for a nation to double its population size, divide the number 70 by its population growth rate. For example, if a nation has an annual growth rate of 3%, it takes about 23.3 years for that nation's population size to double.

As you can see from the map in several nations will see their population size double in this time span if their annual growth continues at its present rate. For these nations, population growth will be a serious problem if food and other resources are not adequately distributed.

Demographers use their knowledge of fertility, mortality, and migration trends to make projections about population growth and decline several decades into the future. Coupled with our knowledge of past population sizes, these projections allow us to understand population trends over many generations. One clear pattern emerges from the study of population growth.

When a society is small, population growth is slow because there are relatively few adults to procreate. But as the number of people grows over time, so does the number of adults. More and more procreation thus occurs every single generation, and population growth then soars in a virtual explosion. We saw evidence of this pattern when we looked at world population growth.

When agricultural societies developed some 12,000 years ago, only about 8 million people occupied the planet. This number had reached about 300 million about 2,100 years ago, and by the 15th century it was still only about 500 million. It finally reached 1 billion by about 1850 and by 1950, only a century later, had doubled to 2 billion. Just 50 years later it tripled to more than 6.8 billion, and it is projected to reach more than 9 billion by 2050.

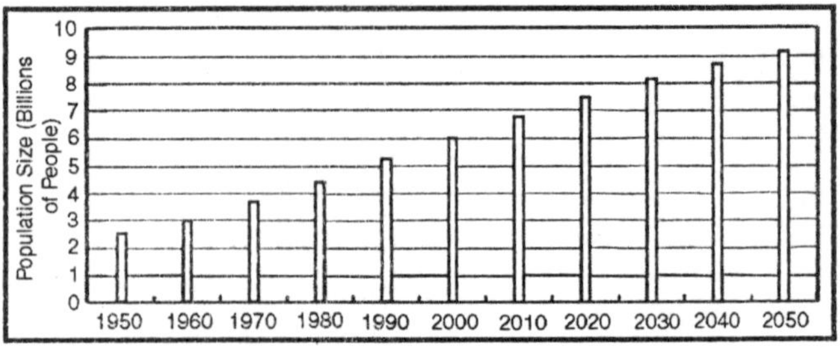

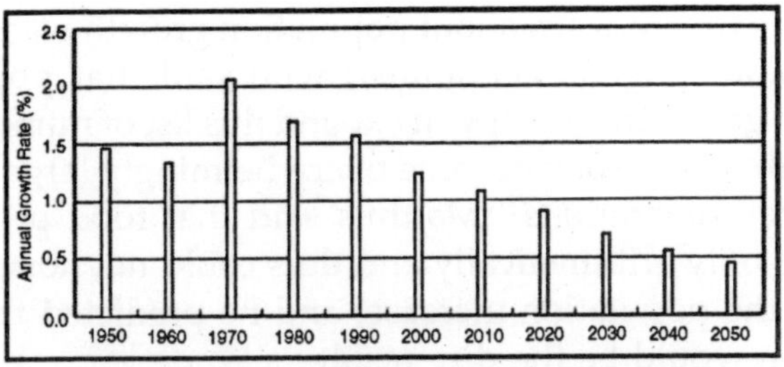

Fig. Total World Population, 1950-2050

Eventually, however, population growth begins to level off after exploding, as explained by demographic transition theory, discussed later. We see this in the bottom half of which shows the average annual growth rate for the world's population. This rate has declined over the last few decades and is projected to further decline over the next four decades. This means that while the world's population will continue to grow during the foreseeable future, it will grow by a smaller rate as time goes by.

The growth that does occur will be concentrated in the poor nations in Africa and some other parts of the world. Still, even there the average number of children a woman has in her lifetime dropped from six a generation ago to about three today.

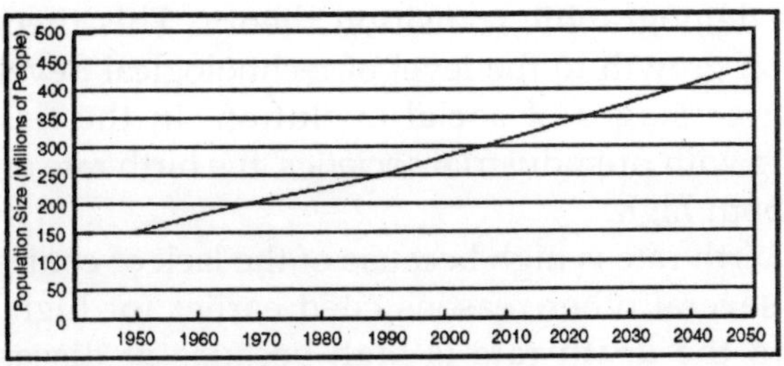

Fig. Past and Projected Size, 1950-2050 (in Millions)

VIEWS OF POPULATION GROWTH

Earlier we talked about the zero population growth movement and concern about overpopulation that received so much attention a generation ago. Social observers have actually worried about overpopulation since the 18th century.

One of the first to warn about population growth was Thomas Malthus, an English economist, who said that population increases geometrically. If you expand this list of numbers, you will see that they soon become overwhelmingly large in just a few more "generations." Malthus said that food production increases only arithmetically and thus could not hope to keep up with the population increase, and he predicted that mass starvation would be the dire result.

Fortunately, Malthus was wrong to some degree. Although population levels have certainly soared, the projections show that the rate of increase is slowing. Among other factors, the development of more effective contraception, especially the birth control pill, has limited population growth in the industrial world and, increasingly, in poorer nations. Food production has also increased by a much greater amount than Malthus predicted, although, as noted earlier, hunger remains a serious problem in poor nations because of inequalities in food distribution.

Demographic Transition Theory

Other factors also explain why population growth has not risen at the geometric rate that Malthus predicted and is even slowing. The view explaining the interaction of these factors is called demographic transition theory. This theory links population growth to the level of technological development across three stages of social evolution. In the first stage, coinciding with preindustrial societies, the birth rate and death rate are both high.

The birth rate is high because of the lack of contraception and the several other reasons cited earlier for high fertility rates, and the death rate is high because of disease, poor nutrition, lack of modern medicine, and other problems. These two high rates cancel each other out, and little population growth occurs. In the second stage, coinciding with the development of industrial societies, the birth rate remains fairly high, owing to the lack of contraception and a continuing belief in the value of large families, but the death rate drops because of several factors, including increased food production, better sanitation, and improved medicine. Because the birth rate remains high but the death rate drops, population growth takes off dramatically. In the third stage, the death rate remains low, but the birth rate finally drops as families begin to realise that large numbers of children in an industrial economy are more of a burden than an asset. Another reason for the drop is the availability of effective contraception. As a result, population growth slows, and, as we saw earlier, it has become quite low or even gone into a decline in several industrial nations.

Demographic transition theory gives us reason to be cautiously optimistic regarding the threat of overpopulation. As poor nations continue to modernize-much as industrial nations did 200 years ago-their population growth rates should start to decline. Still, population growth rates in poor nations continue to be high, and, as the "Sociology Making a Difference" box discussed, inequalities in food distribution allow rampant hunger to persist. Hundreds of thousands of women die in poor nations each year during pregnancy and childbirth.

Reduced fertility would save their lives, in part because their bodies would be healthier if their pregnancies were spaced farther apart. Although world population growth is slowing, then, it is still growing too rapidly in much of the developing and least developed worlds. To reduce it further, more extensive family-planning programmes are needed, as is economic development in general.

URBANIZATION

An important aspect of social change and population growth over the centuries has been urbanization, or the rise and growth of cities. Urbanization has had important consequences for many aspects of social, political, and economic life.

The earliest cities developed in ancient times after the rise of horticultural and pastoral societies made it possible for people to stay in one place instead of having to move around to find food. Because ancient cities had no sanitation facilities, people typically left their garbage and human waste in the city streets or just outside the city wall; this poor sanitation led to rampant disease and high death rates. Some cities eventually developed better sanitation procedures, including, in Rome, a sewer system. Cities became more numerous and much larger during industrialization, as people moved to be near factories and other sites of industrial production.

First in Europe and then in the United States, people crowded together as never before into living conditions that were often decrepit. Lack of sanitation continued to cause rampant disease, and death rates from cholera, typhoid, and other illnesses were high. In addition, crime rates soared, and mob violence became quite common.

VIEWS OF THE CITY

Are cities good or bad? We asked a similar question-is modernization good or bad?- and the answer here is similar as well: cities are both good and bad. They are sites of innovation, high culture, population diversity, and excitement, but they are also sites of high crime, impersonality, and other problems. In the early 20th century, a group of social scientists at the University of Chicago established a research agenda on cities that is still influential today.

Most notably, they began to study the effects of urbanization on various aspects of city residents' lives in what came to be called the human ecology school. One of their innovations was to divide Chicago into geographical regions, or zones, and to analyse crime rates and other behavioural differences among the zones.

They found that crime rates were higher in the inner zone, or central part of the city, where housing was crowded and poverty was common, and were lower in the outer zones, or the outer edges of the city, where houses were spread farther apart and poverty was much lower. Because they found these crime rate differences over time even as the ethnic backgrounds of people in these zones changed, they assumed that the social and physical features of the neighbourhoods were affecting their crime rates. Their work is still useful today, as it helps us realise that the social environment, broadly defined, can affect our attitudes and behaviour. This theme, of course, lies at the heart of the sociological perspective.

Urbanism and Tolerance

One of the most notable Chicago sociologists was Louis Wirth, who, in a well-known thesis entitled "Urbanism as a Way of Life", discussed several differences between urban and rural life. In one such difference, he said that urban residents are more tolerant than rural residents of nontraditional attitudes, behaviours, and lifestyles, in part because they are much more exposed than rural residents to these nontraditional ways. Supporting Wirth's hypothesis, contemporary research finds that urban residents indeed hold more tolerant views on several kinds of issues.

LIFE IN CITIES

Life in U.S. cities today reflects the dual view just outlined. On the one hand, many U.S. cities are vibrant places, filled with museums and other cultural attractions, nightclubs, theaters, and restaurants and populated by people from many walks of life and from varied racial and ethnic and national backgrounds. Many college graduates flock to cities, not only for their employment opportunities but also for their many activities and the sheer excitement of living in a metropolis.

On the other hand, many U.S. cities are also filled with abject poverty, filth and dilapidated housing, high crime rates, traffic gridlock, and dirty air. Many Americans would live nowhere but a city, and many would live anywhere but a city. Cities arouse strong opinions pro and con, and for good reason, because there are many things both to like and to dislike about cities.

Types of Urban Residents

The quality of city life depends on many factors, but one of the most important factors is a person's social background: social class, race and ethnicity, gender, age, and sexual orientation. These dimensions of our social backgrounds often yield many kinds of social inequalities, and the quality of life that city residents enjoy depends heavily on these dimensions. For example, residents who are white and wealthy have the money and access to enjoy the best that cities have to offer, while those who are poor and of colour typically experience the worst aspects of city life. Because of fear of rape and sexual assault, women often feel more constrained than men from traveling freely throughout a city and being out late at night; older people also often feel more constrained because of physical limitations and fear of muggings; and gays and lesbians are still subject to physical assaults stemming from homophobia.

The type of resident we are, then, in terms of our socio-demographic profile affects what we experience in the city and whether that experience is positive or negative. This brief profile of city residents obscures other kinds of differences among residents regarding their lifestyles and experiences. A classic typology of urban dwellers by sociologist Herbert Gans is still useful today in helping to understand the variety of lives found in cities. Gans identified five types of city residents. The first type is cosmopolites.

These are people who live in a city because of its cultural attractions, restaurants, and other features of the best that a city has to offer. Cosmopolites include students, writers, musicians, intellectuals, and writers. Unmarried and childless individuals and couples are the second type; they live in a city to be near their jobs and to enjoy the various kinds of entertainment found in most cities. If and when they marry or have children, respectively, many migrate to the suburbs to raise their families.

The third type is ethnic villagers, who are recent immigrants and members of various ethnic groups who live among each other in certain neighbourhoods. These neighbourhoods tend to have strong social bonds and more generally a strong sense of community. Gans wrote that all of these three types generally find the city inviting rather than alienating and have positive experiences far more often than negative ones. In contrast, two final types of residents find the city alienating and experience a low quality of life. The first of these two types, and the fourth overall, is the deprived. These are people with low levels of formal education who live in poverty or near-poverty and are unemployed, are underemployed, or work at low wages. They live in neighbourhoods filled with trash, broken windows, and other signs of disorder. They commit high rates of crime and also have high rates of victimization by crime.

The final type is the trapped. These are residents who, as their name implies, might wish to leave their neighbourhoods but are unable to do so for several reasons: they may be alcoholics or drug addicts, they may be elderly and disabled, or they may be jobless and cannot afford to move to a better area.

Problems of City Life

By definition, cities consist of very large numbers of people living in a relatively small amount of space. Some of these people have a good deal of money, but many people, and in some cities most people, have very little money. Cities must provide many kinds of services for all their residents, and certain additional services for their poorer residents.

These basic facts of city life make for common sets of problems affecting cities throughout the nation, albeit to varying degrees, with some cities less able than others to address these problems. One evident problem is fiscal: cities typically have serious difficulties in paying for basic services such as policing, public education, trash removal, street maintenance, and, in cold climates, snow removal, and in providing certain services for their residents who are poor or disabled or who have other conditions.

The fiscal difficulties that cities routinely face became even more serious with the onset of the nation's deep recession in 2009, as the term fiscal crisis became a more accurate description of the harsh financial realities that cities were now facing. Another problem is crowding. Cities are crowded in at least two ways. The first involves residential crowding: large numbers of people living in a small amount of space. City streets are filled with apartment buildings, condominiums, row houses, and other types of housing, and many people live on any one city block. The second type of crowding is household crowding: dwelling units in cities are typically small because of lack of space, and much smaller than houses in suburbs or rural areas.

This forces many people to live in close quarters within a particular dwelling unit. Either type of crowding is associated with higher levels of stress, depression, and aggression. A third problem involves housing. Here there are two related issues. Much urban housing is substandard and characterized by such problems as broken windows, malfunctioning heating systems, peeling paint, and insect infestation. At the same time, adequate housing is not affordable for many city residents, as housing prices in cities can be very high, and the residents' incomes are typically very low.

Cities thus have a great need for adequate, affordable housing. A fourth problem is traffic. Gridlock occurs in urban areas, not rural ones, because of the sheer volume of traffic and the sheer number of intersections controlled by traffic lights or stop signs.

Some cities have better public transportation than others, but traffic and commuting are problems that urban residents experience every day. A related problem is pollution. Traffic creates pollution from motor vehicles' exhaust systems, and some cities have factories and other enterprises that also pollute. As a result, air quality in cities is substandard, and the poor quality of air in cities has been linked to respiratory and heart disease and higher mortality rates. Yet another issue for cities is the state of their public education.

Many city schools are housed in old buildings that, like much city housing, are falling apart. City schools are notoriously underfunded and lack current adequate science equipment, and other instructional materials. Although cities have many additional problems, crime is an appropriate one with which to end this part because of its importance. Simply put, cities have much higher rates of violent and property crime than do small towns or rural areas. For example, the violent crime rate in 2008 was 489 for the nation's largest cities, compared to only 205 for rural counties. The property crime rate in the largest cities was 3,352 crimes per 100,000, compared to only 1,681 in rural counties. Crime rates in large cities are thus two to three times higher than those in rural counties.

GLOBAL URBANIZATION

Urbanization varies around the world. In general, wealthy nations are more urban than poor nations thanks in large part to the latter's rural economies. This variation, however, obscures the fact that the world is becoming increasingly urban overall. In 1950, less than one-third of the world's population lived in cities or towns; in 2008, more than half the population lived in cities or towns, representing the first time in history that a majority of people were not living in rural areas. By 2030, almost two-thirds of the world's population is projected to live in urban areas.

The number of urban residents will increase rapidly in the years ahead, especially in Africa and Asia as people in these continents' nations move to urban areas and as their populations continue to grow through natural fertility. Fertility is a special problem in this regard for two reasons. First, and as we saw earlier, women in poor nations have higher fertility rates for several reasons. Second, poorer nations have very high proportions of young people, and these high rates mean that many births occur because of the large number of women in their childbearing years. This trend poses both opportunities and challenges for poorer nations.

The opportunities are many. Jobs are more plentiful in cities than in rural areas and incomes are higher, and services such as health care and schooling are easier to deliver because people are living more closely together. In another advantage, women in poorer nations generally fare better in cities than in rural areas in terms of education and employment possibilities. But there are also many challenges. In the major cities of poor nations, homeless children live in the streets as beggars, and many people lack necessities and conveniences that urban dwellers in industrial nations take for granted. As the United Nations Population Fund warns, "One billion people live in urban slums, which are typically overcrowded, polluted and dangerous, and lack basic services such as clean water and sanitation. "The rapid urbanization of poor nations will compound the many problems these nations already have, just as the rapid urbanization in the industrial world more than a century ago led to the disease and other problems discussed earlier. As cities grow rapidly in poor nations, moreover, these nations' poverty makes them ill equipped to meet the challenges of urbanization. Helping these nations meet the needs of their cities remains a major challenge for the world community in the years ahead.

In this regard, the United Nations Population Fund urges particular attention to housing:

- Addressing the housing needs of the poor will be critical. A roof and an address in a habitable area are the first step to a better life. Improving access to basic social and health services, including reproductive health care, for poor people in urban slums is also critical to breaking the cycle of poverty.

RURAL LIFE AND RURAL PROBLEMS

Before we leave the topic of cities and urbanization, it is important to note that one-fourth of the U.S. population and more than 40% of the world population continue to live in rural areas. The advantages of cities are often disadvantages for rural areas, and the disadvantages of cities are often advantages of rural areas. On the positive side, and focusing on the United States, rural areas obviously feature much more open space and less crowding.

Their violent and property crime rates are much lower than those in large cities, as we have seen. The air is cleaner because there is less traffic and fewer factories and other facilities that emit pollution. On the negative side, rural areas are often poor and lack the services, employment opportunities, and leisure activities that cities have. Teens often complain of boredom, and drug and alcohol use can be high. Rural schools are often small and poorly equipped. Health and Medicine noted, rural areas often lack sufficient numbers of health-care professionals and high-quality hospitals and medical clinics. The long distances that people must travel make it even more difficult for individuals with health problems to receive adequate medical care. In a problem that only recently has been recognized, rural women who experience domestic violence find it especially difficult to get help and/or to leave their abusers.

Rural police may be unenlightened about domestic violence and may even know the abuser; for either reason, they may not consider his violence a crime. Battered women's shelters are also much less common in rural areas than in cities, and battered women in rural areas often lack neighbours and friends to whom they can turn for support. For all of these reasons, rural women who experience domestic violence face a problem that has been called "dangerous exits".

SOCIAL MOVEMENTS

Social movements in the United States and other nations have been great forces for social change. At the same time, governments and other opponents have often tried to thwart the movements' efforts. To understand how and why social change happens, we have to understand why movements begin, how they succeed and fail, and what impact they may have.

UNDERSTANDING SOCIAL MOVEMENTS

To begin this understanding, we first need to understand what social movements are. A social movement may be defined as an organized effort by a large number of people to bring about or impede social change. Defined in this way, social movements might sound similar to special-interest groups, and they do have some things in common.

But a major difference between social movements and special-interest groups lies in the nature of their actions. Special-interest groups normally work within the system via conventional political activities such as lobbying and election campaigning. In contrast, social movements often work outside the system by engaging in various kinds of protest, including demonstrations, picket lines, sit-ins, and sometimes outright violence. Conceived in this way, the efforts of social movements amount to "politics by other means," with these "other means" made necessary because movements lack the resources and access to the political system that interest groups typically enjoy.

TYPES OF SOCIAL MOVEMENTS

Sociologists identify several types of social movements just as to the nature and extent of the change they seek. This typology helps us understand the differences among the many kinds of social movements that existed in the past and continue to exist today. One of the most common and important types of social movements is the reform movement, which seeks limited, though still significant, changes in some aspect of a nation's political, economic, or social systems.

It does not try to overthrow the existing government but rather works to improve conditions within the existing regime. Some of the most important social movements in U.S. history have been reform movements. These include the abolitionist movement preceding the Civil War, the woman suffrage movement that followed the Civil War, the labour movement, the Southern civil rights movement, the Vietnam antiwar movement, the contemporary women's movement, the gay rights movement, and the environmental movement.

A revolutionary movement goes one large step further than a reform movement in seeking to overthrow the existing government and to bring about a new one and even a new way of life. Revolutionary movements were common in the past and were responsible for the world's great revolutions in Russia, China, and several other nations.

Reform and revolutionary movements are often referred to as political movements because the changes they seek are political in nature. Another type of political movement is the reactionary movement, so named because it tries to block social change or to reverse social changes that have already been achieved. The antiabortion movement is a contemporary example of a reactionary movement, as it arose after the U.S. Supreme Court legalized most abortions in Roe v. Wade and seeks to limit or eliminate the legality of abortion. Two other types of movements are self-help movements and religious movements. As their name implies, self-help movements involve people trying to improve aspects of their personal lives; examples of self-help groups include Alcoholics Anonymous and Weight Watchers. Religious movements aim to reinforce religious beliefs among their members and to convert other people to these beliefs.

Early Christianity was certainly a momentous religious movement, and other groups that are part of a more general religious movement today include the various religious cults, Education and Religion. Sometimes self-help and religious movements are difficult to distinguish from each other because some self-help groups emphasize religious faith as a vehicle for achieving personal transformation.

THE ORIGINS OF SOCIAL MOVEMENTS

To understand how and why social movements begin, we need answers to two related questions. First, what are the social, economic, and political conditions that give rise to social movements? They do not arise in a vacuum, and certain macro problems in society must exist for movements to begin.

Second, once social movements do begin, why are some individuals more likely than others to take part in them? Answers to this question usually focus on personality and other micro factors. As suggested, start with these micro factors and then turn to the macro conditions that make movements possible in the first place.

Micro Factors: Emphasis on the Individual

Over the years social scientists have tried to explain why some individuals are more likely than others to join social movements. Their explanations centre on several factors.

The Question of Irrationality

One issue is whether social movement involvement is rational or irrational. Early thinkers such as Gustavo LeBon, a French intellectual, thought that social movement involvement and, more generally, crowd behaviour were the product of irrational impulses. Writing in the wake of the French Revolution of 1789, these thinkers worried that social order was breaking down. LeBon in particular blamed crowds for turning normally rational individuals into irrational and emotional actors who are virtually hypnotized by the crowd's mind-set. American sociologists early in the 20th century adopted LeBon's view.

In so doing, they viewed social movement participation as more expressive, or emotional, than instrumental, or directed at achieving specific goals. Just after the mid-20th century, Ralph H. Turner and Lewis M. Killian presented their emergent norm view of collective behaviour, which downplayed the irrationality emphasized in earlier formulations.

Turner and Killian, when people start interacting in collective behaviour, they are not sure initially how they are supposed to behave. As they discuss their potential behaviour and other related matters, norms governing their behaviour emerge, and social order and rationality then guide behaviour. Adopting this view, most sociologists today feel that people taking part in social movements are indeed acting rationally and instrumentally, not just expressively. Although they have emotions, that does not mean their behaviour is any less rational or political.

Relative Deprivation

Another important line of thought has centered on relative deprivation, or the feeling by individuals that they are deprived relative to some other group or to some ideal state they have not reached. This view was popularized by James C. Davies and Ted Robert Gurr, both of whom built upon the earlier work of social psychologists who had studied frustration and aggression.

When a deprived group perceives that social conditions are improving, wrote Davies, they become hopeful that their lives are getting better. But if these conditions stop improving, they become frustrated and more apt to turn to protest, collective violence, and other social movement activity. Both Davies and Gurr emphasized that people's feelings of being relatively deprived were more important for the involvement in collective behaviour than their level of actual deprivation. Relative deprivation theory was initially very popular, but scholars later pointed out that frustration often does not lead to protest, as people can instead blame themselves for the deprivation they feel and thus not protest. Scholars who favour the theory point out that people will ordinarily not take part in social movements unless they feel deprived, even if many who do feel deprived do not take part.

Social Isolation Versus Social Attachments

A final micro issue has been whether the individuals participating in social movements are isolated from society or very much a part of it. Are they loners, or are they involved in social networks of friends, coworkers, and others? In his influential book The Politics of Mass Society, William Kornhauser wrote that because modern societies are impersonal with weak social ties, individuals who are loners become involved in social movements to provide them the friendships and social bonding they otherwise lack.

Kornhauser's mass society theory was popular for a time, but much research finds that the people who join social movements are in fact very much a part of society instead of loners. They have many friends and belong to several organizations, and these friendship and organizational ties help "pull" them into social movements.

Macro Factors: Emphasis on Social Structure

Structural explanations of social movements try to understand why social movements are more likely to arise in some historical periods and locations than in others. In effect, they try to show how certain social, economic, and political conditions give rise to social movements. We discuss some of these explanations here.

Smelser's Structural-Strain Theory

One of the most popular and influential structural

explanations is Neil Smelser's structural-strain theory. Smelser wrote that social movements and other collective behaviour occur when several conditions are present. One of these conditions is structural strain, which refers to problems in society that cause people to be angry and frustrated.

Without such structural strain, people would not have any reason to protest, and social movements do not arise. Another condition is generalized beliefs, which are people's reasons for why conditions are so bad and their solutions to improve them. If people decide that the conditions they dislike are their own fault, they will decide not to protest. Similarly, if they decide that protest will not improve these conditions, they again will not protest.

A third condition is the existence of precipitating factors, or sudden events that ignite collective behaviour. In the 1960s, for example, several urban riots started when police were rumored to have unjustly arrested or beaten someone. Although conditions in inner cities were widely perceived as unfair and even oppressive, it took this type of police behaviour to ignite people to riot.

Smelser's theory became very popular because it pointed to several factors that must hold true before social movements and other forms of collective behaviour occur. At the same time, collective behaviour does not always occur when his factors do hold true. The theory has also been criticized for being a bit vague; for example, it does not say how much strain a society must have for collective behaviour to take place.

Resource Mobilization Theory

Resource mobilization theory is a general name given to several related views of social movements that arose in the 1970s. This theory assumes that social movement activity is a rational response to unsatisfactory conditions in society. Because these conditions always exist, so does discontent with them.

Despite such constant discontent, people protest only rarely. If this is so, these conditions and associated discontent cannot easily explain why people turn to social movements.

What is crucial instead are efforts by social movement leaders to mobilize the resources-most notably, time, money, and energy-of the population and to direct them into effective political action. Also important are political opportunities for action that arise when, say, a government weakens because of an economic or foreign crisis.

Resource mobilization theory has been very influential since its inception in the 1970s. However, critics say it underestimates the importance of harsh social conditions and discontent for the rise of social movement activity. Conditions can and do worsen, and when they do so, they prompt people to engage in collective behaviour. As just one example, cuts in higher education spending and steep increases in tuition prompted students to protest on campuses in California and several other states in late 2009 and early 2010.

Critics also say that resource mobilization theory neglects the importance of emotions in social movement activity by depicting social movement actors as cold, calculated, and unemotional. This is simply not true, critics say, and they further argue that social movement actors can be both emotional and rational at the same time, just as people are in many other kinds of pursuits.

THE LIFE CYCLE OF SOCIAL MOVEMENTS

Although the many past and present social movements around the world differ from each other in many ways, they all generally go through a life cycle marked by several stages that have long been recognized.

- *Stage 1 is emergence*: This stage is obviously when social movements begin for one or more of the reasons.
- *Stage 2 is coalescence*: At this stage a movement and its leaders must decide how they will recruit new members and they must determine the strategies they will use to achieve their goals. They also may use the news media to win favourable publicity and to convince the public of the justness of their cause.
- *Stage 3 is institutionalization or bureaucratization*: As a movement grows, it often tends to become

bureaucratized, as paid leaders and a paid staff replace the volunteers that began the movement. It also means that clear lines of authority develop, as they do in any bureaucracy. More attention is also devoted to fund-raising. As movement organizations bureaucratize, they may well reduce their effectiveness by turning from the disruptive activities that succeeded in the movement's earlier stages to more conventional activity by working within the system instead of outside it. At the same time, if movements do not bureaucratize to at least some degree, they may lose their focus and not have enough money to keep on going.

- *Stage 4 is the decline of a social movement*: Social movements eventually decline for one or more of many reasons. Sometimes they achieve their goals and naturally cease because there is no more reason to continue. More often, however, they decline because they fail. Both the lack of money and loss of enthusiasm among a movement's members may lead to a movement's decline, and so might factionalism, or strong divisions of opinion within a movement.

The government may also "co-opt" a movement by granting it small, mostly symbolic concessions that reduce people's discontent but leave the conditions that originally motivated their activism largely intact. As noted earlier, movements also may decline because of government repression.

HOW SOCIAL MOVEMENTS MAKE A DIFFERENCE

By definition, social movements often operate outside of the political system by engaging in protest. Their rallies, demonstrations, sit-ins, and silent vigils are often difficult to ignore. With the aid of news media coverage, these events often throw much attention on the problem or grievance at the centre of the protest and bring pressure to bear on the government agencies, corporations, or other targets of the protest. As noted earlier, there are many examples of profound changes brought about by social movements throughout U.S. history. The abolitionist movement called attention to the evils of slavery and increased public abhorrence for that "peculiar institution." The woman suffrage movement after the Civil War eventually won women the right to vote with the ratification of the 19th Amendment in 1920. The labour movement of the late 19th and early 20th centuries established the minimum wage, the 40-hour workweek, and the right to strike. The civil rights movement of the 1950s and 1960s ended legal segregation in the South, while the Vietnam antiwar movement of the 1960s and 1970s helped increase public opposition to that war and bring it to a close. The contemporary women's movement has won many rights in social institutions throughout American society, while the gay rights movement has done the same for gays and lesbians.

Another contemporary movement is the environmental movement, which has helped win legislation and other policies that have reduced air, water, and ground pollution. Although it seems obvious that social movements have made a considerable difference, social movement scholars until recently have paid much more attention to the origins of social movements than to their consequences. Recent work has begun to fill in this gap and has focused on the consequences of social movements for the political system, for various aspects of the society's culture, and for the lives of the people who take part in movements.

Regarding political consequences, scholars have considered such matters as whether movements are more successful when they use more protest or less protest, and when they focus on a single issue versus multiple issues. The use of a greater amount of protest seems to be more effective in this regard, as does a focus on a single issue. Research has also found that movements are more likely to succeed when the government against which they protest is weakened by economic or other problems. In another line of inquiry, movement scholars disagree over whether movements are more successful if their organizations are bureaucratic and centralized or if they remain decentralized and thus more likely to engage in protest. Regarding cultural consequences, movements often influence certain aspects of a society's culture whether or not they intend to do so and, as one scholar has said, "it is perhaps precisely in being able to alter their broader cultural environment that movements can have their deepest and lasting impact". Social movements can affect values and beliefs, and they can affect cultural practices such as music, literature, and even fashion. Movements may also have biographical consequences. Several studies find that people who take part in social movements during their formative years are often transformed by their participation. Their political views change or are at least reinforced, and they are more likely to continue to be involved in political activity and to enter social change occupations. In this manner, writes one scholar, "people who have been involved in social movement activities, even at a lower level of commitment, carry the consequences of that involvement throughout their life".

IMPORTANT POINTS

- Social change involves the transformation of cultural norms and values, behaviour, social institutions, and social structure. As societies become more modern, they become larger, more heterogeneous, and more impersonal, and their sense of community declines. Traditions decline as well, while individual freedom of thought and behaviour increases. Some sociologists view modernization positively, while others view it negatively. Tönnies in particular lamented the shift from the Gemeinschaft of premodern societies to the Gesellschaft of modern societies. Durkheim also recognized the negative aspects of modernization but at the same time valued the freedom of modern societies and thought they retain a good amount of social solidarity from their division of labour.
- A functionalist understanding of social change emphasizes that it's both natural and inevitable. Talcott Parsons's equilibrium model recognized that gradual change is desirable and ordinarily stems from such things as population growth and technological

advances, but that any sudden social change disrupts society's equilibrium. Taking a very different view, conflict theory stresses that sudden social change is often both necessary and desirable to reduce inequality and to address other problems in society. Such social change often stems from intentional efforts by social movements to correct perceived deficiencies in the social, economic, and political systems.

- Several sources of social change exist. These include population growth and changes in population composition, changes in culture and technology, changes in the natural environment, and social and ethnic conflict.
- Demography is the study of population. It encompasses three central concepts: fertility, morality, and migration, which together determine population growth. Fertility and mortality vary by race and ethnicity, and they also vary around the world, with low-income nations having both higher fertility and higher mortality than high-income nations.
- The world's population is growing by about 80 million people annually. Population growth is greatest in the low-income nations of Africa and other regions, while in several industrial nations it's actually on the decline because birth rates have become so low. The world's population reached 6.8 billion by the beginning of the 21st century and is projected to grow to more than 9 billion by 2050, with most of this occurring in low-income nations. The annual rate of population growth will decline in the years ahead.
- Thomas Malthus predicted that the earth's population would greatly exceed the world's food supply. Although his prediction did not come true, hunger remains a serious problem around the world. Although food supply is generally ample thanks to improved technology, the distribution of food is inadequate in low-income nations. Fresh water in these regions is also lacking. Demographic transition

theory helps explain why population growth did not continue to rise as much as Malthus predicted. As societies become more technologically advanced, first death rates and then birth rates decline, leading eventually to little population growth.

- Urbanization is a consequence of population growth. Cities first developed in ancient times after the rise of horticultural and pastoral societies and "took off" during the Industrial Revolution as people moved to be near factories. Urbanization led to many social changes then and continues today to affect society.
- Sociologists have long been interested in the city and have both positive and negative views of urbanization and city life. Contemporary research supports Wirth's hypothesis that tolerance for nontraditional beliefs and behaviours will be higher in urban areas than in rural areas.
- Social movements have been important agents for social change. Common types of social movements include reform movements, revolutionary movements, reactionary movements, and self-help and religious movements.
- Explanations of social movements address both micro and macro factors. Important issues at the micro level include the question of irrationality, the importance of relative deprivation, and the impact of social isolation. Macro theories address the social, economic, and political conditions underlying collective behaviour. Two of the most important such theories are Smelser's structural-strain theory and resource mobilization theory.
- *Most social movements go through a life cycle of four stages*: Emergence, coalescence, bureaucratization, and decline. Decline stems from several reasons, including internal divisions and repressive efforts by the state.
- Social movements have political, cultural, and biographical consequences. Research finds that movements are more successful in the political arena when they use more rather than less protest and when they focus on a single issue rather than multiple issues.

Bibliography

Alan, R.: *The Interrelationships of Economics with the Social Sciences*, Paris: Institute of Economics,1999.

Albertoni, E.A.: *Mosca and the Theory of Elitism*, UK: Oxford University, 2000.

Andrew, M.: *The Tropics and Economic Development*, US: John Hopkins University Press, 2000.

Bartoli, H.: *Economie Unidimensionnelle*, Paris: Institute of Economica, 1991.

Buchanan, J.: *Economics and its Scientifc Neighbours*, London: Westview Press, 2003.

Burke, P.: *Sociology and History*, Paris: Institute of Economica, 2000.

Cahman, W.: *Sociology and History and Research*, New York: Free Press, 2005.

Calhoun, Craig: *Sociology, other Disciplines and the Project of a General Understanding of Social Life*, New York: Routledge Press, 2003.

Dogan, M.: *Fragmentation of the Social Sciences and Recombination of Specialties*, New Haven: Yall University Press, 2001.

Fred, W.: *Development in Social Science Concepts: A Systematic Analysis*, London: Sage Publications, 2001.

Galbraith, J.K.: *Conditions for Economic Change in Underdeveloped Countries*, Paris: Institute of Economics, 2000.

Halliday, T.: *Sociology and its Publics*, New York: University of Chicago Press. 1992.

Hayek, F.A.: The *Dilemna of Specializtion*, New York: Chicago University Press, 2002.

Henry S.: *American Sociology since the Seventies: the Emerging Identity Crisis in the Discipline*, New York: Academic Press, 1992.

Hirshleifer, J.: *The Expanding Domain of Economics,* Paris: Institute of American Economic, 2000.

Huntington, E.: *Civilization and Climate,* New Haven: Yall University Press, 2003.

Inkeles, A.: *Sociological Theory in Relation to Social Psychological Variables,* New York: Appleton Press, 1998.

Intriligator, M.: *Independence Among the Behavioral Sciences,* New York: University of Chicago Press, 2000.

Knapp, P.: *Can Social Theory Escape from History: View of History in Social Science,* Revolutionary Virginia: University Press of Virginia, 1996.

Lewis, W.A.: *The Theory of Economic Growth,* US: University of Chicago Press, 2002.

Marion, J.: *Scientific Analysis is a Subset of Comparative Analysis,* New Haven: Yall University Press, 2001.

Melvin, L.: *Cross-National Research in Sociology,* London: Sage Publications, 1999.

Merton, K.: *Social Theory and Social Structure,* New York: Free Press, 2003.

Rigney, D.: *Patterns of Interdisciplinary Citation in the Social Sciences,* US: Princeton University Press, 1999.

Robert, P.: *Creative Marginality, Innovation at the Intersections of Social Sciences,* Boulder: Westview Press, 2001.

Scheuch, K.: *German Sociology: In Encyclopedia of Sociology,* New York: Macmillan University Press, 1992.

Smelser, N.: *Handbook of Sociology,* London: Sage Publications,1988.

Solow, R.: *Science and Ideology in Economics,*UK: Oxford University, 2000.

Szacki, J.: *The History of Sociology and Substantive Sociological Theories,* London: Sage Publications, 2003.

Tilly, C.: *Big Structures, Large Processes, Huge Comparisons,* New York: Russel Sage Foundation, 1999.

Index